# LIVES AT RISK

# LIVES AT RISK

*Understanding and Treating*
*Young People with Dual Disorders*

Hilary Ryglewicz, ACSW
Bert Pepper, MD

THE FREE PRESS
New York   London   Toronto   Sydney   Singapore

The cases of Bill, Annie, Ellen, and Darrell presented as examples in this book are fictionalized composites. They do not refer to any actual person, living or dead. At the same time, each fact or circumstance described in these composite case studies has been true of at least one real person, and each case represents, in its nature and general characteristics, any number of young men and women we have known. In that sense only, the cases are true stories, illustrating the problems that are the subject of this book.

The authors gratefully acknowledge permission given by the Mental Health Association of Rockland County, Inc., for the use of selected paragraphs originally written for its magazine *Focus;* also the Hazelden Foundation, Center City, MN, for use of a diagram originally published in *Alcohol, Street Drugs, and Emotional Problems: What You Need to Know*, by Bert Pepper, M.D., and Hilary Ryglewicz, copyright © 1994 by The Information Exchange.

THE FREE PRESS
A Division of Simon & Schuster Inc.
1230 Avenue of the Americas, New York, N.Y. 10020

THE FREE PRESS and colophon are trademarks
of Simon & Schuster Inc.

Designed by Carla Bolte

Manufactured in the United States of America

10  9  8  7  6  5  4  3  2  1

**Library of Congress Cataloging-in-Publication Data**

Ryglewicz, Hilary.
    Lives at risk:  understanding and treating young people with dual
disorders/  Hilary Ryglewicz, Bert Pepper.
        p.   cm.
    Includes index.
    ISBN  0-684-82807-3
    1. Dual diagnosis.  2. Youth—Mental health.  I. Pepper, Bert.
1932–  .  II. Title.
RC564.68.R97   1996
616.89'022–dc20                                         96-366
                                                          CIP

For Jack            For Peggy


And for our children


This book has grown from the authors' work together in training and consultation on the subject of dual psychiatric and substance use disorders and community health services. Hilary Ryglewicz wishes to acknowledge Bert Pepper as the leader and guiding spirit of this work and as a prime author of many of the perspectives presented here.

# CONTENTS

# PREFACE

This book is about young men and women who present a growing problem in America today: those who are stuck on the threshold of their adult lives because of serious, persistent mental and emotional problems, in many cases combined with use and abuse of alcohol and other drugs. There are some 25 million such younger adults in America today—people who have reached the age of 24 or 28 or 35 or even 40 without being able to "get it together" or keep it together for very long. By younger adults we mean young men and women in the age group from about 16 to 35 or 40—those years when a person is coming of age and making it or not making it into a fully autonomous, independent life. If 35 or 40 sounds old for that effort, it is. But many young men and women with severe problems continue to struggle during those years with the desire to make a life, to have love and work, to leave home, to graduate from their status of adult child, psychiatric patient, or—to use the latest terminology—consumer or recipient of mental health services, to the more welcome status of ex-recipient or psychiatric survivor. And for some the struggle is not geared to even that toehold in the American dream; it is rather a day-to-day struggle to stay out of the hospital, off the streets, off alcohol and drugs, or to keep a tenuous hold on a low-skilled job, a furnished room, a companion who is almost a friend.

Who are these young men and women? Are we writing about the mentally ill? . . . the homeless? . . . alcoholics and drug addicts? . . . abused children from dysfunctional families? . . . school dropouts? . . . the so-called worried well?—just ordinary people with emotional problems? We have spent our professional lives in community mental health services, and while at times in this work we must think in diagnostic categories, we know that these categories overlap today, and their boundary lines are blurred. Some of the troubled young men and women we have in mind are patients in psychiatric hospitals or clients in community mental health programs. In those settings they may be called dual-diagnosis, dual-disorder, multiproblem, or young adult chronic clients, presenting an interplay of psychiatric and substance abuse problems that are long-lasting and various. Some of these people are passing through shelters or living in the streets, and they are the younger members of that group called the mentally ill homeless. Some are in and out of their childhood homes, where they may no longer be welcome even to the most devoted parents; and some have simply never been able to leave home. Some of these young people are floundering—or holding on tenaciously—in college or in jobs; others are in and out of jail. Some are young adults we might think of as socially maladjusted, delinquent, or in need of supervision—or, looking at the milder end of the spectrum of problems, as immature, having a bad temper, or trying to find themselves—but not yet as men and women who need psychiatric treatment or incarceration. The difference between a troubled young person and a psychiatric patient or substance abuser is sometimes just a matter of time and chance. The disturbed adolescent who falls into the mental health or the criminal justice system may soon take on the identity of "patient," "addict," or "inmate."

We are not writing, then, about just one class or category of people defined by a specific diagnosis or by their status in the mental health treatment system, but rather about a range of people and problems that are confronted by families, mental health and substance abuse treatment agencies, and society itself. These are some of the major "people problems" of today, expressed by a generation of younger adults who are not found in just one place or one category, but pass in and out of the hospital, the jail, the family home, the streets—and in and out of the categories of mentally ill, drug-dependent, dysfunctional, or just barely making it.

Why do we write a book about such a diverse group of young people? Because these are the people our mental health agencies today are trying to serve. And because in today's world it makes less and less sense to ask, as some people do ask about mental/emotional/behavioral problems: Is it drugs? . . . or mental illness? . . . or the breakdown of the family? . . . or a widespread social crisis? Today the answer is likely to be: Some or all of the above. Young people with mental illness get into using drugs, and substance abusers develop mental illness, or the drug effects mimic psychiatric symptoms. Children with emotional problems, some but not all of them from severely troubled families, have problems in learning, drop out of school, get into trouble with the law, and/or overdose on pills or crack. Young women, many of them adult children of people with alcoholism, try to shut out painful memories of abuse or to live out an emotional roller coaster ride by drinking, drugging, cutting their wrists, accepting abusive sex or exploitative relationships, or otherwise endangering themselves. Adolescents who are too troubled and confused to function in school play truant, do drugs, grow into an antisocial pattern, and cycle through the twin revolving doors of state hospitals and state prisons. And people everywhere who care about the quality of public and personal life bemoan the loss of skills, values, and sources of meaning for many of society's adult children, our collective symptom bearers for families trapped in cycles of conflict, abuse, neglect, and what we call dysfunction.

Our book is intended primarily for workers and students in the fields of mental health, substance abuse treatment, and other human services, as well as client/consumers, family members, administrators, and policy makers in these fields. But we believe that anyone who picks up this book can think of a Bill or Annie or Ellen or Darrell—whose disguised and fictionalized, but quite familiar, stories are presented here—or of some other young person who has a problem or is seen as a problem. These young men and women come up in everyday conversation—your neighbor's daughter who can't keep a job . . . your co-worker's son who sleeps all the time, and who she thinks might be on drugs . . . the young man in the paper today who killed somebody on an impulse . . . your daughter's ex-boyfriend who couldn't let go and made those disturbing threats ... your niece's roommate who started seeing the Devil in the mirror ... the strange young man in the subway last night ... the young woman begging in the street. In our experience, nearly everyone knows at least one disturbed or problematic person in the early years of adulthood—late teens, twenties, early thirties—someone who becomes an anecdote, a puzzle, a threat, or perhaps—if the person is in your own family—a lifelong worry.

If you are a parent or other family member of such a young man or woman, you already know better than anyone what mental disorder means and what it does to a person's and a family's life. If you work in mental health, drug and alcohol treatment, or other human services, you know many more than one of these derailed young people. Like family members, though differently, you may be burned out, exhausted with the effort to hold the levee firm against the flood tide of human misery, the pressure of one complex, troubled, sometimes desperate human being after another and another. For the worker in human services the question is not so much: What's wrong with that guy? ... that young woman? ... my son? ... my daughter? It is rather: How can I do my job? What can I do that makes any difference? How should I handle today's crop of seemingly insoluble problems? Or that most daunting question: How can I get this person, my client, to choose living over dying?—or some small measure of success over a life consigned to failure upon failure?

If you are an ordinary citizen, just wishing for a better community in which to live, you may be wondering, Where do they all come from? Why aren't all these people in institutions? What does it really mean when somebody has "mental problems"? Or you may be wondering who or what is really to blame—the family or the TV or the schools or the genes or the drugs or the economy or the values or the whole of society itself.

Today, people on the cutting edge of research into mental illness, addictions, and human development are working toward a more precise understanding of mental/emotional problems, based on a rapidly advancing technology of the brain and expanding knowledge of the biochemistry of psychiatric disorder. There is no question but that we know more each day. Meanwhile, on the front lines, in the trenches of mental health and substance abuse treatment, the problems keep coming, in their relentlessly human, baffling, complex, and urgent forms. How can we translate the new knowledge that is developing into practice—into treatment strategies and techniques that actually help people?

That question would drive everything for the therapist, the case manager, the group home worker, the program director, and the team psychiatrist—if it were not being drowned out by other, even more pressing questions: How can we pay for it all? How can we design and document treatment so that third-party payers will reimburse costs and governmental regulatory bodies license our public agencies? In other words, how can we whose business is helping people manage to stay in business?

What can anyone do about these problems? In spite of the enormous stress of change in the knowledge base, philosophies, and techniques of treatment, in the circumstances of service delivery, and in social values, we believe there is much ground for hope for these troubled young people. The hope, for each of them and for their family members and counselors, is that a failing life can move in a more successful or at least a more stable direction. The meaning of "success" or "failure" may be different for each of the young men and women we will discuss. For one, success might mean beginning a viable occupation; for another, staying out of the hospital or out of prison; for another, being able to move out of the family home into some kind of group setting; for another, going back to school. Some troubled young people are, and will remain, especially vulnerable to the stress of life, to episodes of what we may properly call a psychiatric illness, and to ongoing problems in managing their lives. Some may never get far beyond the hospital walls. Others emerge as capable of changing a downhill pattern, given the kinds of help and support they need.

Most impressive to those who work in the field today is the self-help and mutual support movement of people, many of them younger adults, who are taking their fate and their lives into their own hands and reaching out to help and support one another. These men and women, whether they call themselves ex-patients, ex-recipients of service, consumers of mental health services, or psychiatric survivors, are comparable to the innumerable members of Alcoholics Anonymous (AA) or the hundreds of thousands of family members who have spread the National Alliance for the Mentally Ill (NAMI) across the nation, in their courage and their commitment to helping one another.

The immediate purpose of this book is to help both family members and professional workers to understand and address the everyday and long-term tasks of helping these young men and women to survive and grow. The authors have been working with, learning from, and teaching and writing about young people with mental disorders and their families for a number of years and have paid close attention to new developments in the field of treatment. This book is our attempt to bring together our collective understanding of these problems and how to treat them. The thoughts and principles we offer are based on our own experiences and concerns and those of many respected colleagues, family members, and client/consumers. We hope they will be of value to others who are grappling with mental disorder in their families or working in the field of human services.

If our book has a message beyond this effort, it is that attention must be paid to the causes and treatment of the problems we will describe—because these problems are so pressing and so pervasive. As we write, the availability of health care in our country is decreasing, services are being reduced, the number of uninsured people has swelled to 40 million, and we still grapple with the question of whether mental health care will remain a stepchild in the health care system as a whole. These young people must not remain a concern only to themselves, their families, and their professional helpers. They must be seen and known as our society's adult children, many of whom are currently headed for a lifetime of failure in a country devoted to the ideal of success. Collectively, they signal a current failure of our society to respond adequately to their extensive human needs. At the same time they challenge our ability, as we grapple with the enormity of other social, economic, and human problems, to remember these sons and daughters and to ensure for them the best treatment and support we know how to provide.

# ACKNOWLEDGMENTS

Hilary Ryglewicz wishes to acknowledge Dr. Bert Pepper as the guiding spirit of this book and as prime author of many of its perspectives, including its focus on young men and women with dual disorders. He has been her mentor in the field of community mental health, and has shared freely his broad knowledge and imaginative grasp of issues in treatment, programming, service delivery, and social policy, as well as his zest for teaching and learning and his unfailing gift of metaphor. Over the years, his sense of purpose in furthering progressive treatment has informed her work and that of many others. This book is a culmination of the authors' teaching and writing together. Therefore, there is no page that does not bear in some way the mark of his searching and generous mind.

Bert Pepper wishes to acknowledge Hilary Ryglewicz as his collaborator over 15 years of writing and teaching on the subject of young adults and dual psychiatric and substance use disorders. She has brought to this work her own considerable skills as therapist, teacher and writer, and her own experiences in working with clients, families, and mental health programs. Her ability to grasp, express, and further develop new approaches and ideas, and the warmth of her commitment to working with people, have enhanced the collaboration that has produced this book.

There is no way to name the innumerable people who have contributed to this manuscript. They include client/consumers, family members, teachers, mentors, colleagues, students, loved ones, and other significant others. We each have enjoyed the blessing of good work, good colleagues, and good friends, who have contributed immeasurably to our thinking and experience. We each have found in our relationships with clients and families an ever-deepening warmth of understanding and an increasing respect for the human spirit in its struggle for survival, endurance, and growth. For these contributions we thank all the people with whom we have worked, including particularly the staff, clients, and families of the Rockland County (New York) Department of Mental Health, as well as Dr. Sydney Brandon, who has offered specific comments on this manuscript.

We each wish to thank a loving spouse—Jacob Orbach and Peggy McLaughlin, respectively—whose patience and humor have been a constant support, enabling us to complete this manuscript and to pursue all the efforts of our working lives, as well as bringing us each a constant joy for which we are always grateful.

We wish to acknowledge also the firm and attentive editorial judgment of Susan Arellano of The Free Press and the tireless help and courtesy of our production editor, Loretta Denner.

# PART I

# FACES IN THE CROWD

Chapter 1

# Where Do They All Come From?

How does it happen that so many young men and women today are in some kind of trouble—mentally ill, taking drugs, in trouble with the law, dropping out of high school or college, landing in hospitals or prisons or street shelters or back in their parents' homes—in one way or another failing at life? The question comes to mind for people working in the mental health, substance abuse, criminal justice, public assistance, and other human service professions as well as for teachers, employers, and concerned citizens. People working for treatment agencies and in other human service fields are overwhelmed today by the numbers of people they must treat and the severity, diversity, and persistence of their problems. Family members are overwhelmed in different, far more poignant and pervasive ways by the crises and floundering of a troubled daughter or son.

This book is primarily about how to treat and manage a range of mental, emotional, and substance abuse problems of these younger adults—by "younger" we mean a broad age range from about 16 to 35 or 40 years old. It is addressed to the problems that professionals and family members confront in working and living with troubled young men and women, and offers some perspectives, techniques, and directions of hope. But first we need to consider the questions: Who are these young people? Where have they all come from? Why are there so many of them? Why are their problems so confusing and multifaceted?

A few statistics may highlight the problems we are all confronting:

- In 1955 the population of the United States was 170 million. Some 550,000 people, or one in 300 Americans, were in psychiatric hospitals, most of them in state mental institutions. Today, the population of the United States is 250 million, and we have only 90,000 state mental hospital beds. Only one in 2,800 Americans is in a psychiatric hospital today. Many very vulnerable and troubled people, young and old, spend most of their lives in the streets, or in the care of their families, community treatment agencies, or other agencies of social control.
- In 1962, only two percent of our population over 12 years of age had ever used an illicit drug. By the mid-1980s, nearly half of our adult population had at least tried an illicit substance. The number of people thereby exposed to potential drug dependence or addiction has risen from 2.5 million in 1962 to perhaps 90 million today. The typical age of first drug use has descended from high school to junior high school to elementary school ages, and children of all socioeconomic groups encounter the hazard and temptation of alcohol and street drugs by the age of 8 or 10.
- In 1972 we had about 200,000 jail and prison cells in the United States. By 1995 that number had increased to 1.5 million cells. The state of California plans to increase its prison cell capacity to over 200,000; if this plan could be carried out, it would create by 1998 as many prison cells for California as the entire country had in 1972.

In other words, as psychiatric hospital beds have decreased, prison beds have increased, and the problem of social control of mentally ill people has thereby been transferred to the criminal justice system by transinstitutionalization. This does not mean simply that mentally ill people have been imprisoned instead of being hospitalized. Today's prison populations also include a very high proportion (perhaps 70 to 80 percent) of people with alcohol/drug problems whose dependence or addiction has led them into crime.

At the same time, a recent comprehensive study of our population indicates that some one in five Americans has an active psychiatric disorder at any given time—and for the younger population of 16 to 40 we would estimate three in ten, or a total nationwide of some 25 million young men and women. This statistic does not mean that this one person in five is psychotic—out of touch with reality—and needs to be in a hospital. But the estimate does include major mental illness as well as a variety of problems—alcoholism, depression, anxiety, obsessive-compulsive disorder, borderline personality disorder, antisocial personality— all problems that we can expect to be ongoing, or chronic—the medical term for something that doesn't kill you quickly but never goes away. The difference for a person with a severe psychiatric disorder is that it *may* kill you with its complications—suicide, accidents, poverty, a higher death rate for physical illness than for the general population, and certainly a higher death rate for alcohol and other drug abuse.

More recently, the National Comorbidity Study (NCS) (Kessler et al., 1994) has found a higher incidence and prevalence of psychiatric and substance use disorders. The findings of this study indicate that 48 percent of all Americans between the ages of 15 and 55 have had a diagnosable mental or substance abuse disorder, or both, during their lifetime, and that 30 percent, or 9.9 million people in the 14–54 age group, have both a mental and a substance abuse disorder each year. This indicates an increase from 29 percent to 48 percent of our population with a history of a mental and/or substance abuse disorder during their lifetime, and an increase from about 20 percent to about 30 percent of those who have had at least one disorder during the past year.

Twenty or 30 years ago we did not see our city streets flooded with homeless people, nor did we have a high demand for cities to provide shelters for the homeless. Of course, not all homeless people are mentally ill—current estimates suggest that some 70 percent suffer from a major psychiatric illness and/or a substance abuse disorder. But clearly deinstitutionalization—the massive discharge of long-stay patients from public psychiatric hospitals, and the corresponding noninstitutionalization, admissions diversion, and short-stay admissions of today's younger generations of people with mental illness—has dumped many disturbed people, younger as well as older adults, into the streets. Unable to fend for themselves without services, supervision, and support, many are wandering naked in a social and psychological jungle, their movements driven by fear, rage, and the ongoing struggle to survive.

There are other statistics, concerning more domestic matters, that flicker across the TV screen or the newspaper page:

- Since 1950, the number of American children growing up in families with only a single parent (mother) has risen from 5 million to nearly 20 million, with approximately one-fourth of households with children under 18 headed by mother only, and another four percent by father only.
- Since 1970 the number of single parents has tripled, changing from about four million to about 12 million.
- One of every 11 adults is divorced, three times the proportion in 1970, and one of every six children is a stepchild.
- As of 1992, there were more than 14 million children living in poverty in the United States, defined as below a level of $14,763 for a family of four.
- In 1993 an estimated 464,000 children were in foster homes, group homes, or residential treatment centers on any single day, representing an increase of 77 percent in the past decade. (Sweeney, 1995)

These and other statistics underline the fact that vast numbers of children are living with varying degrees of family instability and/or shortage of personal and financial resources, and they are today's and tomorrow's "high-risk" population for the development of mental disorder. Millions of children are growing up without adequate models of womanhood, manhood, parenting, basic humanity. Many of these lack basic cognitive and survival skills. Many more are learning the basics of everyday functioning and how to present a facade of adequacy, but behind that facade is an emptiness, a failing sense of self, a vacuum, and/or a constant turmoil. Anxiety and depression are widespread among adolescents, and one prominent study has found that such feelings, diagnosed at an average age of 15, double the young person's chances of developing alcohol and drug abuse. Many young people with these painful feelings are also at high risk of being victimized, sexually exploited, or drawn into the self-surrender and false security of a cult.

The figures we have cited are but a few of many signals of enormous changes in our society—and our ways of treating troubled people—that have occurred within a very short time, a few decades. We can summarize these major changes in terms of (1) socioeconomic conditions in society as a whole, (2) treatment of mental illness, (3) the availability and impact of alcohol and drug use, and (4) family structures and the raising of children.

1. *Changes in socioeconomic conditions.* Our culture, especially in urban communities, is increasingly complex, competitive, demanding, fast-paced, and technology-dependent. Life in our communities, especially cities, today is very difficult for anyone who is vulnerable because of mental, emotional, psychological, and/or learning problems. The vulnerable person commonly suffers from high expectations and demands; an overload of information, stimulation, and stress; a constant need to learn and adapt to change; a lack of clear guidelines, values, and reliable social supports; increasing diversity of cultural backgrounds in our population; increasing danger in formerly relatively safe places such as schools, streets, and communities; and a disadvantaged position in society as the gap between abilities and expectations becomes too great.

2. *Changes in treatment of people with major mental illness or other severe emotional and behavioral problems.* Deinstitutionalization and the shift from inpatient to community treatment has placed large numbers of seriously disturbed people in the community, where many are untreated or inadequately treated, and all are vulnerable to the demanding social conditions already noted, as well as to the continuing stigma placed upon mental illness. Large numbers of people with mental illness and/or substance abuse disorders are currently transinstitutionalized into prisons functioning as agencies of social control rather than treatment.

3. *Increased availability and impact of alcohol/drug use.* The wide-spread availability of psychoactive drugs as well as alcohol has greatly increased the numbers of people who use, abuse, depend upon, or become addicted to these substances. Alcohol/drug use has become a complicating factor in the lives and treatment of a majority of people with serious mental/emotional disorders, and for many it greatly increases the frequency and severity of symptoms and acute treatment in emergency rooms and hospitals. Alcohol and other drug use beginning at much earlier ages than in the past has major implications for the neurological and psychological development of children, as well as for the mental/emotional stability of those vulnerable adults who are also parents. People needing intensive treatment for alcoholism and other substance abuse—many of whom are also mentally ill or severely emotionally troubled—outnumber the treatment slots available by a ratio of about 20 to 1, and there is no involuntary commitment to drug rehabilitation facilities in most states. As we all know, there are large numbers of people in society, especially in our cities, who are unable to care for themselves and/or to stay out of trouble without help because of their substance abuse, dependence, or addiction.

4. *Major changes in family structures and in the way children are raised, socialized, and educated.* Family structures have been in flux and in many cases weakened even as stresses on the family have become more severe. These changes and the socioeconomic conditions noted above have resulted in moderate to severe deficits in the essential nurturing and socialization of children in many families, and unmanageable psychological and social stress upon many parents.

While these are the major areas in which sweeping changes have impacted upon the lives and treatment of people with mental disorders, and upon the development of mental/emotional and substance abuse problems, there are other aspects of our present society that are making it still more difficult to come to grips with their burgeoning needs for treatment and other types of intervention. For one, we continue to place a high value upon mobility in social and personal life, a mobility that can be healthy and positive for many people, but that for others creates a constant and un-manageable demand for adaptation to change. We continue to value and absorb into our population people of very diverse cultures, but many people who immigrate are not assimilated into a sense of shared entitlements and values; instead, they may add to the numbers of disadvantaged and stigmatized citizens. A serious backlash is developing against the arrival of these new populations, resulting partly from the fact that we are in the throes of an economic and spiritual depression, in which resources are felt to be scarce or shrinking. Attitudes toward illness, disability, care, and support—as well as toward poverty, homelessness, and social disadvantage—have undergone great change. How we will solve these problems remains to be seen; but it is clear that the solutions will require major adjustments in our economy and our thinking, and will severely test our commitment to our traditions of responsibility and compassion, and our ability to adapt constructively to diversity and change.

Meanwhile, our communities, especially cities, have grown increasingly dangerous. In some localities handguns have become commonplace, not only among street criminals but also among ordinary citizens who feel a need for self-defense, and among children and adolescents, who bring them to school. Concurrently, there has been a widespread loss of faith and frequent public "undressing" of leaders and authority figures, from priests and scout leaders to presidents and politicians. It remains to be seen whether a desirable level of confidence in such personal and political leadership can be restored while the media are ever ready to dramatize everything from a long moment of indecision to an outright breach of trust—or, of course, the details of a leader's sexual past. Can we constructively approach the complex problems of our society with such a low level of confidence in government and without a consensus regarding social values?

This cursory list of social and economic factors, any or all of which may impact at some level upon the struggle of a troubled young man or woman today, explains why the concerns of this book are not easy to summarize. None of the social, family, or individual conditions we have mentioned is by itself "the cause" of mental disorder and failing lives. Rather, these factors are among a number of perspectives or lenses—biological, psychological, social, educational—that can be trained on such young people. We find it most fruitful to begin by cutting the widest possible swath, to view these extremely diverse individuals as sharing a common and fundamental quandary: an inability to place and keep their feet on the path of an adult life. The problems can be specified and diagnosed for any one individual. From the individual perspective they may include major mental illness, personality problems, emotional conflicts, or alcohol/drug use and abuse. Seen through the lens of family and/or society, they may show other constellations of cause and circumstance—social disadvantage, family conflict, economic constraints, poor education and socialization, criminality, and social change—that emerge as equally important concerns. But the essential question remains: What can we do about these problems?

Answering that question is the subject of this book—for of course there is no single or simple answer. The chapters that follow will sketch some faces in this crowd of troubled young people, and some of the diagnostic and treatment issues that are raised in each case. Then we will highlight some promising approaches in treatment and services today, and some issues for service systems and for our society.

Chapter 2

# A Modern Case of Schizophrenia

The young man you are about to meet and the other young people who appear in this book are fictional cases based on composites of people we have known or heard about. Although these stories are fictional, they are true to our experience in their outlines and their meaning. They are not uncommon stories. These are faces in the crowd of younger adults who are striving to live with illness, depression, anxiety—with problems keeping their thoughts on track or maintaining a stable mood, with distinguishing reality from delusion, managing high anxiety, governing their behavior, and meeting society's expectations—problems making viable lives in a complex and demanding world.

BILL'S STORY

Our first story is that of "Bill," a young man diagnosed with schizophrenia. The first voice is that of Bill's mother.

> My son Bill just stays in his room all day. I have to leave his food outside the door sometimes, or he wouldn't eat. He went away to college, but he had to come home. If I try to talk to him, he flares up so quick it scares me.

He is a tall, good-looking young man with a gentle, bemused look. He's a bit of a wag, quick to go for a joke, a play on words. He can argue his way around anybody when he's well. He's compassionate, always there if somebody needs him.

> He was always so kindhearted—he still is. When they were growing up, sometimes I thought he was the sweetest one. But everything was all right then.

Bill was born into a loving family, his parents still together after some 35 years. His father is in real estate. His mother is just a bit on the anxious side, so quick to be concerned about anything going wrong with any of her children—all of them now in their twenties, one married already.

> But that's love, isn't it? Isn't it normal to worry about the people you love? . . . Anyway, I wasn't always like this, believe me, not hanging on every word of his. I just took it for granted that they were all OK—all normal, at least.

There were no signs of trouble then, in elementary school, in junior high. It's true he was shy, at first, in a new situation; there were a few weeks, starting kindergarten, then first grade, then middle school, when he didn't want to go. But then he'd get on with it. He did better than average in his work and would make a few friends after a while.

> The teachers always said he could do well at anything. When it was time to think about college, he was able to get into a very good school. But that was where the trouble started.

For about a year, Bill did well in college, too—although there were signs of strain, high anxiety around exam time, staying up all night to write, becoming obsessed with the question of how he was doing, whether he could measure up.

> His roommate said afterward that he had a feeling Bill was just too tense. I mean, everyone was tense, but he seemed to get so worked up over everything, he was always worried. He would telephone when he was writing a paper and ask me, over and over, did I think it was good, did it sound OK? I just thought . . . it was a new situation again,

he always had to worry awhile until he could get comfortable. It was kind of his style, you know?

Then one night his mother called and Bill sounded odd. He would make only the briefest answers to her questions and finally said, "I've taken a vow of silence." It was sometime after spring break, before the last sprint to the end of the term. She called again the next day, and at one point he let slip the remark, "I know about the plan. . . ." "What plan? . . . What do you mean?" his mother asked. "You know. . . . What's going on," Bill replied. He hesitated, then continued.

Now I understand a lot of things I couldn't figure out before. . . . Like, the teachers keep talking about the CIA, and then they pretend it was all about something else. This one guy in class told me, "We're keeping an eye on you," and he, like, winked at me . . . then he claimed he hadn't said anything. But . . . why're you asking me all these questions? I shouldn't even tell you. . . .

That was on a Wednesday. Bill's parents quickly made plans to go up on the weekend. But the very next day the call came from the dean. Bill was sitting in his room, apparently meditating, not answering any questions, sometimes appearing to be in conversation with inner voices. In the hospital a day or so later he told a doctor he had taken no drugs, but had learned some disturbing information, and that now he understood he had a mission in life. He hoped he would be equal to it.

But *did* he take some kind of a drug? I always wonder about that, because since he's been home, he seemed more like himself for awhile . . . but I think he was using some marijuana, and I know he would drink, because sometimes he'd come home from being with this one friend that he still knew since high school, and he'd seem confused and spacey, and if I'd get near him I could smell the beer.

Bill was discharged when he agreed to go home with his parents. Reluctantly, he agreed to take some medication, and after two or three weeks spent mostly in his room he began to seem more his usual self. In a month, with his doctor's rather guarded permission, he went back to college. He no longer spoke about his mission and seemed to have forgotten what had happened. He returned to college in time to salvage his classes by putting on the pressure, staying up all night. But he was unusually quiet, his roommate said, and when he came home again for the summer he just wasn't his normal self. When his parents suggested getting a job, Bill readily agreed. But, day after day, he stayed in his room, and unless his parents insisted, he rarely came out. When September came, he didn't go back to school.

> It's so hard, you know? to say what's really a sickness and what might be just a passing problem. . . . I hear some of my friends worrying about their children . . . how they can't seem to find themselves, or they go through a period of not doing much and not knowing what to do next. But, I don't know, it's different with him. And of course, his father began to get angry about him hanging out and sleeping so late. . . . I suppose it was just his way of showing his worry . . . because sometimes Bill won't even get out of bed, he'll just sleep all day.

### *IS* IT SCHIZOPHRENIA?

Bill's case is not an unusual one. Young adulthood is the most common time of onset of schizophrenia, an illness that presents as primarily a thought disorder, and it often appears after a period of stress, such as the experience of going away to college, starting a job, leaving home. Schizophrenia is diagnosed by (1) an acute psychotic episode, when the person is out of touch with reality and suffers from hallucinations and delusions as well as a derailing of thought process, and (2) prodromal and residual phases before and after the episode, when less active symptoms of apathy, withdrawal, and some confusion may dominate the clinical picture. Specific deficits in brain functioning for a person with schizophrenia include trouble processing or screening stimuli in the environment, maintaining logical thought sequence, modulating emotional arousal and high levels of anxiety, and responding appropriately to "cues" in interaction with others.

One of the key questions for everyone involved when someone has an episode like Bill's is: Will this be a single episode of illness of unknown or unclear cause, or will it be the first episode of many in an ongoing mental disorder, with a deteriorating or at least a lifelong up-and-down course? In other words: Is it schizophrenia? Thirty years ago, and for some 100 years before deinstitutionalization, the answer to this question seemed much easier. Until recently, schizophrenia was the usual diagnosis in public mental hospitals, the justification for lifelong residence. Today, using DSM-IV, the diagnostic bible of the American Psychiatric Association, there are much more strict criteria to be met before a person can properly be given this diagnosis. Bill needs to have shown symptoms of the disorder for at least six months; short of that time span, he might be diagnosed with schizophreniform disorder, based on similar symptoms but not assuming a long-term course of illness. He must show the characteristic active symptoms of the illness: hallucinations, delusions, disordered thinking, and impaired functioning in more than one life role or activity. If he shows a disorder of mood as well as of thought, he might be given a diagnosis of schizoaffective disorder, with different implications for medication and other treatment. If he shows, or others report, evidence of alcohol and drug dependence, that too will be a part of his diagnosis in a progressive hospital.

SCHIZOPHRENIA AND YOUNG ADULT CRISIS

Why are the young adult years—the late teens and early twenties—the typical age of onset for schizophrenia? One hypothesis is a biological one—that perhaps the brain completes its maturation only at this relatively late stage of development, revealing only then a deficit with some earlier biochemical cause. From another perspective, complementing rather than contradicting the biological or neurochemical, we can reflect on young adulthood as a life stage that makes a heavy demand on the growing person's ability to function independently and autonomously. It is generally, in our culture, a time of leaving home, whether for college or to begin a job or simply to fulfill our cultural ideal of the young person signaling his maturity by setting up a separate, independent life. It is also, for some young people even today, the time of the first serious love relationship, and sometimes the first sexual intercourse. In other words, young adulthood in our society is a time in the life cycle that predictably provokes high levels of anxiety as the young person grapples with questions of where to go, what to do, whom to choose as companions and perhaps a life partner, how to separate from family and overcome excessive dependency, how to manage strong impulses and emotions, how to communicate meaningfully with others, and, in short, how to make it in the world.

Such life cycle issues have two major implications in diagnosing schizophrenia: (1) It is sometimes difficult, at least initially, to determine whether symptoms of "high anxiety" signal a life stage crisis or the onset of illness. (2) Given that schizophrenia involves certain specific deficits in brain function and interactive style, it is surely no surprise—whatever other causative factors might be involved—that it emerges in young adulthood, when a heavy demand is placed on the young person to step over the threshold to full autonomy.

In his book *Levels of Schizophrenia,* published posthumously, psychiatrist and family therapist Albert E. Scheflen (1981) discussed schizophrenia from historical, cultural, family, psychological, behavioral, and neurological perspectives, viewing these perspectives or systemic levels as complementary and interrelated rather than as mutually contradictory. Scheflen described the characteristic neurological difficulties of the person with schizophrenia—deficits in sequencing of thought, speech, and other motor behavior, modulation of mood and attention, and, in interaction with others, a commonly seen combination of overdependence on a partner and alienation or isolation from other relationships. Today, based on imaging techniques that are leading to new knowledge of the brain, we would add the characteristic difficulty of the person with schizophrenia in screening out and/or modulating stimuli, resulting for many people in chronic overstimulation and confusion.

Relating these brain or biochemical deficits to the task of the young person entering society, Scheflen pointed out that in our culture there is a high demand for mobility, separation from family, and individualistic action. As he put it, "[In Western industrial society] *it becomes a virtue to accomplish social mobility without psychosis*" (italics his). For a young person with schizophrenia, this means the creation of a demand that cannot be met effectively because she does not have the neurological equipment; it may be difficult or impossible to utilize the social cues we all have learned in order to find out how to act in a new social group, or to arrange tasks and work toward goals in a logical sequence, or even to keep thoughts on track and strong emotions under socially acceptable control. Schizophrenia is commonly a social disadvantage even when the person is not currently in a psychotic episode—that is, a period of being out of touch with reality and suffering from hallucinations and delusions as well as disorder of thought process. Even when the disorder as a brain illness is in remission, the person with schizophrenia may not be able to meet the demands of our culture. As a widely circulated poster puts it, "This life is a test. It is only a test. If it had been an actual life, you would have been told where to go and what to do." As Scheflen pointed out, in a simpler, nonindustrialized society with clear social roles and expectations, and with a strong, firmly holding network of extended family and close-knit community, the person with schizophrenia *would* have been told "where to go and what to do" by observing stable, familiar models of accepted behavior. In our culture, by extreme contrast, there is little of such clear instruction or guidance available for anyone, relative to the complexity and fast-changing nature of the society. There is certainly not enough for the vulnerable person. If that person becomes identified as a "psychiatric patient," he may receive such help, guidance, and support from a treatment agency, a case manager, and so on. But such support generally follows the personal disaster of a "first break" (a first psychotic episode), and the ongoing price for it is being labeled, by oneself and others, as a "mental patient."

## WHAT CAUSES SCHIZOPHRENIA? AN UNANSWERED QUESTION

What distinguishes young adults who are able to make it through the white water of this life stage and those who fall out as people with schizophrenia? That is a compelling question for researchers, for mental health services, and, of course, for families—not to mention young people who are trying to begin their lives. Together with the various hypotheses about what causes schizophrenia, there have been for many years ongoing studies of possible risk factors for developing the illness. A current focus in some research is the identification of populations of people who are vulnerable to developing schizophrenia, apparently because of neurochemical and/or genetic factors, but who may show merely subclinical or nonpsychotic symptoms in the absence of precipitating stress.

What is precipitating stress? In our culture, many of the normal experiences and challenges of young adult development and family interaction would fall into this category. The so-called average expectable environment may include such stressors as leaving home, losses or traumas, alcohol and street drug use, family illness, divorce or conflict, and/or other factors. "Dysfunctional" families and so-called "schizophrenogenic" family communication are no longer thought by most people in the field to be the cause of schizophrenia, although family interaction and communication have been found in studies to have a positive or negative effect upon its course, and this finding has given rise to the new psychoeducational approaches that offer family members information, guidelines, and support in managing schizophrenia. But the model of schizophrenia's etiology—cause(s)—that is widely accepted in the field today involves a neurobiological and/or genetic vulnerability, combined with unknown and diverse factors of precipitating stress and arousal.

Many younger adults are fearful of developing mental illness and hesitate to communicate their true feelings and anxieties through fear of finding out that they are as "strange" or "crazy" in the eyes of others as they may feel within themselves. This hesitation to share anxiety and confusion adds still more stress to an already difficult life stage. Parents like Bill's, whose sons or daughters have had an episode of mental disorder, wonder: Will this pass, like any other phase of development—or will it happen again? But they receive no immediate answer, as none is available even within the mental health professions.

However, schizophrenia is distinguishable from normal life stress reactions as it continues. The criteria for diagnosis clearly distinguish the illness once it emerges full-blown, and only in the initial stages does it masquerade as "normal" young adult anxiety or overlap with the symptoms of toxic psychosis (see below) or other transient psychotic reactions. Unfortunately, mental health practitioners often have to make diagnoses based on a one-shot evaluation in an emergency room. Family history of schizophrenia offers some indication that such a diagnosis might be valid, but often family information is unavailable, and in any case a family history is not definitive evidence that the illness is present or absent for a given individual. So a diagnosis is given based on whatever information is available and whatever symptoms can be observed. Unfortunately, the label schizophrenia, once pasted to the forehead of a person who is confused, incoherent, or overtly psychotic, tends to be a sticky one, used as a defining tag by treatment staff who take over the person's care. The current diagnostic criteria for schizophrenia, carefully applied, are a partial defense against this hazard—but are not sufficient in the absence of further evaluations of the person over time.

## MARIJUANA, COCAINE, AND SCHIZOPHRENIA

Alcohol and street drug reactions are a major cause of diagnostic confusion in the emergency room, as well as in the longer course of treatment. In the case of Bill, for instance, if there is any indication that he might have ingested alcohol or a street drug in the period before his episode—which might be determined by a urine screen or by information taken from family members or friends—the episode might be considered a toxic (drug-induced) psychosis rather than schizophrenia—especially in the absence of any family history of that illness. In the most up-to-date hospitals a drug test may be performed routinely upon admission, especially of a younger adult. If not, at least the psychiatrist should raise the question of whether Bill has taken any substance that could make him psychotic. Again, the information needed may not be available. And, even if the person has used alcohol or other drugs, that doesn't mean he doesn't also have schizophrenia. When people with major mental illness lived for the most part in institutions, and before use of marijuana, cocaine, and other street drugs became commonplace in the larger society, one could reasonably think: Is it drugs or mental illness? Today, there is, or should be, a high index of suspicion of alcohol and/or street drug use among younger adults, including those with major mental illness, and the well-informed clinician must look for alcohol and drug effects even among people who are not seen as substance-abusing, drug-dependent, or addicted.

Bill probably began drinking fairly large quantities of alcohol during his teens, and probably added marijuana to his normal recreational menu soon afterward. Since the 1970s an alert psychiatrist would also wonder about cocaine, by then a recreational favorite of adventurous young people who could afford it. A case of toxic psychosis induced by cocaine is not distinguishable from schizophrenia in the emergency room, for it too may feature hallucinations, delusions, derailed thought process, and grandiosity. Marijuana use also has been known to precede or mimic a first episode of schizophrenia. (In fact, there have been studies suggesting a higher-than-usual incidence of schizophrenia among young people who have made moderate to heavy use of marijuana over a given period of time—a subject to be addressed later.) Hospital staff learn whether a specific episode of psychosis is drug-induced only by observing the person to see whether the symptoms clear, by gathering both recent and family history, and by using the results of drug screening tests.

## THE QUESTION OF BILL'S FUTURE

The most harrowing question for Bill's parents—and probably for Bill himself—is: What's the prognosis? . . . What kind of future will he have? Here, the question Is it schizophrenia?, though still not decisive as a determinant, does become very important. If sufficient time has elapsed, and careful attention has been given to diagnosis, the criteria mentioned above will have been met:

- There have been symptoms of schizophrenia for at least six months.
- A clear pattern of illness has emerged, including prodromal symptoms (those leading up to the acute psychotic episode)

and residual symptoms of the disorder afterward (the passive or negative symptoms of apathy, withdrawal, and lack of motivation).
- There (usually) has been more than one episode of psychosis.
- Effects of alcohol and street drug use have been ruled out as causative factors for both the acute and the ongoing signs of illness.
- There is some indication (in most cases) of one or more family members having had schizophrenia or a related disorder.

If these criteria are not yet met, it hardly makes sense to think of the future as compromised by schizophrenia. If they are met, then it is important to think about how to manage the disorder in such a way as to minimize the damage and limitation caused by this chronic and sometimes disabling mental disorder. The first thing to say about this is that we cannot know, except over time, how this problem will affect a given individual, and neither easy reassurances nor dark forebodings are useful. Schizophrenia is a complicated disorder or (now considered more likely) a group of related or similar disorders, and we cannot know from a still shot of Bill's (or another Bill's) life how his individual future will unfold.

Thirty years ago, say in 1962, schizophrenia was regarded as virtually a death sentence, in terms of being able to lead a normal life. That is, it was the psychiatric equivalent of cancer, an illness about which we were once so phobic that many people would not utter its name. The reason for this attitude is clear in each case: we did not have much, if any, positive experience of people living with these illnesses, nor did we have a range of effective treatment approaches. As cancer was viewed as inevitably a terminal illness, schizophrenia was viewed as inevitably a downward path of deteriorating functioning from which there was no return. From that viewpoint, there was no point in even thinking about discharge from the hospital. Then, it became popular to refer to the "rule of thirds," which held that, among people who develop a mental illness, one third would get better and suffer no recurrence, one third would deteriorate and become increasingly disabled over time, and one third would continue an oscillating course with repeated episodes relieved by periods of remission. Today, we would say that, of ten people diagnosed with schizophrenia, one recovers completely, six recover but have further episodes, and three become disabled and are heavy users of services.

In general, schizophrenia is found to present a more persistent and pervasive problem in social functioning than, say, bipolar disorder (formerly known as manic-depressive illness), for the reason that the person with schizophrenia is more likely to experience, even in remission, residual symptoms that persist and impair the quality of life and of relationships. The person with schizophrenia seems more likely to find himself or herself on a downward path, with a progressive loss of functioning and therefore of status as more episodes occur—a course that may be determined by the neurobiological aspects of the illness as it impacts on brain function, and by the difficulty we have mentioned in processing social cues.

But today, there is much more knowledge about biochemical and genetic aspects of at least some forms of schizophrenia, as well as a much greater range of treatments. These treatments include both medications and ways of helping people during those lengthy periods when, like Bill, they are not experiencing an acute psychotic episode and therefore do not need to be in a hospital. There also have been long-term studies of people who had good care in the hospital and community; these have suggested that many people with this disorder can go on to live productively and without major episodes of illness in later life. But true schizophrenia does require understanding of its nature and implications, so that it can be effectively managed by treatment providers, family members, and the person who has the problem.

WHAT IS GOOD TREATMENT?

It is important to realize that treatment needs change depending upon the person's current condition and stage of illness, and in any case may differ from one person to another. Most important is the difference between acute stages of the illness, when active symptoms (thought disorder, hallucinations, delusions, erratic behavior) may predominate, and periods of remission, when the residual symptoms (apathy, withdrawal, lack of motivation, difficulty with planning and other goal-related functions, difficulty in processing stimuli, flat affect, poverty of thought and speech, social avoidance and isolation) are more prominent. Clearly, the young man or woman in an acute stage of illness may need hospitalization, perhaps involuntarily, and/or some other kind of protection from irrational behavior that may result from the illness, especially if the person has suicidal or homicidal thoughts and/or hears voices advising suicide or homicide. Involuntary hospitalization is also necessary if the person is simply so "out of it" that ordinary judgment and reality testing are impaired—e.g., if the person is wandering in the street without concern for safety. Any of these situations—danger to self or others based on psychotic thoughts, dangerous behavior, or life-threatening lack of judgment—provides legal grounds for hospitalization in most states.

Psychiatric hospitalization is not always easy to accomplish today, and inpatient episodes are kept as brief as possible in most institutional settings. This means that a person may be maintained in outpatient or day hospital treatment even when an episode becomes acute or may be discharged before the episode is resolved. Whether or not the person is hospitalized—and in most cases this does become necessary—medication needs to be prescribed or the dosage of usual medication raised to control the acute symptoms of illness. Also, in or out of the hospital, the person needs to be watched carefully and protected from any external danger and from his own dangerous impulses.

It is often extremely upsetting for families and others—including mental health practitioners—when someone who seems clearly in need of psychiatric care is not involuntarily hospitalized or is permitted to leave while still evidently confused or having delusional thoughts. These decisions on admission and discharge are generally driven by two major considerations: legal and economic. The first rests on a growing concern for the civil rights of psychiatric patients that was one of the major civil rights movements of the sixties. The second has to do with bed utilization review and with reimbursement for the astronomical and mounting costs of inpatient care. The stay of a person on an inpatient unit, especially if involuntary or relating to relatively subtle forms of mental disorder, is subject to the scrutiny of mental health lawyers, regulating agencies, and third-party payers. This often places inpatient treatment teams in a "Catch-22" situation when trying to deliver good care to a troubled person.

Some of the functions of the psychiatric hospital in care, protection, and support are performed today by acute day programs or partial hospitalization, in which the person has treatment and supervision during the day but goes home to family or a community residence/psychiatric group home at night. This kind of supplement to hospital care, combined with effective medication therapy, is really what makes it possible to handle schizophrenia in brief episodes of hospitalization—ranging from approximately one to three weeks. Most people in an acute episode do need to be in a hospital for a brief period, but most are able, with proper support and treatment on the outside, to keep the length of the episode to a minimum and to spend much of the recuperative period at home. This is not true, of course, if "home" is a city street or shelter for the homeless or any other unprotected, dangerous, unsupportive, or simply overstimulating environment. The person who has been hospitalized with an acute episode of major mental illness needs the same attention to recuperation and to the sometimes lengthy process of convalescence as does a person coming out of the hospital after a major operation or serious physical illness. In fact, experts in the field believe that recuperation from an episode of schizophrenia can take from six to 18 months and recommend that the affected person be given the opportunity to come back at as slow a pace as necessary to the activity and demands of everyday life. This may mean, for instance, letting the person sleep a great deal during the day, with only a minimum of household tasks to be performed, for a period of time following a hospitalization, with a gradual increase in activity as recuperation proceeds. This concept of a slow-paced recovery is not in accord with current practices in many day programs and community residences, where the guiding philosophy may call for as rapid as possible a return to full activity.

In our day there is a widespread treatment philosophy that favors very active treatment—the more active, the better—and allowing people to sleep is associated in our minds with a century of neglect of patients in institutional care. Family members and others are also eager to see the person coming "back to himself" as rapidly as possible. But this push for a quick return to normal activity does not suit the needs of the person with schizophrenia. Some of the "revolving door patient" phenomenon can be attributed to discharges that not only occur too early for some people, but send them back to settings that are unable to honor and protect the need to reconstitute at leisure.

In some cases, the family home is itself an overstimulating environment, for reasons that may be beyond a family's awareness or control. In many such situations, the family can be helped through multifamily group or individual psychoeducation and support to reduce the level of stimulation for a recovering person. In other cases the person may manage his illness better in a more neutral environment—although no environment, including treatment programs and group homes, is free of problems of high levels of stimulation and intense interactions.

Good treatment means somewhat different things, not only according to the person's stage of illness, but also depending on the nature of the treatment program. If the program is a short-term inpatient unit with an average stay of, say, 10 to 14 days, then the hospital or emergency room staff should be expected to:

- Make an initial evaluation and judgment call re: whether hospitalization is needed (either through its own evaluation or that of a related crisis service)
- Assess for possible alcohol/street drug use, and do urine and blood screenings
- Perform or arrange a physical examination and refer for any immediately needed medical care
- Observe and protect the person during the period of active psychosis
- Medicate the person to control active symptoms as needed, and reevaluate the diagnosis and medication needs day by day
- Confer and preferably meet with family members and significant others regarding the person's admission and discharge, as well as to explore and address any family or relationship problems
- Provide education re: schizophrenia as needed for both the person in treatment and family members

- Assess the person's life situation and treatment and support needs
- Involve other clinicians—e.g., substance abuse treatment staff —and case managers if needed
- Formulate and facilitate discharge plans, with input from the person and family
- Address current treatment issues—such as what precipitated the episode, early warning signals, and plans to handle similar stressors in future—through individual and/or group therapy
- Refer the person, engaging his agreement, for further treatment and recuperation in a day program or medication clinic, or other program needed or of his choice, and finally
- Refer the family for psychoeducational work—individual or multifamily group if available—to increase skills in managing schizophrenia.

## TREATMENT ISSUES

Clearly this list of functions is a tall order for today's psychiatric unit, which is commonly beset with a range of administrative, fiscal, psychiatric, community, and systemic problems as well as a heterogeneous group of patients and a need to keep hospitalization very brief. Yet—this is what needs to be done. A psychiatric inpatient unit no longer functions as a place where a mental disorder can be "cured." Rather, the goal is to address the crisis; to stabilize the person's behavior, thought process, and emotional state through medication, psychotherapy, and a calming milieu; to reevaluate and stabilize medication; and to engage or reengage the person in more extended treatment. In a private hospital the inpatient stay may be a little longer and there may be some effort to work with treatment issues that go beyond the acute episode. But even here most hospitalizations today are focused on the goals of stabilization, crisis intervention, and planning for discharge. The fortunate patient and family, who have the luxury of access to a good community treatment and support network, go on to an all-day rehabilitation program or some other form of outpatient care.

Day programs vary greatly in their staff and facilities, the number of people they serve, the other treatment and community resources available, and therefore their philosophies of treatment. A day treatment or partial hospitalization program oriented to acute care may be time-limited and goal-focused in its treatment, with goals of stabilization and return to community functioning. This kind of program may be used either as an alternative to hospitalization when possible, or as a transitional program that carries on some of the acute-care functions where the short-stay hospital leaves off. A psychiatric hospital that is linked with a day program has an enormous advantage in being able to offer continuity of treatment, with the inpatient episode itself kept as brief as possible, but without the sudden drop in the level of attention and support that accompanies many hospital discharges.

A day program that is not time-limited may function as an ongoing support center and source of medication and monitoring and supportive individual or group therapy for a person with major mental illness. Even for people who can afford the luxury of a private psychiatrist, a good day program may be a better choice or an important core component of supplementary treatment. Medication generally must be continued indefinitely (though sometimes changed in response to changing needs) in order to control the active symptoms of the illness. But that is only the beginning, for medication does not affect the "passive" symptoms, the person's tendency to withdraw and to have difficulty following a thought process or a course of action. The person with schizophrenia typically needs help in structuring the day and in relating with other people. Individual insight-oriented psychotherapy is generally not indicated, because it is not suited to the nature of the problem. Rather, social and work experiences and skill training in the tasks of daily life and interaction are much more to the point for most people with schizophrenia.

The picture may be quite different for a person with schizoaffective disorder—that is, with a combination of thought and mood disorder that presents as a close cousin of more typical schizophrenia. The person with this form of illness may show many of the same symptoms in an acute phase of the illness but may be much better able to function in everyday situations— school, work, social interactions—in periods of remission. This is both a blessing and a hazard. On the one hand, the need for training or retraining in social and work skills may be much less, and in fact the person may be well able to manage everyday life and pursue education, jobs, and interests. On the other, the person is much more likely to try to deny the illness and the vulnerability that goes with it—and more likely to be involved, like the major-ity of younger adults, in some form of alcohol and other drug use, as well as in social and love relationships—and sometimes mar-riage and/or parenthood—that may become an additional source of problems and stress.

Young men and women who show this combination of a vul-nerability to schizophrenic illness and an ability to do well between acute episodes commonly—and understandably—do not like to be identified or treated as clients in the mental health system. Like other people who are "patients" with a definable illness, they need education about their illness and how to manage it. But they also need access to school and work programs and opportunities that respond to their strengths and interests, while providing needed attention and support when there are signs of overstress. These higher-functioning young people—of whom 'Bill' may certainly be one—are a challenge to mental health treatment programs, and they also signal good directions in treatment for people at all lev-els of functioning—that is, toward treatment that speaks to the strengths and health of people rather than only to their symptoms of illness. There is a need to avoid infantilizing people in treat-ment and underestimating their potential for growth. At the same time, it is important for therapists and family members not to allow their own values and anxieties to pressure a young person to set more ambitious goals than she is currently capable of achieving.

## WHAT ABOUT THE FAMILY?

Good treatment of schizophrenia today must include education and support for families. Most people in the field today have come to regard schizophrenia as a biogenetic vulnerability, acti-vated into an illness by various possible stress factors, but not symptomatic of a so-called "dysfunctional family." At the same time, as we have more knowledge of the nature of the brain dysfunctions in schizophrenia, it has become clear that family members and "significant others" can play a crucial role in helping the vulnerable person to reduce stress in everyday life and communication, and to prevent crises from developing into full-fledged episodes of psychosis. The use of multifamily psychoeducational groups, as well as psychoeducation for individual families, has been shown in a number of studies to reduce rates of relapse and rehospitalization, by helping family members to create a low-stress and supportive environment and to reduce elements of anxiety and agitation in their own communications and everyday management of issues. (McFarlane, 1983) Even short of this specific kind of supportive and educational help, the good treatment system has a responsibility to educate family members about schizophrenia and other mental disorders, and to help families to create supportive mini-communities for themselves and their sons and daughters with mental illness.

This leaves aside the question of family therapy, in the more traditional sense of that term, for families with a member with schizophrenia. In earlier decades (the forties and fifties) there was considerable attention to the presumed role of maternal and family dynamics in the development of schizophrenia, and such concepts as the schizophrenogenic mother, the schizophrenogenic or dysfunctional family, marital schism, marital skew, and the double bind in communication had their heyday, among family systems-oriented theorists and therapists, as possible descriptions of causative factors in schizophrenic illness, and as indicators of what needed correction through family therapy or family-oriented treatment. These conceptualizations reflected a tendency to focus on environmental factors—today we would call them risk factors—in considering the etiology of illness, a tendency that has been greatly modified by the developments in genetic and biochemical research on schizophrenia. The environmental or family-oriented focus is still maintained by some family therapists who take issue with an exclusive focus on biochemical and genetic aspects of schizophrenia and with a corresponding reliance on psychoeducational approaches to family work. A family therapist with this viewpoint would regard family therapy as essential to helping the "identified patient," viewed as a kind of symptom bearer of family dysfunction, by working to restructure family dynamics.

The authors see this position as inadequate to the reality of biologically based illness, applying that term to at least some forms of schizophrenia. We also view psychoeducation as the most effective and most acceptable form of family work for many or most families, and as a fruitful initial approach even for those families and clients who may both need and want a more dynamically focused approach. We will address this among other family intervention and support issues in a later chapter.

## TEACHING ABOUT SUBSTANCE USE AND ABUSE

Finally, good treatment of schizophrenia today needs to include a core element of education and counseling around alcohol and other drug use, for both the client/consumer and the family. A person's substance use and abuse can make the difference between maintaining stability in the community and, on the other hand, coming into the hospital again with an acute episode. Young people with major mental disorders are commonly hypervulnerable to the effects of mind- and mood-altering drugs—and at the same time many young men and women are inclined to use drugs to try to self-medicate for uncomfortable levels of anxiety and depression, or simply in order to be "like everyone else" in their social interactions. A person recovering from a psychotic episode may turn to marijuana or cocaine to help him cope with early attempts to reestablish social contacts. Unfortunately, the person may be so excruciatingly sensitive to drug effects that minimal use may set off a serious relapse.

Providing carefully tailored treatment for mixed disorders of mental illness and substance abuse is a crucial and complex aspect of treatment planning, and the solutions are not simple. The "dual-disorder" or merely extra-vulnerable person is a major concern for mental health agencies today, and we will address it in detail in coming chapters. It is a problem that will emerge even more clearly in our next story.

Chapter 3

# The Rollercoaster

*Major Mood Disorder and Alcohol Abuse*

ANNIE'S STORY

She stands in the doorway of her room in the psych ward, ready to bolt if the conversation gets too hot, although she herself might do the overheating.

> I got really drunk last night. They brought me up to the Crisis Service, and they tried to reach you because I said you're my case worker, right? You weren't there, so they took me down to detox and put me in a sober-up bed. When I woke up this morning they tried to sign me up for a 28-day drug rehab. I told them I don't belong there, I'm mentally ill! They said I'd better sign myself in on the psych side, then. I said, "No way!" Then things got out of hand, you know how I get, and next thing I know here I am, back on the flight deck.

This young woman's history is very different from Bill's. She was always a "live wire with a short fuse," according to her father. Her older sister was an A-plus student in a private school. She herself was always in trouble. Her father said:

It's just her personality. . . . She couldn't take to rules, you know? And she was always full of life, especially as a kid. Later, she got kind of moody sometimes. . . . She always had some temper, I can tell you!

Early in her high school days her father took a new job and the family had to move.

We lived in a small town, and then suddenly she was flailing around in this big suburban high school. We didn't know who her friends were, though she always made friends. . . . That's the way she is, full of beans . . . jumping beans! She always landed on her feet . . . except for the past, oh, I don't know, five years or so.

Was it the move that sent Annie flying, the total, disorienting change of school and friends in those crucial years? This was certainly a factor in her development, but many families have to move and do so without losing their children to mental illness. For Annie, in those high school years, there was something else happening besides the move. Her family was slowly sliding into alcoholism—her father drinking, sunk in his own problems and trying to keep his job, one of Annie's brothers following in his footsteps, her mother unable to deal with it, not wanting to know any of it. Was there physical abuse? Sexual abuse? Such questions come readily to mind today. One answer often given, even without knowing her: Probably, somewhere along the line. But even that wouldn't explain the full range of Annie's problems.

Was it that she got onto drugs when she went into junior high school? Certainly they were there for the taking, on the street corner, in the schoolyard, in the bathroom, and for children much younger than Annie. And maybe Annie, being genetically predisposed to develop alcoholism, was just sliding down a path she was preprogrammed to follow, like her father and brother, from the time she picked up her first drink at age 10 or 12 or 13. By the age of 15 she was a "revolving door" patient, in and out of the sober-up unit and then the psychiatric ward—the only place where she could be held against her will, for long enough to try to help her get a handle on her life. Going into the hospital each time, she was clearly a danger to herself—as she is much more frequently than Bill in his life today. But, like Bill, even in an inpatient unit she couldn't be kept for more than two or three weeks at most.

There, in the psychiatric hospital, all the questions about Annie became still more confusing. She wasn't a "normal" alcoholic. Nobody saw alcohol as the cause of her frantic, manicky "highs," all-night stands of pacing and cursing and talking incessantly on the ward. Nobody thought it was alcohol that brought her in with some grandiose fantasy about touring the country as a rock musician as soon as she would brush up on guitar, or breaking into TV with a way-out script. Nobody thought it was only liquor that led to the increasingly serious suicide attempts she made, cycling through the hospital each time until some of her workers began to dread hearing news of her death.

She was diagnosed as manic-depressive—today we call it bipolar disorder—and given a medication, lithium carbonate, that helps many people to stabilize those wildly swinging moods. Lithium is a medication that must be taken with regularity and monitored with blood tests to be sure the level is high enough to be therapeutic but not so high that it is toxic. In other words, lithium is a medication that requires a compliant, cooperative, sober patient. It will be years before Annie is able to take this role in her own treatment. Jim, one of her caseworkers, says that what gets to him the worst is her awareness, that look of the alert, sentient being in her who sees what she is doing to herself. Maybe that's the vision she tries, again and again, to drown in alcohol or wipe out by suicide. She knows, she sees, but she can't stop that urge to self-destruction from running its course. Maybe, Jim thinks, she isn't getting the right help. Maybe those doctors and social workers just don't understand her. Maybe he's the only one who ... He stops, laughs at himself. She's pretty, too—but give her another five years like this and he fears that that fresh, bright look of hers—and maybe her life, too—will be gone.

"You guys tell me alcohol is a drug," Annie says. "But why are the drugs you give me any better? You say alcohol can destroy my liver? So? Lithium can destroy my kidneys, right? Isn't that why you keep testing me all the time? So you want me to get addicted to lithium, now? No, thanks, I'll stick to my own drugs!"

"But street drugs and prescribed medications aren't the same thing, get that message across," the doctor tells Jim.

"I know, I know," he says wearily. "Tell her."

A goal for Annie, one she sometimes agrees to, is to attend AA and see a therapist in the outpatient clinic once a week. She refused to go to a 28-day rehabilitation facility, although that has been recommended.

> Their rules are too strict. . . . You know I can't take rules! Anyway, they wouldn't take me—they say I'm mentally ill, I'm not welcome in an alcohol/drug program, at least not with my meds. I'll get sober on the outside, thank you.

And she has worked at getting sober. For a time she went to work, had a part-time job in a library, a little too quiet for Annie, but things were much better, it seemed. She didn't think she needed lithium anymore—she was probably just an alcoholic anyway. She stopped taking the meds.

It didn't take long: She began to lose sleep, pace around the house at night, corner her friends with rapid, intense accounts of some farfetched plans. She ran up bills, couldn't take care of her apartment. If anyone suggested she wasn't well, she'd fly into a rage. *She hadn't had a drink . . . or had she?* Later, she might have just one and it would precipitate an episode like this before she even had the chance to get really drunk. Or that black, bleak, irremediable depression would take over and she would try suicide again.

## THE PROBLEM OF DUAL DISORDERS

Annie—even more clearly than Bill—is one of the growing numbers of "dually diagnosed" people—those who have a major mental illness such as a mood disorder or schizophrenia, and *also* have a serious problem of alcohol/drug abuse. Until recently there has been no room for Annie at any of the "inns" of treatment; she isn't wanted anywhere, doesn't quite belong anywhere. She is persona non grata in the treatment systems, especially psychiatric inpatient units and drug rehabilitation facilities, because she doesn't fit neatly into any of the categories of people for whom the treatment is designed. And yet she is only one of a sizable minority—fast becoming a majority—of young men and women who don't fit these categories because they have dual or multiple problems.

It is ironic that during the century of the state hospital, roughly from 1850 to 1950, when public institutions kept mentally ill people locked up for years, maybe for life, people with mental illness could be seen as a truly separate category from those with alcoholism or other drug addiction. Most people had one problem or another—a mental illness or a drug problem, not both. At least, that's the way everyone saw the situation. Today, Annie is unusual only in not being an habitual polydrug user. She occasionally uses marijuana or dips into cocaine, but most of the time she sticks to alcohol—and that plus a major mood disorder is enough trouble for anyone. There is help for each of these problems; the trick for Annie and her helpers is to handle them *together.* When she is able to stay out of the hospital, all it takes is perfect coordination—to keep the lithium at the right level to stabilize her mood and prevent episodes of manic or depressive psychosis, and for Annie to use Alcoholics Anonymous (AA) meetings and her AA sponsor and alcohol treatment program for help in staying sober. But when one problem or another flares up under the wind of some internal or external stress, the interplay of the two disorders can be deadly.

And there is more to it than that. Annie is different from Bill: when she isn't drinking or suffering from her mood swings, she can make her way in the world quite well—unless she gets into a relationship that troubles her and/or starts having flashbacks about the past. Then, even with her medication and AA, she is back into deep trouble. The personality and the social skills that are unlike Bill's—that help her to get friends and jobs and things to do—also add to the possible sources of life stress. She is out there in the world of relationships, competition, and perhaps family life, with its associated memories that are all too clear. So it is a struggle of a different kind than Bill's to get through each night and each day without relapsing into alcoholism or drowning in a tidal wave of painful emotions.

We are learning a lot today about how to help people like Annie—though translating that knowledge into the language of the two very different treatment systems for psychiatric and substance abuse problems remains a challenge. And treatment is a struggle in any case. Because Annie does have additional issues of an emotional/psychological nature, her treatment must include not only medication for her symptoms of mental illness and support for her sobriety, but also psychotherapy, traditionally a process of exploring deeper feelings of deprivation and loss, shame, and a damaged sense of self. Often the work and pain of therapy itself provokes a crisis. How can these diverse forms of treatment be channeled to work together? Annie and her helpers are trying to stay upright on a tilting deck. A new job, a new awareness in therapy, a new toehold is quickly lost in the next slip backward, the slide once again into the cold ocean of a defeated life.

THE INTERPLAY OF ALCOHOL AND MOOD DISORDER

Today our conceptions of mental illness are focused on its genetic and neurochemical aspects. The pendulum of social and professional thinking that swings slowly between heredity and environment as causative factors has swung, today, to an extreme of biological/neurochemical/genetic concerns, in part through the influence of new knowledge and technologies. Studies of families with many members who have developed bipolar illness have been directed toward trying to identify one or more genes as a cause for the disorder, which is seen as primarily a chemical imbalance, to be controlled with medication. Family studies of alcoholism have also sought to identify genetic causes for at least some forms of the problem. One well-known study found that the sons of men with alcoholism were three or four times more likely to develop the problem than sons of a group of nonalcoholic fathers (Goodwin, 1993). Family studies of alcoholism have also found that mood or affective disorders—both nonpsychotic depression and major affective illness such as bipolar disorder (manic-depressive illness)—often coexist with alcohol dependence and addiction, and both disorders are found to run in families. Both major affective disorder—in Annie's case bipolar disorder, formerly known as manic-depressive illness—and some more moderate forms of depression are seen today as caused by or involving chemical imbalances, and surely it is not surprising that a mood-altering substance has a complex, sometimes devastating interplay with a mood-altering psychiatric disorder that is grounded in biochemistry.

The more that is learned about affective and substance abuse disorders, the more the overlapping of symptoms can be seen. So when we ask, Why was this child the one in her family who was so vulnerable to mental illness and dual disorder? much of the answer may lie in her genetic heritage. Annie may "take after" an aunt of her mother's who is vaguely remembered to have had some serious episodes of depression—or her mother's sister, "the wild one," who also was rebellious and given to angry moods and stormy behavior. But, for bipolar disorder as for schizophrenia, the apparent breakthroughs of science are often followed by a retreat or modification based on further studies. Meanwhile, we still do not know exactly how the effects of environment—the family, the school, the child's particular life circumstances—impact upon a genetic load that predisposes someone like Annie to mental illness.

## THE PUZZLE OF DIAGNOSIS AND TREATMENT PLANNING

Although Annie's story may seem unusually complex, it is common in today's treatment agencies, and it is not surprising that service providers wonder: What should we treat first? Given the many factors in Annie's background—genetic, psychological, family problems, alcoholism and possible physical abuse in the family, and her own high school drug use—her doctors and therapists have been plagued with recurrent questions. For instance: Does she really have an illness called bipolar disorder? Or is it, after all, the alcohol that has produced her unmanageable mood swings and wild behavior? Or has her use of alcohol and other drugs actually triggered a fluctuation in her brain and body chemistry that we identify as bipolar disorder? Or is she using alcohol in an attempt to self-medicate? For Annie and other people like her, researchers are just beginning to sort out these questions.

Diagnosing the affective disorders such as bipolar illness can be particularly tricky. When Annie was younger, when she first began to show the "acting-out" behavior that began to terrorize her family and her therapists, she could have been given quite a different diagnosis, such as borderline personality disorder (BPD)—an entrenched pattern of problematic emotional reactions and behavior—complicated by her reactions to alcohol and drugs. Someone with BPD in a severe form can show very strong, unmanageable feelings and swings of mood and the same kind of self-destructive behavior that we have seen in this young woman. A major difference would be that the person usually wouldn't become psychotic—out of touch with reality. There might be brief, transient episodes when she was reacting so intensely and seeing the world in such a distorted way that she could appear psychotic. Even more likely, the drinking and drugs—such as cocaine—could themselves produce psychotic reactions. Someone who has taken a stimulant such as cocaine or amphetamines ("speed") can be "speeded up" in her movements, speech, and sense of time and can lose touch with realities such as the dangers of driving a car at 90 miles an hour. Cocaine-driven excitement and agitation can mimic the manic excitement of the person with bipolar disorder, although the cycles and mood swings are generally slower with bipolar illness. And alcohol can mimic any psychiatric disorder, depending upon the individual's reactions to use and/or withdrawal.

It is noteworthy that today many people are diagnosed with bipolar disorder (manic-depressive illness) at earlier ages than the midlife years that were once considered typical ages of onset. One hypothesis about this shift is that early alcohol and drug use may have a predisposing influence, triggering the cycle of mood swings and attempts at self-medication. A person may have a first episode and may start a medication such as lithium carbonate in the hospital. But then a common pattern is for the person to be discharged, feel better for awhile, stop taking the medication, and then begin a process of mood destabilization that may escalate quickly and often ends with hospitalization. Unfortunately, as the person ascends into a manic state, he is increasingly unlikely to see the euphoria and grandiose thinking as a problem. Or the person may develop an irritable, aggressive mood in the manic phase of illness, perhaps with the added complication of paranoid ideas. Any suggestion that these ideas and feelings are early warning signals of an impending acute episode, as well as any argument for a return to medication or a brief hospitalization, is likely to be angrily rejected. The problem is often aggravated by increasing alcohol use in the manic phase and/or attempts at self-medication to stabilize mood with alcohol and other drugs. In fact, even without the signs of an acute episode coming on, many young people with bipolar disorder tend to drink while on lithium or, if they have been told this is unwise, to stop the lithium over weekends or for longer periods so they can feel free to drink. The fact that bipolar disorder is often experienced as exhilaration during the manic phase makes it very difficult to involve the person in relapse prevention, except in the form of contracts made in advance with a trusted therapist or buddies—and even these are likely not to stick when the manic state begins to build. The fact that people with bipolar disorder, unlike many people with schizophrenia, tend to be symptom-free and well functioning while on medication also makes it very difficult to hold to the protective strategy of staying on medication all the time.

In addition, some researchers today have observed that many young people with bipolar disorder develop a pattern of rapid cycling in which acute episodes of the illness occur with increasing frequency. It has been suggested by Post and colleagues at NIMH that bipolar disorder may be comparable to epilepsy in that successive episodes, as well as periods of alcohol and drug use, may have a "kindling" effect, making the brain ever more sensitive to the acute response—in epilepsy, a seizure, and in bipolar disorder, an acute episode of the manic or depressive type. Certainly this is consistent with what treatment providers often see as an extreme sensitivity to any use of alcohol and drugs, and the kindling phenomenon may also play a role in the earlier age of onset that we see today.

Certainly the diagnostician's task is not an easy one, and the constant flow of new knowledge makes that task more challenging and complex even as it offers new lenses through which to look at someone like Annie. Taken together, Bill and Annie, as examples of young adults with severe, persistent mental, emotional, and substance abuse problems, represent a large proportion of this book's population of concern. Each has a major mental illness plus additional problems with alcohol and/or drug use—in Bill's case the recreational use of beer and marijuana, with maybe a passing acquaintance with cocaine, and in Annie's case the full-blown, life-threatening disease of alcoholism. Both present a challenge in diagnosis because of the combination of mental/emotional/psychiatric disorder with substance use or abuse, though in Annie's case that challenge is more likely to receive its fair share of attention than in Bill's, simply because her substance abuse is more obvious. And both present a number of serious dilemmas in treatment, as clinicians try to figure out which problem(s) to treat first, which are predominant, which treatment system (psychiatric or substance abuse) offers the most relevant help, and how the person in question may be moved to accept it. These questions will be addressed further in Chapter 6.

Chapter 4

# Unbearable Sorrows

### Borderline Personality and
### Post-Traumatic Stress Disorder

ELLEN'S STORY

Imagine another Annie—that is, another adult child of alcoholism and abuse, but one who does not have a major mental illness such as bipolar disorder. She does not have the episodes of breaking with reality, magical and grandiose thinking, pressured speech and pacing, the escalation of the manic state that we saw in Annie. Yet she does have intense and fluctuating moods and reactions and seriously destructive and self-destructive patterns that get in the way when she tries to manage herself and her relationships. She can't make a life, she can't make it work, and her efforts to do so always seem to end in disaster.

Ellen shows the familiar pattern of borderline personality disorder, a constellation of emotional reactions and behaviors that severely hamper both her relationships and her personal emotional control. She feels isolated and friendless, yet, in the budding friendships that she does try to develop with other women, she quickly takes offense, cutting off a new relationship almost before it has begun. In responding to men she flings herself with abandon into a new relationship, idealizing each new lover as a Prince Charming who will carry her away from all her past sorrows.

41

When each man inevitably disappoints her in this romantic over-expectation, she is quick to respond with rage and an acute sense of abandonment. She experiences passion only with abusive, exploiting men, and when she meets someone capable of a kindlier relationship, someone who offers a potential for genuine intimacy, she panics and becomes numb and unfeeling. Lacking a firm, reliable sense of herself, she can barely tolerate the emptiness she experiences when alone, and she will seek almost any company to avoid it. In moments of despair she cuts her wrists and forearms, as if to regain a sense of being alive by having a specific, irrefutable sensation. At other times she finds herself awash in painful feelings, unbearable memories that come to her as flashbacks and evoke the pain and fear of childhood. She uses liquor and other drugs to cushion herself against these feelings, but lately these old friends are losing their power to keep her safe from her own inner world. In dreams, she is fleeing a monster that threatens to overtake and destroy her. In real life, she herself acts out the monster's rage.

## BORDERLINE PERSONALITY: CONCEPT AND SYMPTOMS

What is borderline personality disorder (BPD)? "Borderlines"—as some people disrespectfully call persons with these problems—often provoke a great deal of anxiety, confusion, frustration, and animosity—not only among family, friends, and other people they encounter, but also among mental health professionals. When referred to in training conferences, "borderlines" provoke a groan of recognition. When discussed at team meetings, they often inspire remarks that sound angry, impatient, exasperated, unprofessional. Why? What is the source of these extreme reactions? Perhaps the fact that people with BPD pull on our own hopes, fears, and vulnerabilities.

Ellen and other people with BPD—an estimated 70 percent of them women—characteristically show the following patterns:

*Emotional intensity:* They seem to overreact. They are acutely sensitive to situations in which they can feel criticized, rejected, abandoned, worthless. Their pain and fear may be instantly converted to defensive anger, even to rage.

*Behavioral intensity:* They may act upon these feelings in extreme ways, with temper outbursts, suicide attempts, and self-destructive and out-of-bounds behavior of various kinds. This behavior is frightening, often abusive to self and others. It is often referred to as "acting out" (of emotional conflicts) but responded to as the acting *up* of an unruly child.

*Emotional and behavioral instability:* They arouse a confusing mixture of expectations, for others and for themselves. Their ego states can shift markedly and with great rapidity. A person may seem very "together" at one time—reasonable, insightful, very capable of managing everyday life and even of high achievement—and at another time, not far removed, this same person may "lose it" and show a very different and much more disturbed picture. These rapid and unpredictable shifts can create a great deal of confusion for family members and treatment staff. The high expectations raised by the person's seeming capabilities are not fulfilled. What is promised is often not performed—whether the promise is of stable everyday behavior, carrying out a treatment plan, abstaining from substance abuse, or honoring a suicide contract—because the self who made the promise is not around to keep it. An added factor of alcohol and drug use is often part of the person's self-destructive repertoire and, of course, aggravates many of the problems.

*Splitting:* This is a primitive, unrealistic defense against anxiety and other painful feelings, and it is often characteristic of BPD. Splitting means that others are not viewed as having "good" and "bad" aspects or qualities or as being sometimes frustrating and sometimes gratifying of one's needs. Instead, the other person is idealized or devalued, perhaps both by turns; the other person is seen as *all* good or *all* bad, totally supportive or rejecting, depending on what is happening right now. There are similar shifts in the person's sense of self: a success, large or small, allows the person to feel good for the moment, but this sense quickly gives way to an "all-bad" feeling in response to a failure, a mistake, or simply the underlying "negative chatter" that always waits in the wings for the person with BPD—and this in turn may lead to a suicidal gesture.

The formal diagnostic criteria for BPD, as stated in the DSM-IV (the 1994 version of the *Diagnostic and Statistical Manual of Mental Disorders*) are:

- Frantic efforts to avoid real or imagined abandonment;
- Pattern of unstable and intense interpersonal relationships with alternating extremes of idealization and devaluation;
- Identity disturbance: persistent and markedly disturbed, distorted, or unstable self-image or sense of self;
- Impulsiveness in at least two areas that are potentially self-damaging (spending, sex, substance abuse, shoplifting, reckless driving, binge eating);
- Recurrent suicidal threats, gestures, or behavior, or self-mutilating behavior;
- Affective instability: marked reactivity of mood;
- Chronic feelings of emptiness;
- Inappropriate, intense anger or lack of control of anger;
- Transient, stress-related severe dissociative symptoms or paranoid ideation.

What do these symptoms or emotional and behavioral patterns mean? How do they come to dominate a person's life, wreaking havoc in relationships and engaging the person in such self-destructive actions? The answers are not simple; BPD is one of the more perplexing and disturbing types of personality disorder.

THE PSYCHOLOGICAL/DEVELOPMENTAL PERSPECTIVE
ON BPD

BPD is interesting and perplexing not only in its case material but in the diagnostic conception itself. It was originally conceptualized by Kernberg and others as borderline personality organization and was thought of as being "on the border" between psychotic and neurotic illness. From this perspective it has been viewed as a distortion or failure of early personality development, resulting in specific deficits in the formation of identity, reality testing in emotionally intense situations, and the development of more mature defenses (those that generally come later in development), such as repression, isolation, and intellectualization. Rather, the person uses what are considered more primitive defenses, such as splitting (seeing others as all good or all bad, idealizing and devaluing people by turns, splitting off negative and hostile impulses and experiences from positive ones) and projection (attributing to others one's own negative feelings—as when someone translates feelings of rage about a disappointment or slight into the idea that "She [the other person] hates me"). The personality, in other words, is not able to adapt to the vicissitudes of life with realism, tolerance, and an integrated, realistic view of self and others. The defenses used are so primitive, so extreme, and so poorly related to the world of others that they leave the person very vulnerable to stress and conflict, and to attacks both from outside and from within the self.

For Kernberg, this failure of personality development and maturation may result from an excess of aggressive drive on the part of the child, combined with excess frustration in the family environment during the process of development. For Kohut, founder of "self psychology," the problem lies in a failure or insufficiency of "mirroring" on the part of the parents or other caregivers—a lack of enough of the appreciative praise, empathy, and "cheerleading" with which attuned parents greet the child's exploration and growth. In discussions of treatment, Kernberg and others have emphasized the importance of structure, boundaries, and limits to contain the aggression and to permit the therapist to confront directly the person's primitive and aggressive responses and acting-out behavior. For Kohut and others, the central need is for empathy to make up for the earlier lack of nurturing and mirroring. Most people concerned with treatment have stressed the need for both structure—in the form of a firm contract and limit setting in the therapy—and empathy—a response that unfortunately is difficult for many therapists to maintain in the face of what feels like a barrage of provocative behaviors.

Margaret Mahler and colleagues added to the body of psychodynamic theory about BPD through her observations of infants and her highlighting the stage of separation and individuation between four or five months and 36 months, during which she observed four substages of development in the growing child: (1) Differentiation (four or five to eight months old): in which the infant begins to have a body image separate from the image of mother, based in part on normal experiences of frustration and delay. (2) Practicing (eight to 15 months): in which the child develops motor skills, begins to explore, and gradually moves away from the mother/caregiver for brief but increasing time spans and distances—always based on the stage of developing capacities and on the sense of safety and confidence that the mother will remain in place for his return. (3) Rapprochement (15 to 24 months): in which the child moves closer again to the mother, more insistently seeking a mirroring of his achievements and increasing independence. This stage is thought to include the bringing together of the good and bad experience and perceptions of the mother and oneself into an integrated image of whole persons with good and bad aspects. And finally, (4) On the road to object constancy (24 to 36 months): Based on the previous stages, the child is establishing and maintaining stable, reliable concepts of self and others and persisting whether or not the mother is (a) present and (b) gratifying the needs or wants of the child at the moment. In other words, basic trust has developed, the capacity to remember the (m)other as reliably present and, for the most part, a soothing and supportive presence, and to remember one's own strength and resilience even during a bad spell or experience, so that the child can begin to learn to soothe and reassure himself when necessary.

For those of us who are fortunate enough to have achieved, in development, a sense of object constancy, having a bad day doesn't utterly destroy our fundamentally good sense of ourselves. A disappointment, a slight, a failure, an embarrassment, even a betrayal or humiliation will not obliterate our underlying and fairly constant sense of being able to trust ourselves. We stand on a foundation of predominantly good experience, with a sense of being able to meet our challenges and master our problems, which has been built into us through the positive mirroring of what Winnicott (1965) called the "good-enough" mother or other caregiver, and through repeated experiences of mastering skills and solving problems. We know there is help for us, both from within ourselves and from others if need be, and we expect that things will return to normal or better, maybe tomorrow or the next day. In bad times, we soothe ourselves with that awareness, and we also feel able to make commitments, knowing that the "I" who makes them will still be the "I" who is expected to keep them, tomorrow or next week or even in years to come.

The sense of object constancy is also crucial to our relationships. It empowers us to hold onto positive feelings about another person, so that we don't leave and look for someone else with the first moments of disenchantment or episode of boredom, and even in a fight we don't allow ourselves to cross the line and seriously injure the other person, either physically or verbally. If we have a secure sense of object constancy operating in an adult relationship, we are able to maintain our feelings and our confidence that the other person is there for us, even during a period of separation. In other words, we rely on a sense of basic trust, in ourselves and our significant others, that must be built on the earlier foundation of basic trust or object constancy in our developmental process.

What has gone wrong, then, for the person who doesn't develop this basic trust or object constancy, and later shows the symptoms of BPD as an adult—the inability to be alone, to tolerate separation and disappointment, to soothe oneself, and to modulate the normal mixtures and shifts of good and bad feelings that are present in all human beings and relationships? One theory has been that the mother, because of her own emotional needs, had trouble tolerating the child's moving away from her during the process of separation and reacted by supporting the child when she was fearful and clinging, but not when she was acting more independent and venturing out into the world. Of course, the child in venturing forth and practicing her developing motor skills still needs the reassurance of the mother's encouragement and her "being there" for the child. If the mother (or other caregiver) withdraws emotionally whenever the child follows her own biologically based program of increasing activity and independence, the child, according to this theory, would suffer from an "abandonment depression" resulting from the mother's rejection. This, in turn, would hamper the child's development of a solid, reliable image of the mother, a sense of "object constancy"; instead she would remain at an earlier stage of psychological development, continuing to separate the good (or accepting) image of the mother from the bad (or rejecting) image in her mind and would carry this tendency to split into other relationships.

This interpretation places a heavy emphasis on the psychological aspects of development and of the mother/child relationship. But from a contemporary perspective, many other circumstances come to mind that can hamper a child's development of a secure sense of self and others. Separation from the mother (or other caregiver) early in life is one such possibility, as well as serious illness or hospitalization, physical or mental illness of the parent, a traumatic or preoccupying family crisis, overwhelming needs of another child, a problem of substance abuse or other compulsive behavior in the family, or simply a lack of effective models of how to parent, leading to various forms of deficient, neglectful, or abusive care. Sexual and/or other forms of physical abuse are of course the most overt form of deficient parenting, at one end of an entire spectrum of behavior that may impact upon a particularly vulnerable child as excess frustration, too little mirroring, and/or apparent rejection of or assault upon the growing child.

THE STRUGGLE OF THE CHILD—AND THE "ADULT CHILD"

What does all this mean in the life of a person like Ellen? The family dominated by alcoholism has been highlighted as one kind of breeding ground for the problems of BPD that Ellen presents. Ellen was the eldest in a family with two alcoholic parents. Her mother was a secret drinker, taking her whiskey in coffee cups and easing herself through the day with it, until after dinner she gave in to an irresistible undertow of sleep. It was Ellen who put the children to bed and then put supper on the table for her father, who came home late and usually drunk. It was she who stayed up with him and watched TV and humored him any way she could. When he began to stroke her, at first with a semblance of the affection she craved and then in ways that were unmistakably sexual, she tried to avoid and placate him. When he began using force and threatening what he would do if she ever told her mother, Ellen began to take refuge in a secret place inside herself, where nothing bad was happening. She became adept at closing off her feelings and her awareness of what was going on, until gradually she became someone who could not afford to feel or to remember. Denial and dissociation are skills she uses now instinctively, whenever she seems to need them. Like so many efforts at control, the defenses she needed as a child now threaten to destroy her emotional life as an adult.

A child in Ellen's situation has no escape, no refuge except to deny reality and avoid feeling altogether. As an adult, such a child is often an "overdoer," compliant and perfectionistic, as if constantly working overtime to vanquish a sense of shame. Ellen tries desperately to overcome the feeling of degradation that she feels, and to pretend to herself and others that the intolerable events of her childhood never happened. But the truth is acted out in her inability to trust others, and in the chaos and self-destructive choices of her romantic life. Having been abused as a child, and not having her own childhood needs met, she is likely to choose relationships that repeat the experience of neglect and abuse—as if, through what Freud called the repetition compulsion, she might gain another chance to take control of uncontrollable events in her own life.

## THE CONCEPT OF TRAUMA AND POST-TRAUMATIC STRESS

As an adult child of alcoholic parents and a survivor of sexual abuse, Ellen can also be viewed as having symptoms of post-traumatic stress disorder (PTSD). Her childhood experience represents one category of trauma in its broader definition, including not only one or more specific and shocking events, but an ongoing pattern of traumatic experience that distorts development and has a lasting effect on a person's adult life.

A trauma or traumatic experience is by definition an experience that overwhelms the child or adult personality. It is something outside the bounds of ordinary, expectable experience. It is something unanticipated, unacceptable, shocking, which threatens the person's fundamental sense of safety in the world. It is an experience that arouses strong emotions that overwhelm the person's inner defenses, much as a flooding river overflows its banks or sweeps away flood barriers. The person, child or adult, is unable to pre-vent, control, or moderate the experience. There is no escape.

Thus broadly defined, the concept of traumatic experience can be applied to many different kinds of trauma encountered by chil-dren and/or adults. There are public disasters that are shared at the time by many other people—an air raid, an earthquake, a fire, ex-periences of combat and captivity—and yet each individual has private memories and a unique context of experience in which these memories lodge. There are individual experiences that are traumatic to some degree to any adult—such as rape, robbery, vandalism, a serious auto accident, or witnessing a sudden death, and these generally have psychological sequelae that are common and predictable, such as anxiety, panic attacks, nightmares, and flashbacks. And there are the traumas of childhood that have be-come all too familiar to the contemporary public through the media: those of being threatened, physically and emotionally injured, and/or sexually used and abused by a trusted person, whether on one or more distinct occasions, or over time, as an on-going life circumstance. These various types of trauma are diverse but, as Judith Herman has discussed in depth in her book *Trauma and Recovery* (Herman, 1992), they have in common the basic characteristics of traumatic experience: that it overwhelms the ego and sense of self, fundamentally disturbs the sense of safety in the world, and provokes strong, sometimes unmanageable emotional responses. Treatment for the aftermath of traumatic experience is concerned with helping the person to reestablish a sense of safety and control, to recover a viable sense of self, and to resolve and master the powerful emotions that have been provoked.

For a child, the experience of helplessness before the abuse of adult power is complicated by another factor: the child's immatu-rity and lack of ego defenses, and the fact that the child's personal-ity is still in the process of development. For the traumatized child the only available defenses are those erected in desperation. One such defense is the shield of numbness or dissociation: *I don't feel anything . . . I'm not really here. . . .* Another is the acceptance of pain and abuse as one's just deserts: *I deserve it . . . I'm not worth any-thing. . . .* Still another is the identification with the aggressor that may lead a child to take the path of aggression and abuse as his or her own way out of suffering. Children find ways of surviving childhood—but only to bring the numbness, the self-denial, the rage and fear into their adult lives.

Here is where the syndrome and the diagnosis of post-traumatic stress disorder come in. For many adult survivors of childhood abuse, acute symptoms of this disorder—flashbacks, nightmares, panic attacks, suicidal impulses—continue to destroy any sense of emotional safety, threatening to return whenever the unpredictable stimuli that are linked to buried memories and feelings set them off. When the abuse has been recurrent or ongoing over a period of time during the child's development, such profound and pervasive aspects of personality as chronic depression, inability to trust, self-loathing, and avoidance of intimacy are likely to be ongoing and disabling facts of life.

The most insidious aspect of these problems is that the adult survivor of this childhood victimization may not recall the events that have led to such distortions of normal personality development. If the child has dealt with traumatic experience by dissociation and suppression of memories, there is clearly a heavy investment in keeping these buried memories—and the unsupportable pain and confusion that they contain—under cover, hidden even from oneself. The current debate about the validity of recovered memories of trauma reflects both this important problem in treatment and our new-found social concern with child sexual abuse.

The concept of childhood trauma has been familiar since the development and spread of Freudian psychoanalytic theory as an explanation for mental and emotional disorders. The psychoanalytic method used to recover buried memories was based on the hypothesis that traumatic experience of a single episode or an ongoing pattern of abuse gave rise to symptoms unconsciously designed to manage the person's otherwise unmanageable anxiety. This idea acknowledges the child's developmental immaturity and unavoidable lack of strong, well-developed ego defenses against overwhelming feelings and traumatic events. The intense fear, pain, or shame that may be evoked by a particular experience—or a repetitive pattern of experience—from which there is no escape overruns a child's ego boundaries and drowns any sense of mastery and effective coping. The feelings of helplessness that

result are terribly damaging to development, because our person-
alities develop through and thrive on a growing sense of mastery
in confronting life's problems. When we are forced to evade the
resolution of problems and painful feelings, because these are
simply too powerful for the immature self or ego to master, we are
forced into a loop of avoidance that may consist of substance
abuse, suicidal or other self-destructive behavior, binge eating,
temper tantrums, social withdrawal, depressed sleep and fatigue,
running away, sexual promiscuity, and/or other compulsive patterns, including dissociative states in which feelings and sometimes the sense of reality are cut off, or psychotic episodes in
which hallucinations and delusions become indistinguishable
from reality in a confused flood of stimuli. The specific pattern of
the avoidance and/or acting out of the problem is chosen from the
possibilities available, given a person's age, peer group and environment, and any individual and/or biological factors that may be
present. The avoidant "loop" behavior or aversive mental state relieves, for the moment, the disabling anxiety, despair, or rage that
threatens to flood the self. But it cannot serve to resolve the problem, nor can it allow for personality development and maturing.

THE LEGACY OF ALCOHOLISM AND ABUSE

In family histories of alcoholism, there is a higher-than-usual
prevalence of major mood disorders. Similarly, borderline personality disorder (BPD) is often linked to a history of family violence,
physical abuse, and sexual abuse. Some studies indicate that from
50 to 80 percent of people diagnosed with BPD also report histories of being sexually abused as children (Saunders and Arnold,
1993). These histories, in turn, are commonly associated with alcoholism in the family. Alcohol is a disinhibitor—it softens the
barriers, blurs the boundaries, fades the lines one mustn't cross
over. The alcoholic father is often someone who behaves abusively toward his wife, his children, and various other people. The
angry man or woman erupts into physical rage; the violence and
sexuality leap the boundaries between children and their parents,
their supposed protectors. The alcohol loosens the structure of
the family, releasing each day's potential for chaos and neglect.

The only recourse of children is not to think, not to feel, not to know, not to tell, not to come home.

Of course, there can be reasons other than alcohol for child abuse and neglect—mental illness, emotional states of rage, frustration, and depression combined with poor impulse control, explosiveness, the parents' own histories of being neglected and abused, and the pressure of other needs. Whatever the reasons in specific families, there is an apparent epidemic of child physical and sexual abuse in our society today—or else it is the knowledge and telling of abuse that has erupted, highlighting for our attention these multiple assaults on the trust and bodies of both female and male children. One survey found that 80 percent of female patients applying to a mental health center stated when questioned that they had been victims of incest.

Both adult children of abuse and other adults with post-traumatic stress disorder show a range of characteristic symptoms and behavior patterns, including disturbances of emotional states and of such cognitive functions as memory, attention, and concentration, as well as damaged trust, self-esteem, self-confidence, and capacity to engage in relationships. It has been pointed out that many of these symptomatic patterns coincide or overlap with the criteria used to diagnose BPD, a personality disorder that often involves very unstable moods, self-destructive behaviors, and disrupted relationships. This raises an important question: Are people diagnosed with BPD, many of them women and many with a history of being abused in childhood and/or as adults, merely showing the natural sequelae of these abuse experiences? (Saunders and Arnold, 1993) This question is likely to be explored in depth during the next few years as we continue to struggle with the meaning of borderline personality. Suffice it to say here that the characteristic patterns of BPD, if indeed they can be separated from post-traumatic stress disorder (PTSD) based on abuse, surely complicate the process of managing memories of traumatic experience as they emerge in treatment. An influx of such memories is difficult for anyone to manage, and so is the stress of a crisis situation or traumatic events in the present, such as rape or domestic violence. When such present events and/or past memories flood in upon a person who is especially vulnerable to intense feelings, the level of stress can be devastating—especially when, as often happens, abuse in the present is laid upon the painful ground of abuse in the past. When a woman or man has never achieved a constant sense of self or others, the skills of self-soothing are not readily available, and it may be difficult or impossible, just as in childhood, to "turn off" the floods of panic, self-loathing, and despair.

## TREATMENT PROBLEMS FOR BPD AND PTSD

The personality disorders, BPD in particular, were at one time thought to be untreatable. In more recent years, a substantial body of theory about BPD treatment has developed, most of it relating to psychodynamic interpretations of BPD problems. Most theorists have stressed the key principles of structure and empathy in the treatment relationship. Kernberg's focus on borderline personality organization and the primitive defenses used to manage high levels of aggression has led to an emphasis on structure, limit setting, and confrontation of such defenses as they emerge in treatment. Kohut's self-psychology and focus on the failure of mirroring has led to an emphasis on empathy on the part of the therapist—sometimes required to an exquisite degree as the person's extreme vulnerability to slights and seeming rejections emerges in treatment. Whatever the particular emphasis, most theorists on BPD have assumed a therapeutic process lasting two years or more, with sessions held at least twice a week, and sometimes involving inpatient treatment for adolescents with BPD behavior.

But clearly these assumptions in treatment planning do not match the realities of contemporary treatment. Even before the advent of managed care, treatment for BPD, especially in the public sector, has been severely hampered by these realities, which include:

*1. Brief hospitalization:* Most inpatient hospitalizations today, especially for adults and especially in public hospitals, but also in private facilities once designed to be long-term, are too brief for any meaningful therapeutic work with a traditional psychody-

namic orientation. The hospital has become a brief crisis intervention for most people and cannot offer the groundwork for
deep-seated or far-reaching personality change. This often leaves
staff, especially those familiar with psychodynamic theory about
BPD and its treatment, feeling frustrated, demoralized, and un-
sure about how to intervene. Added to the sometimes frustrating,
alarming, and provocative behaviors of many BPD clients, this
problem often results in blaming the victim.

2. *Diversity of client populations:* In both hospital units and day
treatment programs, the diversity of clients makes it difficult to
target treatment to BPD problems. The needed attention and empathy, combined with consistent structure and limits, are often
not available in the mixture of needs presented by other clients,
some with major mental illness. In the day program, too, the vulnerability and acting-out behavior of many BPD clients may
arouse frustration and hostility in the absence of viable treatment
models.

3. *High cost/low availability of long-term individual treatment:* Individual therapy sessions twice a week for two years or more has become an option only for the affluent.

4. *Screening criteria for group treatment:* Although many people
with BPD patterns may be selected for therapy groups when they
present with anxiety, depression, relationship problems, parenting
issues, and so on, many more—those people with more severe
symptoms—may be seen as too fragile, demanding, "difficult,"
dangerously at risk, and/or primitive in their defenses for traditional group therapy to be effective or even possible.

5. *Staff turnover:* Especially in agencies where there is high staff
turnover, it can be very difficult to establish an effective long-term
treatment alliance with an ongoing sense of trust. Staff turnover
also can lead to discontinuity in the treatment approach, with different perspectives on how to manage the person's therapy.

6. *Inadequate linkage:* Since people with severe BPD problems
are likely to need a range of services, sometimes including case
management, substance abuse treatment, and frequent shifts from

inpatient to outpatient care, the need for consistent goals and treatment methods among various caregivers may go unmet, and the person's own tendency to deal with stress by splitting staff may be seriously disruptive.

7. *BPD symptomatic problems:* Borderline personality disorder itself often involves frequent and serious difficulties in relationships, in reality testing, and in self-management. The person tries to trust and to get help, but is often derailed by fears of closeness and by the primitive defenses of denial and projection, leading to many instances of feeling rageful and abandoned by caregivers. These reactions often result in interruptions of treatment relationships, limit testing, and other provocative behavior leading to rejection by therapists and treatment units and other serious treatment issues. It is often clear that treatment staff are reacting inappropriately to BPD behavior, and at the same time the frustration and stress created by some clients' behaviors are undeniable.

8. *Self-damaging behaviors:* Suicide threats, gestures, and attempts, self-mutilating, dangerous behavior, and physical acting out of rage by hurting or threatening other people or their property can result in hospitalization and/or police interventions that interrupt treatment, distract from therapeutic work, and create fear, rage, and chaos in relationships.

9. *Alcohol and other drug use and abuse:* Many people with BPD and/or PTSD problems make use of alcohol and other street drugs to numb and avoid feelings. This is another of the self-damaging behaviors that can derail treatment, since substance-induced changes in both mood and thinking can impair reality testing, increase confusion, intensify or mask feeling responses, reduce motivation for change, and obliterate the memory of agreements made and limits acknowledged in the treatment relationship. Deficiencies in the ability and willingness of mental health and substance abuse agencies to work together can result in extremely uncoordinated care and/or in mutual rejection of the dual-disorder client.

10. *Denial and rejection by the treatment system:* Even without the specific and extremely common problem of substance use with

BPD, people with this disorder, many but not all of them women, may be rejected by treatment systems as not having a major mental illness. Some state psychiatric institutions reject BPD clients, accepting only people with schizophrenia, bipolar disorder, and other illnesses involving psychosis. Some clinics may adopt a policy not to accept for treatment a client known to be "difficult." These policies and attitudes ignore the serious risk behaviors and equally severe dysfunctions of many people with BPD, some of whom are certainly as seriously impaired in their ability to manage their lives as a person with "psychotic" mental illness. The client identified as having PTSD and not showing severe BPD symptoms or substance abuse disorder may fare much better in the treatment system—which raises again the interesting question: Is BPD only or primarily an overt and pervasive form of PTSD, perhaps as the result of tramatic experience for a person biologically vulnerable to emotional dysregulation?

For people with PTSD, including BPD-diagnosed persons who have histories of abuse and some PTSD symptoms, there may be more empathy and receptivity on the part of caregivers, but there are other concerns in treatment. Part of our heritage from Freudian psychoanalysis is the assumption that, if someone is suffering from a traumatic experience, the way to health lies in dredging up the feelings and memories associated with the experience, including or especially those that have been numbed, buried, and forgotten, "working through" the pain and discharging the emotion as a way of finally letting it go. This concept of therapy as the recovery of buried memories and unbearable sorrows and their relief through a process of catharsis is fundamental to the tradition of psychodynamically oriented psychotherapy. But psychoanalysis also has recognized the importance of pace and timing in that effort. The danger in working with any memory or awareness that has had to be repressed, isolated from consciousness, or buried—and certainly with the highly emotionally charged memories of sexual and other physical abuse—is that of flooding the ego, or the conscious, integrating self, with an overload of feeling that the person is not equipped to handle.

When substance abuse or dependence is also a factor, the hazards of recovered memory become still more serious. Uncovering and integrating the feelings provoked by early experiences of violation is viewed as a crucial task for many ACOAs (the support-group shorthand for "adult children of alcoholics")—and other women and men with PTSD and/or BPD symptoms—and for their therapists. But the timing of direct attention to the hidden, underground level of emotional damage is crucial, especially when alcohol and other drug use is a person's habitual way of dealing with painful emotions. It is vital for the person to gain both support and new skills in managing these emotions before or during the process of stimulating and discharging remembered feelings and events in therapy. When such powerful emotions are revived and explored, that revisiting must be done with careful attention to pace and timing. The person needs to be assured that he can get the necessary support, from the therapist, from a network of others, and increasingly within the self—in order to brave the seemingly mortal danger of confronting the truth of past events and emotions. Without this care in timing it is all too easy—and all too necessary—to plunge again into the eddy of compulsive and self-destructive behavior, in order to avoid the "river wild" and the terrifying plunge over the great waterfall of fully recovered awareness.

This problem of emerging memories or flashbacks—replays of traumatic experience—is probably the worst danger in working with people with PTSD and BPD patterns, both those with dual disorder and those who are not substance abusing but who may have other self-destructive behaviors. The process of emotional reliving can easily trigger a relapse or a suicide attempt, especially when that reliving is taken on too quickly or before the person has learned to manage intense, overwhelming levels of feeling.

How can this concern with timing be reconciled with the idea that the goal of treatment is a catharsis or discharge of the painful feelings, without which not much can be accomplished in therapy, and that the more emotion a person can get at and bring out in therapy, the better? For that matter, how is it possible to control the pacing of the emergence of memory and emotion? In fact, many people with PTSD and/or BPD present flashbacks, panic attacks, raging outbursts, and sudden, unmanageable despair as their most disturbing symptoms, involving unbidden memories that they experience as intolerable.

## SEQUENCED AND MULTIMODAL TREATMENT

One approach to this problem, as well as to some of the other therapeutic and systemic problems we have mentioned, lies in entering BPD and PTSD issues by a different avenue—sequenced treatment, employing cognitive-behavioral and psychoeducational approaches, combined with individual or group psychotherapy either concurrently or in series, according to the needs and capability of the client and the treatment agency. Sequenced treatment basically means therapy consciously arranged as stages or treatment modules that may have different goals and quite different approaches. Cognitive-behavioral, psychoeducational, or skill-training modules designed to teach management of intense and problematic emotions are urgently needed for someone attempting to explore painful problems in therapy and visited with painful emotions in daily life.

A leading innovator and proponent of cognitive-behavioral work with women with BPD is Linehan, who has developed a treatment protocol (dialectical behavior therapy) for BPD that combines individual treatment with a skills-training group in emotion regulation, distress tolerance, and interpersonal effectiveness. Linehan has published a theoretical and research-based discussion of this treatment (Linehan, 1993), together with a *Skills Training Manual* utilizing a number of exercises and handouts, that offers a very useful guide to the type of treatment that is needed for BPD. In Linehan's model, the individual therapy and skills-training groups are concurrent, although provided by different staff—a therapist and a "trainer." The combination of development of new skills and cognitive retraining to be used in the here-and-now with a therapeutic holding relationship to contain and further modify problematic emotions offers a valuable two-pronged approach to BPD problems.

For the individual therapist working alone with a PTSD/BPD client, sequenced treatment may not be available as a team effort. But it may mean that, instead of going directly to the traumatic events or trying to access a flood of painful memories early in treatment, the therapist for someone with post-traumatic stress disorder will maintain a careful balance of empathy, support, and caution, not encouraging the person to "spill" too quickly or to go rapidly into areas or topics that seem to be fearfully defended, yet conveying confidence in the eventual process of gradual exploration. The careful therapist supports and validates the person's ability to slowly gain mastery over the emerging memories and the chaotic tides of emotion that come with them. The therapist also needs to protect the person, insofar as possible, against too rapid a recovery of lost memories, and with them a flooding of intense emotions that are likely to re-evoke the original trauma in all its intensity. Coming too quickly back into awareness, such memories may drive the person to seek refuge in further numbing or acting out of feelings that she has never learned to tolerate, understand, or contain.

Perhaps most important, the therapist needs to help the person with practical, direct, carefully taught strategies for dealing with painfully intense emotions as they arise. This need for skill training in emotion management—again, combined with a genuine, empathetic "holding relationship" with the therapist—may be the most important factor in treatment, especially in the early stages. Whether the problem is clearly one of post-traumatic stress disorder or is a more general difficulty with overly intense emotional reactions and other BPD patterns, the capacity to manage feelings, seek help and soothing from others, and ultimately learn techniques of self-soothing is fundamental to developing trust and experiencing the therapy—both the process and the relationship—as a safe place. It is also fundamental to developing the confidence to deal with life events with a sense of mastery and self-control, whatever the original or underlying basis for the hyperarousal of panic, rage, and despair. Everyday life, and the treatment relationship itself, cannot wait upon the uncovering of underlying problems and buried memories. Emotional reactions and behaviors that interfere with relationships, with personal safety, and with the therapy itself need to be addressed initially, by means of skill development and carefully planned strategies for managing the pain.

Only then, and gradually, is it safe to explore the deep underground of emotion and memory.

These two aspects of treatment—learning to trust the healing and soothing relationship with the therapist, and learning the skills of soothing oneself—ideally are combined and provided over time. When that is not possible, the therapist may offer a way of combining treatment modalities that are more immediately "portable," such as skills training, with the more traditional, slower-acting, and perhaps deeper and farther-reaching forms of psychotherapy.

Chapter 5

# Diagnosis, DSM-IV, and the Biopsychosocial Model

NAMING THE PROBLEM: THE MULTIAXIAL FRAMEWORK
OF DSM-III, IIIR, AND IV

Looking at the faces of these three young adults—Bill, Annie, and
Ellen—we need to look through a number of lenses to see every
feature of their problems. One lens is that of psychiatric diagnosis,
which itself has offered us, for the past 15 years, a much more
multifaceted picture than before. In the United States our standard instrument for diagnosis has been the *Diagnostic and Statistical
Manual of Mental Disorders* (DSM) published by the American Psychiatric Association. Between the second version (DSM-II) of this
manual and the third (DSM-III), published in 1980 and followed
by DSM-IIIR (Revised Edition) in 1987 and DSM-IV in 1994,
there was a giant leap into the multiaxial or five-axis framework
for diagnosis. This multiaxial system invites the clinician to look
at and utilize all aspects of a person's problems. Unfortunately, the
opportunity to look at everything is often not used when diagnoses are made, but we should appreciate how far we have come
from the DSM-II, which, like physical medicine, sought a single
diagnosis to account for all of a person's symptoms.

Basically, the multiaxial system invites or even requires us to look at each person as a human being—not just as a mental illness such as schizophrenia or a presenting symptom such as anxiety or depression. You are looking at a human being, the manual reminds us, with ongoing personality traits and sometimes disorders, with physical problems in some cases, and with ongoing life stressors and sometimes extremely stressful events. Do not try to explain everything in terms of an illness. Recognize the human face and the surrounding world in which the illness or symptom occurs.

Briefly, the axes of DSM-IV and its predecessors are used as follows:

*Axis I.* Clinical syndromes and V codes—e.g., schizophrenia, major affective disorder, other dysthymic disorder, anxiety disorder, adjustment disorders, eating disorder, substance abuse, marital or parent/child problem

*Axis II.* Developmental and personality disorders

*Axis III.* Physical disorders and conditions

*Axis IV.* Severity of psychosocial stressors

*Axis V.* Highest level of adaptive functioning

One useful way to think of DSM-IV is to regard each axis as the axle of a truck. Let's call it the Assessment Express. Axis I is at the front—the presenting symptom or illness that brings the person to seek help. The Axis I disorder develops sometime during life and can be seen as having an onset at some point, be it abrupt or slow and insidious. Serious, ongoing, and disruptive disorders that often impair a person's entire life (ability to have a family, hold a job, finish school, live independently) are referred to as major mental illness and often involve acute episodes when the person has to go into a hospital or have some other form of crisis care. Two of the major mental illnesses—schizophrenia and bipolar disorder (previously called manic-depressive illness) are recorded on this axis—and so are major depression, dysthymia (milder depression), the anxiety disorders, and various other presenting problems that are considered the primary diagnosis—the

one to be treated—and many Axis I disorder(s), including those
we have mentioned, are treated with medication as well as other
therapies. But that first axle can have more than one set of tires,
and if the truck is heavy it usually does. Axis I is also the place for
disorders of substance abuse, dependence, or addiction, and the
person who has a psychiatric disorder and a substance abuse problem is one of the "dual-disorder" clients to be discussed in the
next chapter.

Axis II, the axle that also supports the cab of the truck and helps
to set its direction, represents disorders that develop early in life
and continue to shape the person's experience throughout life.
These fall into two broad categories, one of which is the developmental disabilities, including mental retardation, learning disabilities, physical impairments, and so on. The other Axis II category,
more central to the subject of this book, is that of the 10 personality disorders. (Chapter 4 has given a case example of borderline
personality disorder [Ellen], and Chapter 7 will present a man
with apparent antisocial personality disorder [Darrell].) Earlier
thinking in the field held that these personality disorders, though
intractable or even untreatable, were not as serious as the major
mental illnesses such as schizophrenia, and on this basis people
with borderline personality disorder are sometimes denied admission to state psychiatric hospitals. Yet today we are beginning to
recognize that personality disorders, particularly if they are min-
gled with alcohol or other drug abuse, can produce devastating
impairments, as much misery as a major mental illness, and sometimes the fatal outcome of suicide.

Axis III and Axis IV, the trailer axles, further reflect and refine
the manual's use as a guide to treatment planning. Axis III asks for
any medical conditions that should be kept in mind. Not only do
physical conditions add stress to the person's life, but also many
medical conditions—diabetes, thyroid disorders, Alzheimer's disease, multiple sclerosis, AIDS—may result in serious psychiatric
symptoms at certain stages of the illness.

Axis IV continues the holistic approach of DSM-IV by making
room for other stressors, both recent and long past, which may
contribute to the diagnosis and to the severity of symptoms. For
example, the death of a parent or spouse just two months ago

might be a severe stress, precipitating or worsening the symptoms of a depressive or anxiety disorder. On the other hand, a person exposed to severe and unusual trauma in childhood—such as witnessing a murder, suffering an accident, or the ongoing stress of being a refugee in wartime or enduring sexual abuse—might later experience lasting problems with anxiety, depression, and fearfulness, perhaps leading to a diagnosis of post-traumatic stress disorder, delayed onset.

Axis V, the axle that brings up the rear, assesses on a scale from 10 to 90 the person's level of functioning, using global indicators in personal and social life. This serves as a reference point during the person's progress through illness and recovery.

DSM-IV is now widely used by insurance companies, federal agencies, and managed-care panels. As a result, mental health professionals need to fine-tune their understanding of this multiaxial diagnostic system. Its use has supported better communication among researchers and clinicians, not only in the United States but abroad as well, where the DSM-III and -IV editions have been quite popular with mental health professionals. By bringing level of functioning, level of stress, and related medical disorders into the picture, as well as ongoing personality traits and problems of long standing, the psychiatric symptoms and disorder are placed in a broad psychological and social context. DSM-IV speaks to the complexity of every person and every life situation.

## DIAGNOSIS AND EPIDEMIOLOGY: THE ECA AND NCS STUDIES

Beyond its uses in individual treatment planning, another use of diagnostic categories lies in epidemiology, the study of the incidence and prevalence of various disorders in society—in this case, mental/emotional disorders. *Incidence* means the number of new cases of a disorder appearing in a given time period, usually one year. *Prevalence* means the number or proportion of people who have a particular illness at a given time. *Lifetime prevalence* means the number of people who have the illness at some time in their lives. *Twelve-month prevalence* means the number who have had the illness at some time in the past 12 months.

Epidemiology plays a crucial role in public health—and in this case, mental health—planning and service delivery. From the counting of people with a given disorder, which in turn depends on the naming or diagnosis and its criteria, comes the identification of treatment needs in society as a whole or in a given community. And this sequence of naming and counting can offer indications of unmet treatment needs—that is, of how many people, with what kinds of disorders, are going without needed treatment.

During the past decade the Epidemiologic Catchment Area (ECA) Study (1991) has been the major source of data on the prevalence of psychiatric disorders and service utilization in the United States. The ECA study, by means of a series of five community epidemiological surveys, interviewed more than 20,000 respondents. The operative word in that sentence is *community;* that is, the people surveyed were the public at large, not merely those who had shown evidence of having a mental or substance use disorder. The ECA study utilized 30 diagnostic categories and found that one or more of these disorders had been experienced at some time in their lives by 32 percent of the sample, and 20 percent, or one in five people, had an active disorder at the time of the survey.

More recently, another study, called the National Comorbidity Study (NCS), surveyed more than 8,000 people nationwide, using a somewhat younger age group than the ECA study (15 to 54 years old instead of 18 and older). The NCS study found that nearly 50 percent of respondents reported at least one lifetime disorder (a disorder occurring at any time in the person's life), and close to 30 percent reported at least one disorder in the past 12 months. The most common disorders were major depressive episode, alcohol dependence, social phobia, and simple phobia. As the ECA study had noted, women were found to have higher rates of affective disorders (except mania) and anxiety disorders than men, while men had elevated rates of substance use disorders and antisocial personality disorder. Most disorders declined with age and socioeconomic status—that is, they were less prevalent among higher age groups in the cohort and among those persons with higher socioeconomic status.

The high lifetime prevalence (50 percent, or one in two people, having had a diagnosable disorder at some time in their lives) was considered an important new finding of the NCS study. Even more striking was the finding that more than half of all lifetime disorders occurred in the 14 percent of the population with a history of three or more comorbid (concurrent) disorders at one time. This group of people, roughly one-sixth of the population, also included the majority of people with severe disorders such as schizophrenia and other psychotic illness. The study highlights the need for research and program development for people with dual or multiple disorders—the subject of the next chapter.

Even more striking than the high prevalence of mental disorder and comorbidity found by the NCS study was the finding that less than 40 percent of persons with a lifetime disorder had ever received professional treatment, and less than 20 percent of those with a recent disorder had been in treatment during the past 12 months. Furthermore, among the one-sixth of the population who had a history of three or more comorbid disorders and the most severe disorders, less than 50 percent had ever received specialty mental health treatment (that is, treatment by an agency or person working in the mental health professions, as distinguished from, for example, treatment by a family physician or services by a shelter for homeless persons). This highlights the need to pay close attention to outreach and to barriers to treatment, especially for people with dual or multiple disorders.

## DISORDERS AND THEIR CAUSES: THE BIOPSYCHOSOCIAL MODEL

As DSM-III and -IV acknowledge the complexity of human problems, they also reflect an important framework or model that is part of the thinking of most mental health clinicians today: the biopsychosocial model of human behavior. This rather daunting term simply refers to the multiple aspects—biological, psychological, social—of a person and/or a problem. The term itself reflects a discarded understanding of what it is to be human: that is, it suggests a dichotomy, a separation between body and mind that is no longer viable. Most of us believe today that, Descartes to the contrary, the mind as a psychological entity is not separable from the brain as a biological entity. Rather, researchers are busy relating brain function and, for instance, the action of neurotransmitters to our feelings and behavior. According to contemporary understanding of the brain, the biological aspect of our experience is different from the psychological only for purposes of discussion. That is, we experience changes in brain function and in the action of neurotransmitters as psychological symptoms, and psychological problems and conflict may trigger biochemical changes. It is artificial in one sense to describe any of these functional changes as this statement does, seeing the biological and psychological aspects as separate. Rather, all human experience, seen in terms of functional events, has more than one aspect, and we can understand it in more than one language and theoretical framework.

Currently, for instance, both schizophrenia and major affective disorder are seen as brain disease and/or dysfunction of the neurotransmitters, produced in some measure by genetic factors. Yet these genetic factors are seen as vulnerabilities that may or may not be activated by a specific psychological and social context. The biological aspects of schizophrenia seem to play a predominant role, and treatment today includes the use of psychotropic medications as its most important tool, preferably combined with close attention to family education and support. Such approaches are intended to reduce stress and overstimulation for the person with schizophrenia, who has difficulty processing information and adapting to complexity and change. Major mood disorders, both bipolar and unipolar (e.g., episodes of major depression without episodes of mania), are also seen as predominantly biological and treated predominantly with medication. Depression and anxiety that fall short of major psychotic episodes—that is, breaks with reality—are also treated with medication whenever possible and appropriate, but clearly involve other factors seen as psychological and/or social—as when a series of losses or serious problems in relationships may trigger a biochemical process that can lead to physical illness and/or to a clinical depression with biological symptoms that can become overwhelming.

Again, even to speak of biological versus psychological or of physical versus mental systems belies the contemporary view of the human being as an organic entity, seen through the lenses of different systems and terminologies. The more we learn, the more difficult it is to avoid either oversimplifying or overcomplicating any description of human experience. But we cannot grasp its unity and its complexity and change our way of thinking and speaking all at once. Meanwhile, the biopsychosocial model, a term coined by George Engel in an attempt to integrate these three aspects of human problems and their causes, and a step in understanding the concept of organic unity, continues to serve as a basic framework for considering how to help a person with a problem. Simply put, it means the viewing of human problems through the three major lenses of biological, psychological, and social perspectives in order to see the problem in three dimensions and respond appropriately to each aspect. If this seems too basic to be belabored, we might reflect on how often the biological aspects of alcohol and other drug effects have been ignored in an assessment of depression or anxiety by mental health professionals untrained in substance disorders, or how profoundly an individual's social support network can affect illness and recovery, without the family or other significant others necessarily being included in the treatment.

Relating the biopsychosocial model to DSM-IV, we can see biological factors reflected in both Axis III (physical disorders) and Axis I, where schizophrenia and major mood disorders are both seen as having biochemical components that are predominant factors in the illness, and less severe depression and anxiety at the least present biochemical symptoms. Many people today also see a biological substrate for such Axis II problems as borderline personality disorder, and of course biological factors are predominant in the other Axis II category, the developmental disorders. Psychological factors are also seen as present in many Axis I problems, including depression and anxiety, as well as in the Axis II problems of personality disorder. Social aspects of problems are reflected on Axis IV as recent stressors, and to a degree on Axis V, where baseline functioning is rated. Unfortunately we have yet to relate individual diagnosis and disorder to a rating system for marital and family systems and their functioning that would be widely known and utilized outside the specialized field of marriage and family therapy. DSM-III and -IV also have not attempted to rate the support networks of individuals with disorders, even though this can be a major factor in the course of psychiatric illness and recovery. The more extended concern of community psychiatry with the capacity of communities, mental health systems, and social policy to aggravate illness or support recovery is constantly explored in the form of epidemiology, program and system development, and service delivery issues, but it has no place in the formal diagnostic framework. Yet this more extended "diagnosis" of a person's life situation is a crucial aspect of any assessment of that person's condition and treatment needs.

## WHAT'S IN A NAME? BEYOND DIAGNOSIS

But what does diagnosis really mean? And what about the rumor that up to 10 percent of diagnoses are changed at some point in the psychiatric history? This disconcerting news is true—but there are reasons for it: the fact that people present themselves differently at different times, that new symptoms may appear or old ones disappear, or that a clinician may take a new look at someone or wish to try a different medication, and that an illness itself can be in a different stage as a person grows older. Diagnoses should not be taken as absolute. At best, they are a guide to treatment, especially to medication; they offer some degree of predictability about the probable course of an illness and how severe and long-lasting it is likely to be; they give the treating clinician and the client a place to begin to understand what is happening and to develop some guidelines for mental health treatment and for managing everyday problems; and they are, of course, essential for third-party reimbursement and other administrative purposes.

Today, our diagnostic system represents tremendous effort, experience, and research devoted by leading clinicians and researchers to refining our conceptions and understanding of the various types of mental and emotional disorders. The effort to identify common and diverse elements in the nearly infinite variety of profiles of disturbed thinking, feeling, and behavior has an extraordinary history, and we now have elaborate paths through the wilderness of nosology—the naming of disorders—that was once explored with only the compass of a few observant clinicians. Each new effort at naming draws upon a vast pooled experience and observations of individuals with their own specific symptoms of illness, yet with overriding commonalities with others with the same illness and diagnosis. Yet, with all the refinements of our present system, diagnoses are still not absolute truths, and they cannot present a total and reliably accurate picture of a human being.

Chapter 6

# The Many Forms of Dual Disorder

O ur previous chapter discussed how the multiaxial diagnostic system (DSM-III, -IIIR, and -IV) has provided for diagnosis on more than one axis or dimension of a person's problems. We also referred to the diagnosis of dual or multiple disorders on Axis I, the axis reserved for presenting problems. Such dual or multiple diagnoses may be, for instance, a combination of a major depressive episode and bulimia, or an anxiety disorder and a marital problem, or post-traumatic stress disorder combined with substance dependence, specific to one or more drugs, each with its own diagnosis. Any of these diagnoses would be placed on Axis I and might be accompanied by an Axis II disorder such as borderline personality or "personality disorder not otherwise specified."

But the term *dual disorder* or *dual diagnosis,* especially in referring to a treatment population, is usually used today to mean the combination of mental/emotional/psychiatric problems with the abuse of alcohol and street drugs. The term *dual diagnosis* formerly was used for the combination of psychiatric problems and mental retardation, and it is still so used in the mental retardation field. The changed meaning of dual disorder or dual diagnosis that is now more widely used reflects the fact that the major area of overlap in mental/emotional disorders today is between mental disorder, alcoholism, and drug abuse, as attested by the ECA and NCS studies cited in Chapter 1 (Robins and Regier, 1991; Kessler et al., 1994).

There was a time in our society when "mental patients," "alcoholics," and "drug addicts" were three very separate groups of people. Mental patients were in institutions, where (unlike today) they had little if any opportunity to get involved with street drugs. Alcoholism was not yet recognized as a disease but was rampant at all levels of society, where it was not identified as a major problem until far along in its course. Drug abuse was regarded as a problem of a small minority of people, most of whom were criminals or in some way marginal in society. Neither mental patients nor alcoholics did drugs, still less the general population. Of course, those times are long gone. A generation or two of young men and women with serious problems have been caught in the intersection between deinstitutionalization on the one hand and the widespread availability and use of street drugs on the other. Deinstitutionalization, which began in the late seventies and rapidly grew into a tidal wave, discharged large numbers of long-stay institutional patients into the community—and its corollaries, admission diversion (avoiding an admission whenever possible) and short-stay hospitalization (keeping inpatient stays as brief as possible) have resulted in a community-based life for millions of seriously disturbed young men and women. The spread of drug availability and use into all the interstices of our society since the sixties has made that community a dangerous and sometimes overstimulating place for vulnerable people, such as young children and people of any age with mental/emotional disorders. These are major reasons why the mentally ill, alcoholics, and drug addicts should no longer to be thought of as separate populations. Rather, they are groups of people with overlapping and interacting problems.

But the agencies providing treatment are still playing catch-up, and most are only at the beginning of the game. The single-problem population is long gone, but a treatment agency—a mental health clinic or drug rehabilitation facility—still defines itself as offering treatment for psychiatric *or* substance abuse problems, because the barriers between the psychiatric and substance abuse treatment systems are firm, long-established, and supported by the existence of separate administrations and funding streams. The fact that this structure no longer fits the reality of people's treatment needs is a major challenge to the human service professions of the nineties. Today, it is not uncommon to hear that some 60 percent of a mental health clinic's clients use or abuse alcohol and/or other drugs. It is startling but not unlikely that some 70 to 80 percent of the admissions to a state psychiatric hospital are occasioned by an episode of alcohol/drug use by a psychiatrically vulnerable person. The dually diagnosed (meaning diagnosed with both psychiatric and substance abuse problems) or MICA (mentally ill chemical-abusing) client group—also known in some agencies as CAMI (chemical-abusing mentally ill) or SAMI (substance-abusing mentally ill), or by some similar acronym—dominates the scene in mental health service delivery today as a population of concern that is difficult to engage, to motivate, to treat, to follow, or to help. In a sense this large and still-growing population is our albatross today, and it will follow our ship until we learn more effective ways to be of service to the people who comprise it.

## FOUR SUBGROUPS OF DUAL-DISORDER CLIENTS

But who *are* these people? In our view, the discussion of dual diagnosis must not be limited to those who (like both Bill and Annie) have a major mental illness, nor to those who (like Annie) have a major, clearly identified problem of substance abuse, and especially not to those who have already been diagnosed with dual psychiatric/substance abuse problems. We believe that the most useful understanding of these problems lies in the broadest possible view of their scope, at least as a context for understanding individuals. From this perspective, people with dual diagnosis —or, as we prefer to call it, dual (or multiple) disorders—can be thought of in at least four subgroups, as those diagnosed or diagnosable with:

*Group 1. A major mental illness and a major problem with alcohol and/or drug abuse, dependence, or addiction.* This group would include Annie, but not Bill. Her dual disorders are bipolar disorder (formerly manic-depressive illness) and alcohol dependence.

*Group 2. A major mental illness and a special vulnerability to the effects of alcohol and other drugs.* Bill would belong to this group, with dual disorders of schizophrenia and substance abuse.

*Group 3. Personality disorder and/or other mental/emotional problems that are complicated and aggravated by alcohol and/or street drug use or abuse, but no major mental illness that in itself would produce psychotic episodes or require hospitalization.* This group would include Ellen, with Axis I diagnoses of post-traumatic stress disorder, bulimia in partial remission, and substance dependence (marijuana and co-caine), also in partial remission at present.

*Group 4. Diagnosed or identified alcohol/drug abuse, dependence, or addiction, plus personality disorder or other mental/emotional/cognitive problems that are masked by the substance use and may increase during withdrawal.* This group would include Darrell, the man we will discuss in the next chapter.

Just to indicate these four subgroups may suggest the complexity of the problem of dual diagnosis. These are four roughly defined groups of people who are very different in their degree of mental/emotional stability, the symptoms they develop under stress, and their ability to cope with everyday life. Depending on the nature of their mental/emotional problems and their own vulnerability, they may be variously affected by even small amounts of the various street drugs to which they may have access as a usual part of their everyday lives. And in most treatment systems people in each of these groups face hazards of misdiagnosis and inadequate treatment at every stage, from the emergency or crisis evaluation through the long-term day program or community residence.

Group 1 and Group 2 people have a mental illness such as schizophrenia or bipolar disorder (formerly called manic-depressive illness) that involves acute/psychotic episodes (psychotic meaning a loss of contact with reality and/or extreme confusion). People in these groups could be expected to have at least brief periods of hospitalization from time to time, and most need to take medication on an ongoing basis to prevent or at least control their most severe symptoms. For schizophrenia, the more active symptoms would be hallucinations, delusions, derailing of thought process, and/or paranoia, and the medication might be a neuroleptic or a more recently developed medication such as clozapine. For bipolar disorder, the symptoms would include pressured speech or behavior and perhaps wild elation, euphoria, grandiose ideas, aggressiveness, and/or paranoia—or, in the depression episode, a profoundly depressed and/or agitated mood, or perhaps slowed-down speech and movements, as well as persistent thoughts of suicide—and the medication to stabilize moods and prevent these extremes might be lithium carbonate or one of the anti-epilepsy medications used for people with rapid cycles of bipolar disorder: Tegretol (carbamazepine), Depakene (valproic acid) or Depakote (divalproex sodium), sometimes combined with antidepressants.

Either of these major mental illnesses might be reasonably well managed during the periods between episodes, at least for someone who is responsive to the medication, helped also by other forms of treatment and support, and willing and able to acknowledge the illness and the need for appropriate care. Schizophrenia is, in general, the more disruptive of everyday life of these two disorders, and people with this diagnosis, like Bill, are likely to show some impairment of their functioning even between episodes, and in some cases a deterioration over time—although some long-term studies suggest a much more positive prognosis than was usual in the past, provided the person has good treatment. People with bipolar disorder, on the other hand, may function particularly well if they are responsive to medication, continue to take it, and do not neglect their illness. Still, occasional acute episodes requiring hospitalization are likely to happen when medication is reduced or interrupted or at times of more than usual stress on the vulnerable person.

But add to these pictures the wild cards of alcohol and street drug effects on a given individual, and they become much more complex. The Group 1 person may turn to alcohol and other drugs in an effort to control troubling symptoms of anxiety and confusion, to a degree that may seem to "work," but often at a price. The person in Group 1 or Group 2 may also pick up a beer or a joint or move into habitual substance use as a way of fitting in with others, viewing the use of alcohol, marijuana, and sometimes cocaine as part of what a young person in our society normally does. Whatever the reason, (1) the expectable acute episodes requiring psychiatric inpatient care are likely to increase in both number and severity, and (2) the person with a mental illness is at least as much at risk as anyone else of becoming psychologically or physically dependent on the substance used.

In the process of getting treatment, the picture is still more complicated. Bill, who does have an illness called schizophrenia, may receive excellent care for that illness. But if the hospital doesn't do a urine screen for drugs, or the test results are not available before his discharge, or no traces of drug use show up at that particular time, he may receive no education or advice about how drinking and drug use may affect his recovery, and certainly no referral for treatment or involvement in Alcoholics Anonymous (AA). The recommended treatment will be in a mental health day treatment program, and Bill will be lucky if the program includes some close attention to his alcohol and drug use—because Bill is a Group 2 person who doesn't use "that much" and therefore may not be seen as needing education and treatment around substance abuse.

Unfortunately, Bill is vulnerable to drug effects, and "not that much" is *too much* for him. When he goes out to a bar on a Friday night to be with other young people and try to make friends and has a few beers or a joint, he may start to decompensate—that is, to become confused and disorganized, to lose his cognitive and emotional balance, and perhaps to have trouble making sense of things, begin to hear voices, or have strange thoughts—a recurrence of the active symptoms of schizophrenia. These effects of a mild-to-moderate amount of drinking or drug use are all the more likely to be neglected by clinicians and denied by Bill himself, simply because the amounts are moderate, and no one would call Bill an alcoholic or a "druggie."

For Annie, a Group 1, or MICA, person who *does* clearly have a major problem with alcohol in addition to her bipolar disorder, getting the right treatment is a problem for at least two other reasons. One is the lack of a single clinic or agency that can provide, in one place and with a coherent approach, all the forms of treatment that she needs—the medication, the education and counseling around alcoholism, the carefully timed psychotherapy for post-traumatic stress disorder. Many or most substance abuse treatment agencies will not accept a client who needs ongoing medication, because for some clients that flexibility could confuse the issue of becoming drug-free—although attitudes are beginning to change as substance abuse counselors become more knowledgeable about the medications used for psychiatric disorders.

A second reason is that at AA meetings, Annie is still more likely to encounter a lack of understanding and perhaps hostility about her "other" illness and her need for medication. The psychiatric and substance abuse treatment systems have been, historically, very separate and very different in philosophy, methods, and staff backgrounds, and bringing them together is a complex and challenging task in our fields today. Yet only a unified, integrated approach to Annie's problems will give her a chance of learning to handle the combination of a major mood disorder, the disease of alcoholism, and the fallout from her traumatic childhood experiences.

For the Group 3 person such as Ellen, the situation is still more complex, for this is a group with great variety among its members. People in our Group 3 do *not* have the kind of mental illness that usually would result in a hospitalization—unless it were for a suicide attempt, as has happened in Ellen's case, or an especially extreme aggressive outburst or violent incident. The Group 3 person might be someone who is anxious, impatient, angry, impulsive, aggressive, with temper outbursts that fall short of violence—except when liquor or cocaine is involved. Or that person might be a young woman who becomes sexually provocative and promiscuous when she takes drugs . . . or a boy with learning disabilities who avoids school and mellows out on marijuana, and gradually takes on avoidance as a way of life . . . or a woman with borderline personality disorder who uses drinking and drugs as one of several forms of self-destructive behavior. The alcohol may also serve as a disinhibitor, allowing her to "let loose" with raging outbursts or suicide gestures and attempts. Or, as in Ellen's case, drinking and drugging may be a way to numb and deny feelings and memories that are unbearably painful.

Why do we call these examples of dual-disorder problems rather than simply alcohol/drug problems? Certainly the dividing line is not always clear, for alcohol and drug effects themselves can mimic any of the disorders of thought, mood, and behavior that we might otherwise define in psychiatric terms. But what we have in mind in discussing Group 3 is the recognition that there is a large, heterogeneous population of people whose problems are carried to the point of crisis or severe dysfunction only by their use of alcohol and other drugs. The Group 3 person is someone who has difficulty coping with daily life, but has no major mental illness that involves psychotic episodes; and yet, in combination with the effects of alcohol and drugs, that person is driven over the edge into violence or suicidal acts—and into a hospital or a jail—or crosses over into a condition of unremitting dependency and hopelessness.

And what of the person in Group 4? In a sense, this is not a group but rather a way station. The Group 4 dual-disorder client emerges in a substance abuse treatment program—or in the streets, like "Darrell" in the next chapter—with a major substance abuse problem plus psychiatric symptoms that interfere with treatment. He can't easily tolerate a group, because of feeling too pressured to let others talk, or too preoccupied with an inner world to pay attention, or too withdrawn to interact with others, or too easily threatened by any confrontation. The Group 4 person may feel too depressed to get out of bed and come to the alcohol day program or the AA meeting, or too anxious to stay in the room once a meeting begins. Instead of becoming more clearheaded as the effects of alcohol or marijuana wear off, he may experience more severe symptoms, may start to hear voices or to feel an urgent preoccupation with suicide, or be ambushed by frequent flashbacks of traumatic experiences. These may be symptoms that the alcohol or other drugs have been masking, against which the person has no other defense.

The Group 4 person is very likely to leave substance abuse treatment because the program seems much too demanding, or to be ejected for not being able to follow the rules. The requirements of a program for substance abusers are generally quite rigorous, and their apparent rigidity is necessary to help the program and the individual client to stand firm against the insidious power of alcoholism and drug addiction, and the denial and rationalizations that are part of either disease. But the person with dual psychiatric and substance abuse problems is likely not to be able to handle this rigorous a structure.

The person with schizophrenia such as Bill, for instance, may not be able to follow the content and pacing of the educational part of a substance abuse treatment program, and he may become overstimulated and "flooded" by the stories about childhood traumas and domestic violence that people often tell in AA meetings. Confrontation about alcohol and drug use or continuing dependence on parents may be too threatening to handle. The person with bipolar disorder such as Annie may be too excitable, too easily stimulated by the groups that are central to alcohol and drug treatment programs and to AA and NA (Narcotics Anonymous). She may get too wound up and demand all of the group's attention by delivering a life story in a seamless dramatic monologue. Drug treatment programs are beginning to accept the need of people such as Bill or Annie who have a major mental illness to continue their medications and other psychiatric treatment. But it is still very much the exception to find a hospital where a double track of concurrent treatment, complete with medication for mental illness and training in abstinence and sobriety, is available to the person with dual disorders. Instead that person may become a dropout or "kickout" from the treatment program and show up in one of the other groups being served in the mental health treatment system—often without proper attention to the problem of alcohol and drug use.

Clearly the problems involved in treating dual disorders are not simple. We make a beginning by thinking about the subgroups we have outlined. It is important to realize, for instance, that people with major psychiatric illness in addition to their substance abuse—Group 1 and Group 2 people like Annie and Bill—have treatment needs that are determined by that illness—the need for medication, case managers, day programs, support in the community. Other people without a major mental illness—and who do not have any other form of dual disorder—can manage without these kinds of help, once they are able to stop using alcohol or other drugs. And people who are, in a sense, between these groups—who are adult survivors of childhood physical or sexual abuse with serious symptoms as sequelae of trauma and/or present severe, entrenched forms of personality disorder—Group 3 people such as Ellen, whether male or female—need extra help of another kind, most commonly psychotherapy plus self-help support groups and/or some cognitive therapy. Later in this chapter we will discuss an approach to treatment planning and some ways of combining or sequencing treatment for people with these different combinations of dual or multiple disorders. But first comes a crucial question: What is the person's motivation for alcohol/drug treatment?

## LEVELS OF MOTIVATION AND DENIAL

Alcohol and drug dependence are, in their very nature, diseases of denial. That is, the person denies that she "has a problem"; denies the quantity, frequency, and/or compulsive quality of her use of the substance; denies the degree to which obtaining and using the substance drains time and money; and denies as well the other negative effects of use—physical, psychological, interpersonal. In fact, one of the defining criteria for the diagnosis of substance dependence is the person's continuing use *in spite of* negative consequences. Compulsive behavior, especially when it becomes physiologically as well as psychologically addictive, is defended at any cost. And denial of the problem is the first line of defense—too often the bottom line in a treatment effort.

In a program designed to treat alcoholism or other substance abuse, it is usual that some people are more motivated than others, and more or less denying of their illness. In addition, some people are attending because they want to, and some because they have to—that is, because they are under court order or some other kind of external duress. But in spite of these differences, at least it is clear to all participants what the program is about: that it is directed to the goal of abstinence and ongoing sobriety. By contrast, client/consumers in a mental health treatment program typically do not view their alcohol or drug use as a problem, nor do they view their use or abstinence as a legitimate concern of the program staff. After all, that's not what the mental health program is about. In order to appreciate the relevance and value of any kind of substance abuse treatment, a person in mental health treatment needs persuasion, often in the form of education. Many people are motivated for or resigned to having psychiatric treatment—for medication to help with the experience of hearing voices, for unmanageable anxiety or depression, for severe marital and family problems—but they are distinctly *not* motivated or available for treatment or even discussion of substance abuse. We have come to call such people, often younger adults, premotivated clients.

The premotivated client who is compromising his mental status and treatment by continuing to use alcohol and other drugs can present a major problem to a mental health treatment program. What is the responsibility of the program? How can clinicians help people to reach an understanding that the problems they *know* they have—auditory hallucinations, confusion, emotional pain, trouble in their relationships—are in fact related to or aggravated by using alcohol and other drugs? When people are unable to see or resist seeing that connection, they generally find it easy to deny, downplay, or quickly forget actual incidents of losing their temper and becoming violent or experiencing psychotic delusions or confusion when they have used a substance—even if the use has led to another episode in jail or in a psychiatric hospital.

This means that the mental health treatment program must decide whether to provide treatment at all when a person is denying the fact of alcohol/drug use and refusing to address the issue, to have treatment for substance abuse, to try abstinence, and/or to remain abstinent. Usually the decision has to be based on a complex tangle of risk factors. If the client is a Group 1 or Group 2 person, the need to provide medication and monitoring for psychotic episodes may be overriding; the person *has* to have treatment to prevent psychotic episodes. But if the person is in the Group 1 category—that is, makes heavy use of alcohol/drugs—and also needs psychotropic medication, prescribing such medication may be too risky. If the person is a Group 3 dual-disorder client, the choice depends on the severity of the person's problems—whether they are life-threatening and/or so all-pervasive that ongoing treatment is essential. If not, or if the substance abuse is clearly the major cause of dysfunction, the most legitimate choice may be to refuse mental health clinic treatment—most likely individual or marital therapy—until the person accepts at least a substance use evaluation as a prerequisite. And so it goes. The worst hazard in making such decisions is that the risk factors may cancel each other out, or the treatment decisions may be made without taking all factors into account, because of the characteristic blind spots of each of the treatment agencies.

## DIFFERENTIAL TREATMENT PLANNING FOR DUAL-DISORDER CLIENTS

Before the growing awareness of dual-disorder problems, client assessment and treatment planning tended to focus on the question: Which problem is primary? or Which problem came first? The answer to this question often depended upon the training and work setting of the intake worker. A therapist in an outpatient clinic might see the person's anxiety or depression or marital problem as primary, and the use of alcohol as a secondary effort to relieve the pain. A worker in a day treatment program might pay attention to a client's symptoms of schizophrenia but see his marijuana use as just an effort to self-medicate, to "mellow out," or to pursue a normal social life. An alcohol or drug counselor would be more likely to see the substance use as primary and any relationship problems or even psychiatric symptoms as just part of the territory of alcohol/drug effects.

This "either/or" or "primary/secondary" way of thinking has been required in part by the administrative separation of mental health and substance abuse agencies and treatment programs. When the question is: Where should I send this person for treatment? and the choice is between one single-problem, self-contained agency and another, or even one or another treatment unit in a larger agency, it is almost inevitable that this either/or thinking should persist. At best, the question becomes: What kind of treatment should come first? The trouble with this line of thinking is that, for one thing, experience in the field tells us that concurrent treatment of both psychiatric and substance use disorders has the best chance of interrupting the deadly interplay of the two problems. The notion that someone can profit from substance abuse treatment first and psychiatric treatment second, or the other way around, ignores the difficult truth that the two problems play into one another, and that neither major mental illness nor substance abuse can be "cured" by a dose of time-limited treatment.

Second, and no less important, even if we could determine what kind of treatment should come first, there would still be no guarantee that the person would go along with the treatment plan. As noted earlier, denial is inherent in most patterns of substance abuse. More often than not, the person in "double trouble" with mental illness and substance abuse will acknowledge one problem but not the other.

In assessing problems and planning treatment, then, we need to consider not only the four subgroups or combinations of dual disorders suggested earlier, but also where the person is on the path of motivation for treatment. One way of grouping people in these terms is to identify the person as (1) *premotivated*—not yet seeing alcohol and drug use as a problem; (2) *motivated*, but preabstinent—seeing the use as at least potentially a problem but at present still continuing to use; (3) *currently abstinent*, but not yet well established in a sober/abstinent lifestyle, and subject to slips and possible relapse; and (4) *committed to sobriety/abstinence*, having already made a substantial commitment to a changed life-style, and continuing a path of increasing commitment and ongoing relapse prevention.

Osher and Kofoed (1989) have suggested four stages of treatment, corresponding roughly to these levels of motivation: (1) engagement, (2) persuasion, (3) active treatment, and (4) relapse prevention or maintenance. It is useful to reflect on how different the approaches and time spans devoted to these stages of treatment may be when working with a person with dual disorders. It is central to dual-disorder treatment today to expect a fairly lengthy period of engagement and persuasion before active treatment can begin—that is, before the person is ready or willing to consider abstinence as a goal. Clearly the treatment approaches and often the setting of treatment must depend on how far along the person has come on the motivational path. The more a mental illness, a major personality disorder, or a disabling level of anxiety and depression interferes with a person's thought process and/or stability of mood, the more difficult it is to gain a commitment to a major change in habits and attempted coping. A person whose thinking is confused finds it difficult or impossible to hold onto goals or thoughts about goals. A person whose mood is deeply depressed or whose feelings are chaotic and painful feels an intense need for relief, and often any excitation is translated into a craving for a drug, be it alcohol or cocaine, marijuana or heroin, caffeine or nicotine. The more severe and pervasive the disturbance in thinking, or the more overwhelmingly painful the feelings, the more difficult it is for the person to gather the strength and clarity that are needed to undertake abstinence. This is true, albeit for different reasons, whether the person is a casual user or occasional abuser of drugs and alcohol or a clearly substance-dependent or addicted person. If the person is physically and/or psychologically dependent on a drug, then obviously abstinence looms as a very difficult or virtually impossible undertaking. If the person is "only" a casual or occasional user, then the tendency will be to downplay the amount and frequency of use and to forget any bad consequences.

To a degree, such denial and resistance are present in the initial stages of all substance abuse treatment. The difference in dual-disorder treatment lies in the greater interference of thought disorder, apathy and withdrawal, overwhelming depression, or anxiety with the process of developing motivation. This interference is in many cases so great that only gradually, with the help of a very low-key approach and considerable patience and repetition, can the person begin to entertain thoughts in any continuous way about the negative effects of substance use and the possible benefits of abstinence. The process of emotional conversion that often marks the beginning of substance abuse treatment, sometimes with the aid of strong confrontation and intervention by family members and other people who are important to the substance abuser, may be much too intense and threatening for the dual-problem person. The way in is likely to be the more gradual path of low-key education or "psychoedu-cation," often in a group or classroom setting, about alcohol and drug effects, and an ongoing invitation to consider these in the context of personal experience. Such educational groups do not require self-identification as an "alcoholic" or "drug addict," or even as someone who has "a problem" with alcohol and drug use. In this way they bypass the more familiar categories of substance abuse, dependence, and addiction, which are all diagnostic categories that address a pattern of substance use, and instead they can address nonjudgmentally the subject of drug effects.

## A SAMPLE TREATMENT PLAN

Considering Osher's stages of treatment as they correspond to levels of motivation for abstinence, then, we can consider some options in planning treatment. The task is to provide an appropriate blend of education, treatment interventions, and supports at each level of motivation, for each of the suggested subgroups of dual-disorder clients. The framework offered in Table 6.1 suggests a way of thinking about treatment plans for the four groups of clients we have defined, in intersection with their levels of motivation for treatment. Of course, these levels of motivation, as well as the treatment plans, are affected by other factors. In extending this framework we will want to incorporate also a person's level and patterns of substance use, abuse, dependence, or addiction, as well as the stage of treatment—e.g., how many times the person has passed through the revolving door of the psychiatric hospital or drug rehab, and whether he or she is currently in inpatient or outpatient treatment. Clearly a hospital treatment team must confront the issue of substance use more strongly than an outpatient clinician may dare to. The hospital episode has great potential as a crisis intervention, and it should include helping each person to raise the question: How did I get in here . . . and how can I stay out next time? The outpatient program or clinician, lacking the constant availability of the client and the hospital's potentially powerful leverage, may be most concerned with keeping the person coming back to the clinic or drop-in center, in the hope that motivation for abstinence may develop over time.

How, then, can the person's substance abuse be addressed? The authors believe that to fail to address it is to "enable" or feed into the substance use problem—that is, to allow it to continue by looking the other way or protecting the person from its consequences. Therefore, the treatment program, whether mental health or substance abuse treatment, should refuse to treat someone when that person is drunk or is known to have used alcohol or street drugs that day. But we believe as strongly that to treat dual-disorder clients in mental health programs with premotivational attention in the form of psychoeducation about alcohol and drugs is *not* "enabling" in most cases, but rather is legitimate treatment for the person's motivation and direction toward abstinence.

Suiting the setting and components of treatment to the subgroup and motivational level of different clients is a complex task, and clearly depends upon the resources available in a specific community for its specifics and its success. In our framework we assume that a person is already in outpatient treatment. But, applying this framework to Annie, we will begin where the reader has already met her, in the hospital.

Annie, with both a major mental illness (bipolar disorder) and substance dependence (alcohol), would be considered a Group 1 client. She probably would begin at Level 1, as a premotivated client, who might acknowledge, at least some of the time, the need for treatment for her mental illness, but not acknowledge her alcoholism as a problem. What would be the options in her treatment? If she is seen in a psychiatric emergency room during an acute episode, possibly after already having medical clearance and/or spending the night in a sober-up bed, she would almost certainly be hospitalized. In the hospital, (1) the first goal would be to stabilize her symptoms by starting or reinstating medication—in her case lithium carbonate. (2) At the same time, during the two-week hospitalization, she would be "drying out" in a brief period of involuntary abstinence from drinking. (3) Ideally, during this time, she could be given an educational or psychoeducational experience, preferably a group/class meeting daily or several times a week, about the effects of alcohol and other drugs, and about alcoholism as a disease process. (4) The hospitalization should also include one or more family meetings to assess the

Table 6.1. *Treatment Suggestions for Client Subgroups at Different Levels of Motivation*

| Dual-Dx Subgroup | *Level 1 Pre-Motivated* *Engagement* | *Level 2 Pre-Abstinent* *Persuasion* | *Level 3 Abstinent ?* *Active Tx* | *Level 4 Commitment* *Relapse Prevention* |
|---|---|---|---|---|
| 1 Major Mental Illness and Substance Abuse | *MH Tx Program* unless SA too risky. Provide some services—e.g., drop-in case management center Use psychoeducational groups re drug effects Don't allow attendance when drunk/drugged Don't make an issue of use | *MH Tx Program* Encourage client to keep a log re use, temptation. Use PE groups w/more personal material Begin to discuss use, low-key | *MH Tx Program* with SA enrichment. *SA program, adapted* AA, with help in utilizing program as needed | *MH Tx Program* PE groups, w/senior status |
| 2 Major Mental Illness and Substance Vulnerability | *Same,* plus Encourage client to keep a log | *Same* Specific education re substance vulnerability. | *MH Tx Program* with SA enrichment. AA, with help as needed. | |

| | MH Tx Program | MH or SA Tx Program, adapted to individual client | Continue psychoeducation re emotion management & stress |
|---|---|---|---|
| 3 Personality Disorder, Axis I Disorder, and Substance Use/Abuse | *MH Tx Program* or Depending on severity, refuse to treat until SA evaluation and Tx are part of the plan. For high-risk clients, treat, but with ongoing, increasing attention to substance use issue For post-traumatic stress disorder, anxiety, depression: Use psychoeducation *re* managing feelings before/while undertaking abstinence as goal | AA, with help if needed........... Don't push "therapy" issues while working for abstinence | Continue psychoeducation *re* emotion management & stress |
| 4 Substance Abuse and Psychiatric Symptoms | Refer to MH Program if indicated by psychiatric symptoms........... Intervene with caution and promise of help for psychiatric symptoms........... Use psychoeducation *re* SA vs. "emotional conversion"........... | *SA Program,* adapted as needed Don't view psych Sx as resistance Provide help for problem Sx— meds as needed | *AA, with help* and MH Tx as needed MH Tx Prog Meds for psych Sx |

substance use of other family members; to learn about relevant family history in substance abuse and mood disorders (many families with a high incidence of substance abuse also have a higher-than-average incidence of mood disorders, and vice versa); and to share and reinforce the information about alcohol with Annie's family, who ideally would also have access to psychoeducational groups or programs. ("Psychoeducational" in this context is different from simply "educational" in that it focuses on psychiatric and psychological content and serves and/or supplements the purposes of treatment.) If such programs were not available in the psychiatric hospital, they should be accessed from alcohol services, and Annie should begin attending AA, armed with any needed help and guidance about, for instance, her need to take medication on a regular basis. At the same time, she should be connected with an alcohol counselor and an AA sponsor who could continue her education about alcoholism and support her if and when she is ready to undertake abstinence. All this assumes a state-of-the-art hospital unit, with adequate staff time and a good network of services in the community.

Leaving the hospital, Annie ideally would go to a day treatment program with an active thrust, which would monitor her medication, continue to reinforce her education about alcohol use, and help her, through the use of group as well as individual and family therapy, to consider her problematic emotional and behavioral patterns. The program would see her through the process of getting her life back on track by addressing her work, schooling, housing, social, and treatment plans for the immediate future. If this outpatient plan proved inadequate, given Annie's frequent bouts of heavy drinking and her fragile emotional condition, an alternative might be a period of treatment in a hospital with a special unit for dual-disorder clients, or perhaps, if her psychiatric symptoms had cleared, an inpatient alcohol rehabilitation program . . . if one could be found that would support her taking lithium for bipolar disorder.

But what if she won't go to day treatment? Or a rehab? Or an alcohol treatment program? Or AA? Treatment plans, however well conceived and supported by program resources, often go awry at the hospital exit, where the treatment staff lose their leverage because the person has already been discharged. It is at this point that our multistage framework begins, because this is where the person spends most of her treatment time—in the community, where being engaged in any kind of treatment is a matter of personal choice. Annie might pick up on any of the good options mentioned above—but at some future time, after a few more times around the merry-go-round of acute episodes and revolving-door hospital treatment. In the meantime, how can her needs be even partially met?

In the community, she is likely to begin some kind of mental health or psychiatric treatment, in order to have access to her lithium—that is, as long as she continues to acknowledge that she has a mental disorder for which she needs medication. She might go to an outpatient clinic, drop-in center, or psychosocial club that offers medication together with a low-key schedule of activities. In that setting, there would be an opportunity for a low-key beginning or continuation of the "engagement" process for undertaking abstinence, through the use of psychoeducational groups or classes on alcohol and drug effects. The approach taken by such a group needs to be quite different from an inpatient educational program in an alcohol treatment unit. A group of this type in a voluntary community setting cannot assume that those who attend will in fact choose to give up their substance use. Rather, the goal is to provide a knowledge base and an opportunity to exchange ideas and increase awareness about how the substance affects the person's symptoms and, in some cases, results in more frequent hospitalizations and other negative consequences. When Annie reaches this understanding, she may be able to make use of AA and other treatment more specific to substance abuse problems than what the mental health system can offer. But the path of abstinence requires, at the outset, a person who is able and willing to make a decision, at least for the moment, to pursue that path. Until that point is reached, there is no such thing as a "slip" or a "relapse"; the person has not yet decided to give up drinking or using other drugs. The "engagement" and "persuasion" stages are not just a preamble to treatment. For the dual-disorder client they contain much of the work of treatment, without which nothing further can happen.

As her treatment progresses, what is Annie to do with her legacy of post-traumatic stress disorder? For some clinicians, and traditionally in psychodynamically oriented psychotherapy, there could be no progress until her childhood traumas were un-earthed, relived, and put to rest. In our view, while such an ap-proach might be desirable and possible in a structured, protected setting, where she could be kept safe from the self-destructive be-havior that accompanies her intense emotions, there is no such safe place available to Annie or her clinicians, and therapy itself is too stressful. We would see rather, as a positive first step, psycho-education not only about alcohol and alcoholism, but also about alternative ways of managing painful emotions. A cognitive ap-proach to present symptoms, together with the use of SSRI's (Se-lective Serotonin Reuptake Inhibitors, such as Prozac and its cousins) is often the best approach at the beginning of treatment.

For Annie, and also for a Group 3 person, male or female, such as Ellen, the issue of how to handle the aftermath of traumatic experi-ence is a major concern. It is as if the subject of the trauma were a hot stove, too painful to approach, and yet, for the burned child or adult, too preoccupying to ignore, for one is always in danger of stumbling into it and being painfully burned again. The only seem-ing refuge is an emotional numbing that is both deadening and im-possible to maintain. The subject can be uncovered in therapy—the hot stove can be approached—but only slowly and with great care, and perhaps only as the most risky and self-damaging symptoms begin to come under some control. For the person whose major mode of avoidance has been substance abuse, bulimia, and/or suici-dal behavior, the first task is to place these behaviors "off limits" as ways of responding to painful feelings, and to establish other ways of managing extreme emotions, such as anxiety, rage, and self-loathing, that are the aftermath of traumatic experience.

## CONFLICT AND MISMATCH BETWEEN THE TREATMENT SYSTEMS

This chapter would not be complete without a few more words about the mental health and substance abuse treatment systems as they impact upon the dual-disorder client—for any plan for integrated treatment brings us up against conflicts between the systems. These conflicts are well grounded in history. Again, it is no news to people in the field that alcoholism and other drug addictions are diseases of denial. It is in the very nature of substance dependence and addiction that people protect their compulsive behavior by every possible means, and the first line of defense is certainly to deny that the alcohol or other drug use is a problem. *I don't drink that much . . . I only smoke a joint once in a while, just to relax . . . I party on cocaine, but just for something to do . . . It's not really a problem, not at all. . . .* There was a time, and not long ago, when people working in mental health, without any training in alcoholism or substance abuse treatment, were easily convinced by these denials. We weren't thinking about drug dependence; we didn't expect alcoholics to enter our programs, disguised as ordinary people with problems or major mental illness. Or if we did think such a person had an alcohol/drug abuse problem, we might refer that person to a substance abuse treatment program only to have the referral seen as inappropriate because the person denied the abuse—or because he had other major problems such as mental illness. The tragicomedy of treatment for many client/consumers with dual disorders and their families has been the pingpong effect—being bounced back and forth between the mental health and substance abuse treatment systems because neither system was prepared to treat dual or multiple problems.

This quandary is more widely recognized today, but it cannot become history until we find new and effective ways to treat dual disorders—and to share responsibility for such clients. In most communities, neither the mental health nor the substance abuse treatment agency is ready for the dual- or multiple-problem client, and there are some serious hurdles to be confronted before the two systems can work together. In other words, fully coordinated dual-disorder treatment is a problem whether it is addressed within a single mental health or substance abuse treatment clinic or through an effort to coordinate treatment by two separate agencies.

The difficulty faced by mental health and substance abuse treatment staff trying to work together springs from several sources. Each, but especially the substance abuse treatment system, represents an approach developed for a specific population with psychiatric or substance abuse problems, not with the combination and interplay we have described. The two systems have different philosophies, views of causality, methods and approaches, and training and credentialing of clinicians. For instance, (1) a psychiatric/mental health treatment program may downplay substance use or abuse as a factor in treatment, or look at the use as "self-medicating," with the assumption that substance use will disappear once psychiatric symptoms are controlled or emotional and interpersonal problems are resolved. A substance abuse team may identify the alcohol/drug use as primary, or else may not consider the Group 2 person—using drugs minimally but vulnerable to drug effects—to be a potential client. (2) In either case, the person with marked psychiatric symptoms such as a thought disorder is often found inappropriate for the treatment program, and the heavy user of alcohol and drugs is similarly rejected by mental health programs. (3) The use of psychotropic medications is not acceptable in many substance abuse programs, particularly in inpatient rehabilitation facilities, although a more informed and therefore accepting attitude is developing regarding use of such medications as neuroleptics for schizophrenia. In mental health treatment there may be an overreliance on antidepressant and anxiety-reducing medication, with insufficient awareness of their implications for substance-abusing people. (4) Substance abuse programs are often seen as taking a "hard line," as is required by the power of substance dependence and addiction and the denial and rationalization that go with the territory. Mental health treatment tends to be more individualizing and to allow or even encourage dependency and a low-demand approach. (5) Finally, the substance abuse treatment program begins with the acknowledgment of alcohol/drug dependence as a problem, and with abstinence as a clearly identified goal. The psychiatric/mental health program, however, is mandated to treat the premotivated and the preabstinent dual-disorder client and therefore may be seen as "enabling" by tolerating the continued use. (6) In many or most treatment programs, these philosophical and methodological differences are reinforced by the lack of training of each discipline in the other's expertise. The single-problem treatment program commonly has staff who are substance abuse counselors or mental health clinicians, and each group may be uninformed about or insensitive to the other dimension presented by the dual-disorder client. Although there has been a marked increase in the past few years in programs identified as offering treatment for dual diagnosis, these are still scarce and variable in quality and tend to serve primarily the Group 1 person with long-established and overt dual-disorder problems.

To bridge these differences and correct these limitations is a challenging goal for both mental health and substance abuse treatment programs. In our view, the greater burden of responsibility rests with the psychiatric/mental health program, which *must* provide treatment for people with severe psychiatric symptoms, which already provides a range of psychiatric/mental health services and requires a wide range of clinical knowledge and experience, and which is alone in providing involuntary inpatient treatment. It is probably easier in most cases for mental health programs to adapt to the needs of dual-disorder clients, by offering initial treatment directed to developing motivation, followed by appropriate accessing of substance abuse services. Substance abuse programs are likely to have a more difficult time adapting the treatment program to the needs of dual-disorder clients without weakening the strong didactic thrust, the demand for abstinence, the confrontation of denial, and the firm structure that are essential to their approach to the larger population of substance-abusing or substance-dependent clients.

But for each arm of the larger network of treatment services there are adaptations to be made, in order to cooperate even minimally in dual-disorder treatment. In our view, the psychiatric/mental health program needs to:

- *Establish the expectation of a basic knowledge base* in alcohol/drug effects and vulnerability to substance use effects, as well as in the dynamics of alcohol/drug dependence and addictive illness, for all mental health clinicians—and provide or access training in these areas if needed.

- *Include basic alcohol/drug assessment, education, and/or initial treat-ment*, at whatever level of use and motivation is appropriate, for all clients in mental health programs.
- *Educate/raise consciousness* among psychiatrists and other physi-cians about the hazards of specific prescribed medications (pri-marily antianxiety agents) for dual-disorder clients.

For the substance abuse treatment program, the corresponding adaptations would be to:

- *Train clinicians in a basic knowledge base* regarding the major men-tal illnesses and other psychiatric diagnoses.
- *Provide an informed assessment and/or diagnosis of psychiatric disorders and treatment needs* in addition to substance abuse treatment, with accessing of other services or referral as needed.
- *Increase awareness of adaptations in treatment approaches* that are needed for certain clients, based on psychiatric disabilities—e.g., a slower-moving or lower-impact program for people with schizophrenia.
- *Accept the use of psychotropic medications* for dual-disorder clients, based on their psychiatric disorders and treatment needs—e.g., neuroleptics for people with schizophrenia, antidepressants for unmanageable levels of anxiety and/or depression that exceed the withdrawal period.

These are but a few, and the most sweeping, of the adaptations that need to be made between the treatment systems in order to develop fully coordinated approaches to the needs of people with dual disorders. Until there is both psychiatric and substance abuse expertise on both sides of the wall that remains between these sys-tems, dual-disorder clients will continue to be at risk even within our treatment agencies. Providing coordinated and comprehen-sive treatment will not be the total answer, but it will give us a solid ground to stand on together in trying to respond to a major problem of the 1990s.

Chapter 7

# The Child in the Man

## *A Multi-need, Multi-system Client*

DARRELL'S STORY

> And this is the man you've been waiting to meet and are afraid to
> meet—the one who breaks into your car and steals your radio—the
> one who pulls a knife and demands your money, or strips off your sil-
> ver earrings, or pulls you into an alley and . . . Isn't he? He must be,
> because he's big, he's black, he's homeless, he's mentally ill and he's
> on drugs. . . .

Darrell grew up in one bombed-out neighborhood, and now
he lives in another. His father deals crack, his mother was a drug
addict who worked the street before she died. As a child, he went
the full route—the special class, the truant officer, getting arrested
for mouthing off and then for breaking and entering. But he is so
much at the mercy of impulse that one gets the feeling he hardly
knew what he was doing, that his life has been some kind of bad
dream.

Darrell knows very little about his childhood—he remembers a
grandmother, or maybe an aunt, who took care of him for a short
time, but she got sick or moved away—he isn't sure which. He
was then raised in a foster family with several other children.

*Maybe they didn't want him?* What is it to "want" a child when life offers no resource for its raising? Darrell's and his family's lives have been lived under constant siege from the multiple stressors—poverty, unemployment, drugs, crime—that have threatened their health and safety in an urban slum. Today, in the halfway house where he is living, no one comes to visit him on family day.

It seems, from fragments of stories that Darrell tells, that he was a constant truant, suspended for fighting in school, for stealing from his classmates, once for hitting a teacher. Then he became an early dropout and continued another schooling in the streets. He had already learned to do drugs, and although he was sent to a rehab facility once during his teens, the treatment didn't "take," perhaps because there was no follow-up and he went back to the same life. He learned more about breaking and entering, and for each of these crimes he served time in prison and is still on probation. Once, he was convicted of rape and was himself a victim of homosexual rape during one of his prison terms. He has made money as a male prostitute in order to buy drugs. Twice he's been hospitalized in psychiatric institutions, with diagnoses of schizophrenia, paranoid type, and antisocial personality disorder as well as substance abuse. Before he came into the house where he lives now, he was making heavy use of crack cocaine, marijuana, and alcohol. What other drugs he's used over the years isn't known, as much of Darrell's life is not clearly known, but seems to swim in his memory like some flashing, elusive life form. At last he came into a halfway house designed for homeless, mentally ill, drug-addicted men.

## A QUESTION OF SOCIALIZATION

The halfway house is a new world, a new culture to learn. When Darrell has lived in the house for a few weeks, he begins coming to the AA or "double trouble" meetings held in the living room. He's shy, sidling in and hovering at the edge of a group. They won't want me, he thinks. If you ask him a question, you get a one-word answer. If it's time to talk in the meeting, he says some kind of nonsense, as if he's somewhere else, in his own head.

Once, he went into the next room and ate some of a cake that was brought to celebrate somebody's anniversary. When this trespass was discovered he insisted, "I didn't do it!" with the crumbs all over his face . . . the way a child would, before learning how to behave, or even what would stand up to scrutiny and work with other people.

The problem seems to go deeper than mere immaturities or deficits in socialization, down to the building blocks of human interaction. Darrell can't concentrate on anything for more than a minute or so—if he's under stress, maybe only a few seconds; if you try to talk to him, you see him glancing all over the room. He's confused; he gets more confused in the middle of a sentence, as if he's stumbling over his own thoughts. He has trouble with his memory; sometimes he can't remember what was just said, how a sentence began, so he asks you to repeat. Maybe that's why he's confused, because he can't remember or follow a thought. So it's hard for Darrell to communicate, to manage in a social situation, to understand what he's supposed to do on a job or hold onto the instruction to do it. And with all this, he seeks attention—he's needy, greedy for it, the way a child might be.

Darrell is isolated from the other residents; sometimes he says that people are picking on him. He gets paranoid sometimes; he thinks, for instance, that people plan for things to go against him; and he thinks he himself has certain "powers" that can do people harm or affect, for instance, their choice of where to sit in the group room, or that his passing thoughts can cause them to change seats. Sometimes he believes that he can control, with his thoughts, who comes to the halfway house and who leaves. This is one way, perhaps, that a person might try to control an uncontrollable, unpredictable world—with special powers, with magic, with such good magic that one can steal before someone's eyes and not get caught, with taking and violating on impulse, before the beginnings of guilt or a regard for the world of others.

For many people, Darrell represents a faceless group—"the homeless," "addicts," "street people," "blacks," "rapists," "sociopaths"—who are often discussed in the *New York Times* and in polite company—but from a safe distance. How can we read his face in the middle of this crowd? He *is* homeless, crack-addicted, black, and convicted of several criminal acts, including rape. But is he a sociopath?

There are people in this world who can fairly be called sociopathic—or, to use the more current term, people with antisocial personality disorder—another of those personality disorders that are rampant in our diagnostic scheme, our way of looking at things today, as well as in our social and personal lives. The person currently defined as having an antisocial personality has shown, even before the age of 15, a pattern of what is called, at that age, a conduct disorder—being truant from school, running away from home, getting into fights, using a weapon, destroying property, being physically cruel to people or animals, forcing someone to have sex, lying, stealing, fire setting—three of these behavior patterns are considered evidence of a conduct disorder; Darrell did nine of these things before he was out of junior high school.

But that earlier conduct-disorder history is only part of the picture, the foundation for the adult evidence of an antisocial pattern. For an adult, antisocial personality means someone who doesn't work consistently, doesn't ever make an ongoing relationship, behaves aggressively (a criterion that now includes wife or child beating), breaks the law, is impulsive, reckless, vagrant, lying, conning, failing to honor obligations, squandering money. . . . Darrell makes enough marks to pass these criteria, too. We should note, though, that a salient feature of the antisocial personality—and we don't know this yet about Darrell—is the lack of remorse, the seeming lack of a conscience, of an internalized sense of "knowing right from wrong,"and an inability to care when one *has* done wrong.

Darrell and his brothers- and sisters-in-arms—people living in the margins of our society, some of them often stepping over the boundaries, the foul line of the law—are often referred to as "unsocialized." Actually, they are very well socialized, but to a subculture of our society which, for a child growing into manhood as Darrell did, represents the adult world and offers few alternative means of survival. It's not, perhaps, that there are literally no alternatives. But can *this* individual with *this* personal and social equipment take hold of them? And, in any case, do the alternatives appear to the growing young person in time—before he is drawn off onto another track, into an antisocial life? What encourages a person to think or feel that there might be alternatives—that the easiest, most accessible thing to do or get drawn into doing might not be the best or the only thing? What is needed for someone to develop and hold onto a self that is able to say, "No, that's not for me . . . That's wrong . . . I draw the line here . . . I don't hurt people or rob or rape or steal . . . I don't break the law"?

Looking at Darrell, we can see no source of such a message, but rather a social world lacking in both opportunity and nurture, in which the social and the psychological/developmental failures are so thoroughly enmeshed that we can't separate the strands. The addicted mother, the drug-dealing and addicted father have been themselves as much neglected as neglectful, as much abused as abusing. The consistent care and the tender mirroring of growth that are thought to feed and shape the inner self have been as far out of reach for these parents as for their children. Their parenting, like Darrell's, was a fragmented mirror, a "holding environment" that could not hold him, except in the instant between one passing impulse and another.

*Darrell! . . . Stop that, Darrell! . . . What makes you so evil?*

The foster mother has too many children, her own and others'. She bends over him in a fury, hits him across the face. Then her attention wanders to another. If she thinks of him later, she thinks how he doesn't seem to learn right, he can't seem to follow along like the others, he's always off in his own world or else tormenting someone, wanting too much attention. He's up at night, after bedtime, screaming for a bottle though he's much too old for that. He screams for his mother, maybe, or is it his aunt he screams for? And if she goes in and tries to comfort him, he just keeps on sobbing under his breath, until he falls off to sleep.

That's at least potentially a good story, that story—for the child to be able to cry for who and what he has lost. Did it ever happen in Darrell's life, and if so was he ever comforted, or is it just a passing fiction, something we might imagine should happen, if a child loses his mother? If he could cry for her—the first mother, and the second mother, and the third now-clearly-a-stand-in-mother—instead of just closing a thin, stiff, impermeable skin over an open wound . . . if he ever had her, so that he could lose her and cry for her, instead of having had just an empty space, an unmade connection ... then that might be a good thing. The growth of a self that can enter this world alone depends on that as a foundation—the taking in of that early knowledge of someone close, someone who responds to the cries of needing and wanting. The fact that Darrell has survived means that he had physical care in the beginning of his life, as well as some degree of close human caring and stimulation—for, as was discovered decades ago in a study of infant orphans in institutional care, human infants literally die without the specific attention of someone who cares for them and interacts with them as they enter the world.

Something else about Darrell holds out a hope. Now, as an adult, he shows that he cares about how people feel about him in the residence where he lives, what is known as a modified "TC"—a therapeutic community that is breaking new ground in housing and treating people with dual (psychiatric/substance abuse) problems. When he has the chance, he tries to relate to other people. He values their praise and attention. He shows distress at their reproach. He wants to stay in the house, not to be thrown out; he wants to learn to go by the rules, to learn to live in this little society of homeless people who also are struggling to learn their way. Given a firm structure, a group of staff *in loco parentis* who are consistent, limiting but supportive, both structuring and nurturing, he shows in various ways that he wants to learn to get along in a way that is fair and respectful of others and himself.

This sense of human connection is crucial to learning to be a member of society. If there is no basis for wanting and needing others—no basis in having had at least one good human connection early in life—then a person with Darrell's record of antisocial behavior, as a child and as an adult, could well continue on the same path, despite efforts at treatment. The capacity for remorse, for shame, for wanting the liking and regard of other people, is the leverage that helps people—whether as children or as adults—to grow into an adult role in human society. The person who does harm without remorse, or perhaps with a feigned concern that is one more way of conning people, may be for all practical purposes past help, or past any help that there is a way to give. But a man like Darrell, if he is lucky enough to land in a home like this, has a chance to change, if only he and the people who work with him can stick with the effort.

Being able to stick with it depends, perhaps, on the merest thread or nub of self, and who knows the ultimate source of that sense in a deprived child? We believe, certainly, that the foundation of selfhood rests always on some basis of trust, some good experience of life, however rudimentary, however transient. People write about the so-called "undefeated child"—the child who survives disasters of early upbringing and yet, inexplicably, grows and thrives and achieves. But Darrell is not one of these. And yet somewhere back there—in his first knowledge of the mother, in the few years with the aunt who was at least kin, however reluctantly—somewhere back there was someone and something good, a seed for late-blooming trust—though it was a long time between that early planting and even the most minimal chance for the tree to grow.

## A VICTIM OF CRACK/COCAINE: THE BIOPSYCHOSOCIAL FALLOUT

Darrell, among his other disadvantages in life, represents a population of growing concern—that of infants born to alcohol- and drug-abusing mothers. The child of cocaine has a triple threat against him—first, the damage done prenatally by the drug or drugs. Cocaine exposure through the mother's use during pregnancy affects the fetus both directly and indirectly. Constriction of blood vessels in the uterus results in lack of oxygen and nutrients to the fetus, slowing its growth. Low birth weight, in turn, "increases the risk of infant mortality and (makes) the child vulnerable to illness and neurobehavioral conditions. . . . Drug-exposed infants are twice as likely to be of low birth weight." Evidence is less consistent for certain problems at birth, such as congenital malformations, cerebral damage, and seizures, because some studies have not controlled for effects of use of drugs in addition to cocaine. (Grossman and Schottenfeld, 1992)

Ongoing, postnatal effects are also difficult to isolate. The authors cited also report that ". . . there is some evidence of persistent central nervous system dysfunction and problems in attention regulation and state control [maintaining a stable state of perception and affect]. Anecdotal and media reports, classroom observations, and increasing referrals to special education are suggestive of long-term learning and developmental deficits . . ." on the part of cocaine-affected children. Yet the authors add the caution that ". . . many of these long-term behavioral problems may result from impaired parent-child interaction in multiproblem families where substance abuse continues throughout childhood."

Darrell was born before the outburst of social concern about "crack babies," and he probably shows the neuropsychological effects of fetal alcohol syndrome as well as those of his mother's cocaine abuse. Some researchers today observe that "crack babies," while they show severe symptoms of overstimulation and dysregulation at birth and in early infancy, if they are given appropriate care, appear to outgrow these symptoms as they move into elementary school years, whereas fetal alcohol syndrome, by contrast, seems to do long-lasting damage to brain function.

For Darrell, the neurobiological effects of his mother's cocaine, impossible as they are to tease out completely from effects of his family and social learning, may contribute pervasively to his problems in everyday functioning. Focusing attention, regulating one's emotional states, tolerating tension and the frustration of impulse—these are requirements of social living that depend heavily on the basic capacities of the organism, the ability of *this* infant, this child, to achieve a balanced, peaceful rhythm of activity and rest, tension and its relief, arousal and satisfaction. This rhythm, and its uniqueness in each individual, begins with our biological heritage and only on that already-imprinted slate imprints further the many-layered patterns of early and later learning—the rhythms of hunger and feeding, rest and stimulation, the rhythms of the self and the surrounding world. Whatever soothing and regularity was available to Darrell had to be impressed on an organism with limited capacity to respond and to integrate its lesson.

An infant who is "born addicted" is hyperactive to stimulation and may not be able to be soothed, just as a "colicky baby" may not be able to sleep, or a small infant that feeds every two hours cannot sleep through the night. Tension and its relief is a normal rhythm of infancy—but tension as craving for a specific, chemical form of relief plays havoc with the rocking of that cradle. The experience of being soothed—the normal experience of babies—is a foundation for the future capacity for self-soothing, and for the later self-regulation of impulse and emotion. But it is normally part of the experience of oneness with the mother, the body warmth of another human being; the comfort is on a human scale that cannot match the abnormal tension of craving. Insatiable craving, unmanageable anxiety, unsatisfied hunger are stimulations that are intensely painful for the immature (or the addicted adult) organism, and the rhythm they excite is chaotic and unrelenting; the relief or "soothing" may be available only in the numbness of apathy, the artificial euphoria or "mellowing" of drugs, the oblivion of sleep.

So the drug-damaged infant is born with at least one strike against him, the *bio* part of bio-psycho-social—impaired neurophysiological equipment for forming the structures of perception and self that are needed to make sense of life and manage its stressors day by day. What about the next strike, the second threat of the trio, the impact of this problem on Darrell's *psychological* development? Today, if a child is born with neurological impairments that become evident as he begins to grow and to learn, parents can be advised about how to compensate—how to adapt their handling and education of the child to help him to grow up as normally as possible. Children with these problems need very careful, attentive handling—direct, not overly complex communications, an even, low-key emotional tone, consistent structuring and discipline, gentleness, constancy. The second threat to Darrell is inconstant parenting—the repeated losses and sudden changes of "mothers" and the difficulty of building into himself the experience of a good, loving figure, as a foundation for his own sense of self. Yes, probably there was someone and something . . . perhaps something partial and fragmented. But what Darrell—or any infant who is biochemically and/or neurologically compromised—needed more of, Darrell could hardly get at all. That was the psychological part. Any of these unavailable experiences—of nurturing, of constancy, of structure—would have helped Darrell. These are the building blocks of what we call socialization—the learning through repeated experience of time and its rhythms, of how space is structured and defined, of how people treat each other and what comfort is. Lack of any one of these—especially for this particular child, and indeed for most children—would have been devastating.

That's without the *social* part of the picture—the third threat: grinding, unremitting poverty, the familiar fate of the marginal or unskilled person in this time and place in society, the effects on children of disasters in the lives of parents, the closed and open doors in our society for a man like Darrell, with plenty of opportunity to act on the promptings of untrammeled impulse, his biological and psychological and social heritage in a life short on resources otherwise.

## THE MULTI-PROBLEM PERSON: FALLING THROUGH SYSTEMS

Of the three cases we have highlighted, Darrell represents most clearly the crisis that is currently confronted by our systems of health care, education, human services, and social control. He emerges first as a victim of a social, community, and family problem, a failure of both the public health and the criminal justice system to conquer the drug traffic at the national level, drug dealing at the community level, and patterns of drug abuse, dependence, and addiction within families. As a drug user before he had a choice, as an abused and undernurtured child, a target of drug dealers and a student of his local street and family life, he is clearly overdetermined to be a victim of addiction and of neurobiological damage.

In terms of this concern with the fetus and infant affected by alcohol and drug use, and specifically by cocaine, how many "Darrells" are growing up now in our society? Issues of methodology and sample selection within the rapidly growing data base on substance use generally, and cocaine use by pregnant women in particular, make the statistics available somewhat confusing. Various sources (referenced in Grossman and Schottenfeld, 1992:374, 375) report as follows:

There has been a marked increase in the number of women addicted to cocaine (U.S. Department of Health and Human Services, 1988). . . . In a nationwide survey of 36 hospitals . . . it was estimated that 11% of the deliveries (or an estimated 375,000 infants) were exposed to illicit substances. (Chasnoff, 1989). . . . The projections for cocaine exposure range from 100,000 infants affected each year (U.S. General Accounting Office, 1990) to reports that there will be about four million cocaine-exposed infants and children in ten years who will need special services (Wheeler Clinic, 1991). . . . Across studies, the rate of cocaine use among pregnant women averages approximately 10%–11% . . . with rates approaching 50% in some centers (Chasnoff, 1989; Jones & Lopex, 1990). . . . Hospitals that used rigorous testing procedures had rates three to five times that of hospitals with less systematic methods (Chasnoff, 1989).

Clearly the problem of drug-affected infants and children is widespread, especially in poverty-stricken inner-city communities like Darrell's, where the problem of substance use is commonly intergenerational and pervasive in the neighborhood culture. At the same time, treatment and other social resources are either nonexistent or very sparse relative to the need. People concerned with public policy in this field stress the need for a very broad-based and multifaceted approach to services in communities. People outside the field may take a different attitude, demanding to know why society should help and support not only the cocaine-impaired infants, but their mothers, who have "freely chosen" to use drugs. In recent years there has been a move to criminalize drug use by pregnant women as a form of child abuse. Unfortunately this approach, like the insultingly simplistic slogan "Just say 'No,'" begs the question of where people are to turn for alternative, healthier forms of relief from the ongoing, overwhelming internal and external stressors of their lives—lives largely unsupported by psychological strengths and social resources that are taken for granted in other strata of our society. Clearly the first system failure affecting Darrell, and the source of the most fundamental handicaps this man has borne into adult life, is the drug-ridden family and community he was born into, and the shortfall of resources devoted to reversing the direction of such lives.

A broad-based approach to these problems would include interventions ranging from more effective interference with the drug traffic and local drug dealing, through a spectrum of inpatient and outpatient treatments in much more adequate supply. These would include some involuntary inpatient treatment slots for people meeting specific criteria, as well as much more attention to aftercare and relapse prevention in the community. Adaptation of such treatment for the growing numbers of people like Darrell, with combined problems of mental illness and substance dependence, will be discussed below. Finally, a full spectrum of interventions would include intensive support of all kinds to families and communities, so that a child like Darrell would have at least a chance of starting life without confronting the triple threat of biopsychosocial factors overdetermining the damage of alcohol and street drugs.

At the next stage of Darrell's life, following the complex interplay of prenatal neurobiological damage and psychological deprivations of early childhood, the educational system had its opportunity to address his needs. As a child, Darrell, in a "special class," may have had some specialized help in learning; but he was probably thrown in with a group of other children with various and multiple needs, in a classroom and school situation where teachers and other staff were hard-pressed just to contain and protect children, let alone to further their educational needs. Today, the wildfire spread of guns in both elementary and high schools, converting what was once a safe place for children into another battleground, has blurred the distinction between school and street life. For Darrell it was a short step from childhood into the world of drugs and increasingly antisocial, and finally illegal, behavior. Between the two, as another turning point to take a young Darrell in another direction, there is a place for the residential treatment center and the drug rehabilitation facility, and also for programs such as Outward Bound and VisionQuest, which have offered youth an arena where physical challenge and excitement could replace the false challenge of substance use. The fact that Darrell was never referred for such treatment speaks of the overwhelming numbers of youth and adults in need, and the extreme shortage of services available, both within and outside school systems.

Once moving from the educational into the criminal justice system, Darrell encountered still another school, in which he learned more about sexual assault and drug-related street crime. A recent study in the state of Washington found that 80 percent of prisoners had a diagnosable problem of substance abuse, and 80 percent of those prisoners who were substance abusing also had a diagnosable mental illness. This study and Darrell's case reflect the widespread phenomenon of transinstitutionalization, the reduction of the number of psychiatric hospital beds vis à vis the increase of prison beds in this decade and the inverse relationship between the two. Each of Darrell's three terms in prison represents a lost opportunity to engage him in treatment. Jails and prisons have what treatment staff may wish for—a population that stays around and can be obliged to follow a specific regimen. What they lack is an established mission of offering treatment, and the commitment, resources, and expertise that would go with it. A promising approach now being explored in some systems is incorporating intensive drug rehabilitation into the prisoner's last year before anticipated release or parole—a prophylactic for discharge into the street, though it is unlikely to have a lasting effect unless there is attention to follow-up care and linkage to treatment, support, and self-help groups such as AA (Alcoholics Anonymous) and NA (Narcotics Anonymous). Another positive trend is toward bringing mental health agency services into local jails.

Finally, the psychiatric treatment system: Darrell had three involuntary hospitalizations for symptoms of mental illness and was diagnosed with schizophrenia, paranoid type and antisocial personality disorder in addition to substance dependence on alcohol and cocaine. But here, too, the opportunity for assessment and integrated treatment for his psychiatric and substance abuse problems was lost. Although Darrell's drug problem was noted among the diagnoses, it was not put first, and his symptoms in the emergency room, like his paranoid thinking in the halfway house, may or may not have been signs of schizophrenic illness. That judgment could not be made with certainty until or unless there had been a period free of alcohol and other drug use. During his hospitalizations Darrell was able to obtain marijuana from other patients and sometimes from staff; he never showed a drug-free picture, and even now has taken many months to clear his system of the effects of marijuana. The reason for this is that marijuana, often regarded as a relatively harmless drug, has a half-life of seven or eight days; this means that half of the substance used is still in the body a week after use. For the frequent and/or heavy user, there is a buildup of the substance over time, without an opportunity for symptoms to clear—symptoms that can resemble certain signs of a major mental illness. The psychiatric ward, like most hospital units and other mental health services, did not provide alcohol and drug treatment and would have been unable to refer Darrell for inpatient drug rehabilitation, even had they made drug dependence the primary diagnosis, and even if he had been willing to sign himself into treatment, because of his evident signs of thought disorder and his possibly incorrect diagnosis of schizophrenia. Only a closely controlled hospital unit, offering intensive and integrated treatment for both psychiatric and substance abuse problems, and able to keep him in the hospital for a more extended stay than the usual two or three weeks, could have met Darrell's real needs. Instead, his symptoms cleared as much as anyone expected, and he was discharged once again to the street, where he soon reentered the endless cycle of jail, prison, hospital, and shelter for the homeless.

Why don't these multiple systems work for a man like Darrell? Because they don't work together. Because Darrell shows up by turns as a medical emergency, a psychiatric emergency, a homeless person, a street criminal, a drug addict, and each system treats him with its own services but has limited authority or opportunity to bring in the resources of other systems. The Darrell who comes into the psychiatric ward needs drug treatment and containment in a truly drug-free setting. The Darrell who comes into a drug rehab needs some way to come to grips with unmanageable anxiety and confusion and needs the psychotropic medications he may or may not be allowed to take. The Darrell who comes into a shelter or into jail needs not only shelter or correction, but also treatment for both his mental/emotional and his drug problems. Except for a few exemplary initiatives, there has not been a way out of this endless cycle, nor out of the limitations of each system's perspective on Darrell's problems.

## THE THERAPEUTIC COMMUNITY: SHAPING AND RESHAPING PERSONALITY

The house where Darrell lives is an example of a program designed to interrupt and perhaps redirect the downward path of such a life. The house is a form of therapeutic community that is adapted to the needs of the dual-disorder, multi-problem person. Therapeutic communities have long been a familiar concept in substance abuse treatment, especially for people still in the adolescent or young adult years, who have been seen as needing a radically structured approach to reshaping personality and values. The power of the group, the power of the milieu to establish and maintain new norms of conduct and interaction, is a social analog of the usual instrument of socialization, the family. For a man like Darrell, as well as for younger adolescents who have not experienced an effective socializing force that honors the values of the larger society, this is the crucible of growth.

The resident in this halfway house encounters the same thing a child encounters in a well-functioning family: reliable, ongoing support that is as strong as the person needs at the time, combined with immediate, decisive feedback and confrontation when he breaks the rules. If anything, the feedback is more consistent, the rules more clear than most families can provide. But that is necessary, because this resocialization process has to hold the line against so much learning from the past, so much experience of being able to get around the rules or not being able to abide by them or even figure out what they are. And it must hold the line, as well, against the overwhelming force of substance dependence and addiction, the habits of denial and manipulation that are part of addictive illness, and the sheer lack of practice in finding any more approved way out of restless anxiety, unmanageable rage, grinding depression, and other distressful emotions. These are, after all, human feelings that all people learn in growing to manage somehow, with increasing maturity or in increasingly destructive ways. A man or woman in Darrell's situation has learned only the outlets of impulsive and compulsive behavior, culminating in drug addiction and criminality.

Watching Darrell in the group home—laying aside for the moment the mantle of the street criminal and rapist, and looking instead for the hapless and undernurtured child—we can find surprising commonalities between what would be normal in the child and what emerges as a grievous lack in the adult. Take the cake, for instance—Darrell denied having snatched a piece of someone else's anniversary cake, even as the fresh crumbs on his face betrayed him. Who does this? A child of a certain age, with a child's magical thinking or lack of appreciation of the power of adults to "see through" his motives and behavior. But if a child does this, people recognize it as childlike and smile to themselves; it is even endearing, for each of us recognizes in it the urges and wishful fantasies of our own inner child. If a child does this, and what he steals is cake, we understand. But what if a child lives in the powerful body of an adult and controls what that adult man does?

As we noted earlier, Darrell's history contains ample evidence for the diagnosis of antisocial personality disorder—the personality of the entrenched criminal or sociopath. But in the shelter of the group home, it's the child that people keep seeing in him. He shows, for instance, the following behavior:

*Impulsive behavior:* Much in the process of growing up and becoming socialized has to do with the restraint of impulse. Freudian theory developed extensively around a problem confronted by any society or civilization: How do you teach a child enough self-control to live in society and yet allow the life force— for Freud, the libido, or sexual/aggressive energy—to survive as a fuel for love and work? In almost any society there are reasons to say that more or less restraint of impulse would be desirable. In the Victorian society that was the context of Freud's thinking, it was easy to find that harm was done by *too much* restraint of normal sexual and aggressive drives. In our society today, most people find *too little* teaching of self-control, especially in a world like Darrell's, where there has been little room for consistency and structure.

Of course, impulsive behavior is partly the fruit of biology, as we have seen—it may result from an excess of aggressive drive and/or a deficit in regulation of affect (feeling), mood, and impulse—as well as from the failures of social nurturing and psychological development. Whatever the mix of reasons, certainly one we can see in Darrell's life is a simple failure of socialization—a lengthy, complex, multifaceted process without which the man remains an impulse-ridden child.

*Low tolerance for frustration:* Ideally, as children grow and mature they have innumerable experiences that help them to develop an ability to wait, to put up with disappointment, to tolerate frustration. You can't always get what you want: that is a fundamental lesson of human life in any society. Ideally, these experiences of living with frustration are more or less tolerable, in fact are graded and progressive, corresponding to the increasing tolerance and maturity of the growing child. Attentive parents with time and resources try to arrange life so that there is not too much frustration at any point. As with the task of learning to tolerate the parent's absence—the growing child needs a little bit of frustration, then a little more, then more still, but in accord with her capacity to handle the experience without unbearable anxiety, pain, and rage. If life were never frustrating—if the milk were always there at the first twinge of hunger, if whatever we want could be conjured up at the instant of wanting—we would never develop the ability to live with frustration and work or wait for its end.

But Darrell's life is a very different matter, the opposite situation of severe, repeated loss, frustration, and pain—the flooding of the immature organism with panic-level anxiety. Such anxiety is the joint product of the biological impairment—the effects of the mother's drug use on the developing fetus—and of the social/psychological frustration of waiting too long, too many times for what one wants and needs. Too much frustration, too soon, and on levels that are fundamental to the sense of bodily well-being is bad news in the development of any child, and at the level of infancy and early childhood it is limiting frustration that needs to be the major concern. The repeated experience of painful, grinding hunger or panic, the flooding of rage and frustration, the experience: *I am always hungry,* or *Help will never come*—these experiences don't teach the infant or child to tolerate frustration; they teach, if anything, that it *can't* be tolerated. We can surmise that, like the overactive alarm system in post-traumatic stress disorder that we can see in Annie's case, these experiences of unbearable frustration teach the child to respond with panic, anxiety, and rage, the moment frustration is threatened, because any frustration, any delay, suggests the intolerable. Such experiences make it impossible to learn in a tolerable, graduated way how to wait, how to soothe oneself as a parent would, how to ease the experience of waiting and the disappointment of not having what is wanted. For Darrell, "she"—the parent who might have taught this, if she could—has been gone a long time now. Too long and too soon. His tolerance of frustration is that of the early child, the infant flooded with panic and rage.

*Shallow affect:* You get a sense, with a child/adult like this, that feeling doesn't go very deep. And what follows from that is that relationships don't go very deep, and that it's hard to help the person with painful emotions, hard to take hold of anything, and to plant the seeds of genuine liking, deep caring, and trust. In the true antisocial personality, the lack of remorse speaks of a lack of the fundamental sense of connectedness between one human being and all others, based at first on the deep bond of need and trust with the mother/caregiver and developed further with other significant others in the child's immediate, intimate world, and based finally on the conscience—or what Freud called the superego, the internalized values that have been taught by modeling or example as well as by precept or stated value. The capacity for remorse and the presence of conscience are founded on relationships that are important and abiding, and that is where people begin with the professional helping or corrective relationship—by forming a bond of trust, a therapeutic alliance.

If you haven't learned to bond with another person—or have learned that it's too dangerous, too disappointing to place trust in a mother, only to have her disappear or turn on you—then it is difficult, more than difficult, to make a trusting relationship later in life. This is a key to why one of the criteria for antisocial personality disorder is the lack of any important long-term (even a year-long) relationship with a person of the opposite gender. The close, one-to-one connection early in life is both the model and the basis for our later connections, both in intimacy and in the cooler, yet vitally important zone of our connection with a group and with the human race as a whole.

If you feel this sense of connectedness with other human beings, a number of things follow: you don't want to hurt another person physically, or even emotionally, if the relationship is close; and you don't want to break the rules, spoken and unspoken (if you know them) that modulate people's relationships with one another, because you may be "punished" by being cast out—out of a single relationship or, worse yet, out of your group. A person who has never learned to feel that sense of connectedness or relationship or has been taught not to trust, already *is* "outside" in a fundamental sense. That person may not feel remorse; the feeling that one must not hurt another is lacking, and so is the vulnerability to being punished by rejection or being "cast out." The person is outside all that, and in that sense may feel above all that, at once grandiosely superior to these usual human restraints and, on another level, threatened and forced to rely only on himself and his own wits.

But this picture is not a picture of Darrell. His affect is shallow—he does not show the depth of feeling or relating that one finds in the mature adult. But he does show a genuine, open concern with "doing better," with meeting the standards of his group. He seeks attention and praise, and people feel good when they help him because he is responsive to the help. Although he expresses some doubts about how he's doing and how far he can go in developing himself, he also expresses a fervent wish to learn, grow, and become more capable. In the true antisocial personality this expressed wish would be another form of con job. Coming from Darrell, it is clearly sincere—and one may wonder, then, how does this person who shows an openhearted, even naïve desire to learn the rules of human connection get involved in so many antisocial actions, some of them, such as rape, among our currently most widely condemned offenses?

One key to this is that the sense of connection and the seeking of praise and attention have been directed to a social group very different from the larger society—the also large, but so far minority society of the outsider, the criminal. There, too, there are rules, standards, mores—and according to that set of standards Darrell falls short, not because of his antisocial actions, but because he is inept, unskilled at criminality—he hurts others but also himself; he is not a "smart" criminal; rather, he stumbles into criminal behavior through his lack of judgment and self-control—and because, like a very young child, he goes where he is wanted and accepted and has not yet formed a strong and deep sense of connection, based on deeply formed emotional relationships with others that would bind him to the moral and legal standards of the larger society. He hasn't had the chance to form that kind of relationship—and it is on that kind of relationship, with a loved and trusted parent who models the social values to be formed, that what we call "conscience" is founded.

*Sensitivity to rejection:* The person who is in the early throes of feeling loved and accepted—who has only a tenuous hold on such love and acceptance, and never is given the foundation of a steady, reliable flow of this good milk of human connectedness—can be easily hurt and can be highly sensitive to rejection. It is as if each single incident of criticism or blame, however trivial in itself, means a total rejection of the person. People who give advice about child rearing are likely to stress that one should condemn the act but not the child himself—that the message should not be: Darrell, what makes you so evil? but rather something like: I don't like what you just did. The message, of course, is conveyed not just in the particular words that are said, but rather in the tone, that is accepting or rejecting of the child itself even as the parent teaches the rights and wrongs of particular actions. For some parents, including one who is driven by another set of needs and concerns, such as those of substance abuse or of narcissism, the "bad action" is merely one that irritates the parent. That is, the child cannot discern any difference in weight between violating the more serious moral concerns—about lying, for instance, or hurting others—and simply being seen as bad because the parent is annoyed. The basic message, either way, is that the child is naughty, nasty, annoying, not loved, not wanted.

When Darrell hangs back from coming into the group room, he will say, "They don't want me there." This is perhaps his most fundamental experience—not being wanted, not being accepted. But one must feel accepted in a fundamental way—first by the parent/caregiver, and then, internalizing that sense, by one's own inner self—in order to have any reason not to violate that acceptance and bring on the pain of one's own guilt and the pain of rejection. Someone who feels rejected all the time, or rejected by the smallest slight—someone who feels guilty and "bad" all the time—has little or no motivation to avoid doing wrong and the punishment that follows. Indeed, some people seem to seek punishment, as if to bring on the retribution from outside that their internal sense of guilt requires. It is a touchy matter, conscience, and even concerned and attentive parents can overdo or underdo its teaching. For Darrell, rejection has come all too easily, often for reasons he could not fathom—and he has that same experience in the group home—except that here he can rely on trusting relationships that are developing with certain staff, in which he does feel accepted as himself. The sensitivity to rejection doesn't go away, but he can be supported as he tries to learn how to gain equally reliable acceptance from his group.

*Lying to avoid punishment:* A child of a certain age normally lies to avoid angering the parent. "I didn't do it" is a refrain often heard, and heard with skepticism, by parents. What is involved is not only the lack of a developed conscience, one that prohibits lying—and lying to avoid punishment is often one of the last prohibitions to be mastered. But also involved is the young child's lack of discrimination about what is plausible. When Darrell says, "I didn't take any cake," ignoring the crumbs that inform everyone of the truth, his denial rests on a degree of magical thinking, the kind of thinking that can make a child feel invisible if he closes his eyes. It is not only a matter of not having integrated the prohibition: I shouldn't lie (or, for that matter, I shouldn't take this cake). It is also, even more inappropriately, not having learned: They won't believe this. The lie as well as the deed it attempts to hide is that of a young child, a child perhaps five years old.

One aspect of learning not to lie is learning what is plausible. Another is developing a conscience, an internalized parent, that punishes us with guilt if we lie, especially to someone who is important to us. And yet another, without which the learning really is not workable, is learning to "face the music"—learning how to survive the disapproval and blame, perhaps the rejection that follows if one admits to having done something "wrong" or foolish. Of course, the criminal will say, "I didn't do it" in order to avoid going to prison; yet some people give themselves up to the law because they recognize the consequences of not owning up to their action—a self-imposed prison of guilt, or a life of hiding and running away. When someone lies about a small offense, it has to do with not knowing how to face the purgatory of the other person's anger and rejection. As we grow and mature, normally we learn to stand up to what we have done and to take whatever consequences are involved. If the learning of the prohibition against lying is weak, if the sense of reality that says, "This won't work . . . They won't buy it" is also weak, and if the person dreads rejection above all things—then even the adult, who has not become a fully mature adult, may lie as a child might. When the child does it, we laugh indulgently at the naïveté of the denial. When the adult does it, we find it antisocial. Of course, this has something to do with the mistakes or actions involved. The more blatantly foolish the mistake, the more blatantly "evil"—that is, in violation of the unspoken social contract with other human beings—is the action, the more difficult it is to admit to it. For Darrell, or for another Darrell, the act of taking the cake might be too childish to own up to. The more serious the act, the more dire the consequences—whether prison or the emotional exile of a lost relationship—and the more difficult it is to tell the truth and to tolerate what follows. This means too that the impulsive person, the person who has not learned control, is more likely to have to give in to the impulse to lie; both the actions that are done and the way of dealing with the fact of having done them are the ways of a child, focused on what is easier at the moment, unable to muster the strength and maturity to cope with the impulse to do or the impulse to lie, and lacking the alternatives to both the action and the attempt to deny its reality. The ultimate form of this denial, of course, is lying to oneself, the psychological defense of denial as an internal mechanism for blotting out the truth.

*Testing the limits:* It's not very surprising that Darrell is always testing limits. If you haven't been given, in growing up, a map or a clear set of signposts—"Off Limits!"—you continue, as an adult, stepping over the boundaries, trampling on other people's territory, trying to find out where your rights end and those of others begin. If there is no one there to keep showing the child where the limits are—repeatedly, consistently, without confusing mixed messages and jarring absences and unexplained reversals of how things are done—the behavior of the growing person goes out of bounds, one way and another . . . until the trampling of boundaries becomes too blatant, the social or the statutory law is broken, and the child-cum-adult is punished. Then, is the limit learned? By some, perhaps . . . and some have to learn it again and again.

And what if the child-in-a-man's-body doesn't learn it, but does land in a new kind of place—a place where rules are clear, consistent, even rigid, and strictly, conscientiously enforced? Then there is reason to test, to try to find out: Are these the rules? Are these really the rules? How far can I bend them? Will they still stay in place? What can I get away with? If I push hard, will people give in? If I sneak something, will they see? Can I find some way to do what I've always done?—because, if I can't do what I've always done, what can I do now? Natural questions . . . that is, questions that are natural to the child in the process of being socialized to a given family, a given class or social group, a given society. These are Darrell's questions in this new place, this new family.

*Delaying gratification:* This too is something that has to be learned, and over time, not overnight—why you should ever consent to wait for pleasure; why you should ever want the kind of pleasure you have to wait for; how to wait and work and look forward to it without giving in to easier pleasures, more immediate rewards; how to survive the waiting, when the wanting is so intense it brings tears to your eyes, or how to maintain the wanting, when the waiting is so dismal and so long? Darrell takes the cake blindly, on impulse, without a thought, probably. If he thought about it, he might try to wait for the cake—if he feared the punishment of rejection or ridicule, if he wanted the pleasure of praise or of eating with the others, if the wait wouldn't be too long, if he weren't too hungry that night, or too despairing.

*Working for a distant goal:* Darrell starts a job in the group home: he's expected to vacuum the living room. He does about a third of it, and the vacuum cleaner shuts off; the bag has to be changed. But Darrell is hungry, and he wants to quit working and go in to lunch. Finish the job, you can eat when you finish . . . Finish your homework before you go out to play . . . Finish practicing before you get on the phone to your friends: These are the lessons of parents who are attentive to structuring time and building useful habits in a child . . . the demands of a society that values productiveness, goal-directed action, work before play. This is the demand: to delay gratification and let the good feeling, the pride, the satisfaction be part of your reward. But the news of this demand has not reached Darrell before, and even now it may require too much of him. Any time you have a delay in seeking pleasure, you need to be able to control your impulse to jump over that delay, to push it aside, to smash it with the force of your wanting. You need to be able to keep in mind the other, larger goal, and you need to be able to see far enough ahead and far enough behind to remember and trust that you'll get to the pleasure in the end, to remember that you'll feel good about yourself if you finish what you should finish first. These are lessons of experience, of consistent experience with delay and its rewards—but not lessons of Darrell's life, until now.

A turning point comes when Darrell is asked to mind a booth at a fair; to sit and watch people coming and going but stay at his post, and wait for his snack until break time. Another turning point, another hopeful sign, is when he works at tiling a bathroom for an hour without giving up in the middle. What does it represent, this mustering of persistence, stick-to-it-iveness? A thousand mini-decisions, a thousand little moments of self-denial, self-reminders or reminders by others to stay with it, to have patience, to keep going, to wait for the end of work time. More of the lessons that children learn much earlier in life, if they're lucky, and use every day, without thinking much about it.

A TC, or therapeutic community for substance abusers, a group home for adolescents, a residential school—these are places to learn the basic lessons of childhood: the structuring of time and space and work and play, the boundaries between self and others, the ways of living through intolerable feelings, unmanageable levels of anxiety and rage. Some children, such as Darrell or Annie, who grow up troubled have the luck of a second chance at learning these childhood lessons. For a young man like Bill there are ways, too, of learning to cope and compensate for the deficits of a major mental illness, and learning one or another degree of the simple, yet very complex skills of making a life in this world. For a troubled or impaired young man or woman there are many ways of getting lost in this society, and there are also a number of ways of being found and finding oneself. But a traditional TC or halfway house for people with alcohol and drug problems is not usually a recourse for those with dual or multiple disorders, unless it is adapted, as this house is, to such clients' special needs and sensitivities.

Historically, therapeutic communities were heavy hitters, using humiliation and coercion as a means of breaking through the entrenched defenses of the drug addict. Today's TCs are typically more moderate in their approaches, while maintaining the kind of firm, even rigid structure that allows no room for evasion and getting around the rules. The adapted TC, directed like Darrell's house to both mental/emotional and substance abuse disorders, must take into account not only the habits of drug dependence and addiction, but the full range of the person's impairments. In Darrell's case, as we have seen, that range may include some magical and paranoid thinking, some distortions in how he perceives events, some real difficulties with such cognitive functions as memory and linear thought process, as well as the deficits in social learning and the drug-related problems that the halfway house is primarily addressing. We do not yet know the outcome of this kind of milieu treatment for a man like Darrell, but it offers at least a chance of addressing a multifaceted failure of socialization—for this man and how many more?

## COGNITIVE/BEHAVIORAL TRAINING AND REHABILITATION

At the other end of an imaginary spectrum, relating to cognitive as well as social and emotional deficits, is a type of therapy sometimes called *training* or *focused rehabilitation,* or—in the context of contemporary psychiatric programs—*intensive psychiatric rehabilitation.* Where the therapeutic milieu or therapeutic community addresses socialization in a broad sense, focused rehabilitation or cognitive/behavioral training addresses specific psychological, behavioral and/or educational skill deficits. For a man like Darrell, a two-pronged approach, offering a supportive yet limiting "family" for resocialization on the one hand, and a specifically targeted skill training program on the other, may offer new circumstances for functioning in the world. A noteworthy aspect of a skill-based approach is that it need not be confined to the kinds of specific skills that are often identified in social and vocational rehabilitation programs. Such a program can also include emotion management, self-esteem building, anxiety control, problem-solving and interpersonal communication as topics of training, together with more cognitively based areas such as memory and attention—depending upon how the person's problems are assessed and what are his own choices of areas to target. The major difference between skill-training methods of rehabilitation and traditional psychotherapy lies in the method and perspective on the person's problems in living. In general, cognitive/behavioral methods are based in the here-and-now and involve specific practice of new approaches or underdeveloped skills, rather than exploration of the "whys" and the feelings involved in the pervasive problems of a man like Darrell. For this reason such approaches, together with the resocializing power of the therapeutic community, may offer the best hope for people like Darrell, who have lost their birthright, the right to be children and to be taught and nurtured and helped to grow into a healthy, mature adulthood.

We have chosen Darrell to illustrate the extreme effects of early deprivation, neglect, and delinquent socialization. His combination of biopsychosocial disadvantages has been presented at length to illustrate two points. First, few individuals are beyond help; to label Darrell a "sociopath" is to condemn him to repeating his cycle of despair until his early death or life imprisonment removes him from society. Analysis and understanding of his problems do offer a possible, though long and painful, road to acceptable functioning in society—though unfortunately his role in society is still likely to be marginal. Secondly, Darrell's experience can be recognized in many people who are less disabled and come from less disrupted family backgrounds. Recognition of these elements offers a clue to remediation of the otherwise unexplained and unacceptable behavior of an outcast. If a commitment to the small, consistently reinforcing society of the TC can be learned, and if the basic skills of ordinary life can also be learned, and if there is then any next step in the form of services and supports and job possibilities, then there could be hope for a young man like Darrell or his female counterpart. If not, we will have to rely on continuing to multiply the numbers of prison beds in a vain effort to keep up with their occupants, the homeless, mentally ill, and drug-addicted young people who have landed in the "treatment" milieu of last resort.

# PART II

# A MULTI-LENS PERSPECTIVE ON PEOPLE AND PROBLEMS

Chapter 8

# The Making of Personality

*Development, Disorder, and Immaturity*

Whilte the shaping life experiences of Bill, Annie, Ellen, and Darrell are diverse, they can each be seen in terms of a common unifying model of personality development. Each of these individuals brings into life a very specific genetic profile, an encoded map for development that we are only beginning to learn to read. Each presents a unique and complex set of variations on the basic program of growth and development that is our common human heritage. Each person then confronts a great variety of experiences that are nurturing, shaping, challenging, traumatizing, as it may happen in a particular family, culture, and set of circumstances. These experiences are integrated in various ways with the inner program of growth and development. Each person makes a complex array of adaptations to both the inner and the outer world—to the neurochemical signals of the brain as well as the interpersonal signals of the environment.

The crucial question in a person's life, first as a child and then as an adult, is: What is the match (or mismatch) between what the person needs and can offer, on the one hand, and what the environment demands and can offer, on the other? The DSM-IV Axis I presenting problems of anxiety and depression often reflect a mismatch, either transient or ongoing, between What I need and What I can get, or between What I can do and What is expected of me. The Axis II patterns of personality disorder represent in part the person's defensive strategies, developed over time, for coping with an ongoing mismatch between the person and what is offered and demanded in his world.

Darrell, a child trying to cope with a heavy load of neuropsychological, emotional, and social disadvantage, couldn't tap into extra resources in his environment to meet his special needs and learn to cope with a demanding, undernurturing, and hazardous social world. He didn't have an attentive parent, a special teacher, a calm home or school environment in which he might have been able to struggle more effectively with the learning and perceptual problems resulting from disorders in his brain functioning. He became evasive and impulse-ridden, unable to muster an inner strength to compensate for his deficits. In Darrell's case the tasks of personality development stand out as essential to his rehabilitation. But his personality style, in turn, seems directly related to the cognitive problems of a child who couldn't pay attention, couldn't remember, couldn't learn, couldn't calm himself. The world he couldn't deal with—at home and at school, and in the inner world of his own feelings—became, in each case, a place he had to escape from, into drugs, magical thinking, and impulsive and sometimes violent behavior.

In Bill's case we met someone seemingly very different—a young man who was born into the lucky circumstances of an attentive, stable middle-class family and had a good education in relatively trouble-free schools, only to fall off the track of his life when he developed a major mental illness. Unlike Darrell, he was able until then to do well, in spite of a tendency to be shy, hesitant, and anxious in approaching anything new. In a supportive environment that rewarded what he was able to do, he could build up the personality characteristics that go with success: some sense of mastery and self-confidence, some ease and humor in dealing with other people. The blow, when it came, was a cruel one—an illness only slightly less stigmatizing, and in some ways even more disabling, than Darrell's drug addiction and criminal behavior. But at least Bill came into young adulthood equipped with all the social and learning skills he had built up in his growing years, and these will give him a much better chance in going on with his life than if he had been afflicted with schizophrenia since childhood or had complicated his problems by getting into alcohol and marijuana at an earlier age.

Annie shows a mixture of factors shaping her personality. She had a family that was once attentive, but became dominated and eventually devastated by alcoholism, unemployment, and poverty, with loss of family cohesion and parental supervision and related patterns of physical and sexual abuse. She was bright and successful in school, up to the point where trouble at home began to show up as missed assignments, falling asleep in class, and an unhappy, angry, disruptive, or tuned-out mood. Then she took an early plunge into her own alcoholism—a product of her biological heritage of vulnerability, the social pattern of experimental drinking among very young teens in her peer group, the familiarity of her parents' use of alcohol, and her anxiety and depression, which have been found to double the risk of a young person's developing alcohol and drug problems. Her alcoholism was overdetermined by biological, psychological, family, and social factors. Her mental illness, bipolar disorder, had a genetic basis, and some evidence of it turned up in her family history. It is not uncommon in such family histories to find an overlap of affective (mood) disorders and alcoholism or other drug addiction.

Ellen, with a background something like Annie's but a different problem, diagnosed as borderline personality disorder, is spared the extreme mood swings and psychotic episodes of bipolar disorder, but does show a very intensely reactive pattern of feelings and behavior. While BPD has not yet been identified as biologically or genetically determined, nor as involving a clear-cut "chemical imbalance," it is believed by many people to to have at least a component of biological difficulty in regulating intense and shifting moods and/or aggressive states, with effects on the person's psychological and interpersonal experience—and the development of personality—at every stage of growing. Someone like Ellen, if she does have a mood disorder or an emotion-regulation deficit, is likely to have a difficult course of development, with problems in managing both personal tasks and relationships. Superimposed on this, for Ellen, were the wild cards of traumatizing experience from an early age. Both problems feed back into a continuing cycle of stressful and sometimes unbearable emotions, which Ellen is only now in the process of learning to manage.

Peter D. Kramer, in his book *Listening to Prozac* (1993), observes that moods, emotions, and behavior patterns can be modified by certain medications to such an extent that the modification looks like personality change. He raises the question: What, then, is personality? There is controversy about both the validity and the meaning of Kramer's observations on the effects of Prozac. But increasingly people in the field do recognize the unity of biological, psychological/developmental, and social elements in the creation of the human being. So the questions: Is it mental or physical? Is it heredity or environment? Is it the family or the genes? lose their meaning, reflecting a time when less was known and understood about the complex interplay of neurobiology with both cognitive and emotional phenomena. Today, personality is a picture seen through multiple lenses, and seen as much more fixed, in biological and genetic terms, than it was believed to be a few decades ago.

## THE MEANING OF PERSONALITY

Personality is a familiar, yet elusive concept. We use the word very readily: She has a great personality . . . He doesn't have much of a personality . . . She's a lot of person . . . and on into: I don't like her personality . . . or: It was a personality conflict. But what does personality really mean?

What we mean by it is the relatively stable pattern of thinking, feeling, and behavior that defines and describes that person's unique self to the outside observer. When we know someone and have a sense of his or her personality, we may say, "That isn't like her," or "He's always like that when something goes wrong." Or—hearing an anecdote about a friend, or reading a novel in which we've become well acquainted with the characters—we may smile knowingly because we recognize yet another instance when the person was "just being herself"—that is, demonstrating the personality we have come to recognize.

In Oliver Sacks' engaging book *The Man Who Mistook His Wife for a Hat* (1988), the subject of the title story was a man who, for neurological reasons, lost the capacity to recognize a face, to put together the visual information he received into a comprehensible pattern he could identify as the face of a friend or of his wife—or, indeed, as a face at all. Normally, we recognize the constellation of a friend's face or bodily form very readily—the more readily, the more intimately we know the person. And the same is true of personality: we recognize and in general adapt to—or at least come to expect—those aspects that are relatively constant in a person's way of dealing with the world. We may recognize a friend walking a block ahead of us by some peculiarity of gait, gesture, angle of the head or left arm, long before we can recognize her facial features. We may recognize someone we know on the telephone as soon as that person says, "Hello," by the unique identifiers of timbre, pitch, and intonation of that single word. Knowing the person well, we can also sense her mood from the tone of these two brief syllables.

Without these patterns of behavior and response—including the person's speech and gestures and facial expressions—there would be little predictability in our dealing with one another. But the impact of personality goes beyond the cognitive, beyond our conscious awareness and expectations—what we think people will do or what we perceive about their motives. We also take in many more messages emotionally, unthinkingly—our sense of who a person is, the special flavor of each individual, our feelings of ease and warmth or discomfort and tension in that person's presence. This kind of knowledge and recognition is taken in through every pore—the more intimately, the longer and more closely we know the person.

Much of this more "emotional" knowledge, while it is conveyed in the mini-messages of everyday communications, is based on much broader aspects of personality. These underlying aspects are not merely superficial identifiers; they affect dominant patterns of behavior and important, repetitive life choices. These deeper aspects of personality include fundamental attitudes toward oneself, toward others, toward life experience in the present, past, and future. They incorporate issues of self-esteem, of optimism versus pessimism, of empowerment versus helplessness and hopelessness, of entitlement and grandiosity versus humility, self-denial, and self-abnegation. Such underlying attitudes are expressed in our everyday choices and interactions, though they usually do not break the surface of our conscious awareness; they are the ground of our basic sense of ourselves and others, and of what we can do in the world.

Even 20 years ago it was common to assume that personality traits and characteristics—both fundamental personality style and minor idiosyncrasies—were largely the product of upbringing and environment. Our society, including the schools of postgraduate education in the helping professions, went through a period of focusing almost entirely on the social environment as a determinant of the individual life. The dominant belief was that the influence of environment far outweighed that of heredity in human life. This view was actually a source of optimism; it offered an illusion of control to parents and to society. We could write the future by programming the behavior of the growing child. It was the cumulative experiences of the child that would form personality from an infinite reservoir of possibilities; experience would write its messages on a blank slate, the *tabula rasa* of the unformed organism. It was this view that gave rise to the supposition that mental illness could be eliminated from society through the preventive services of community mental health centers—that, once deinstitutionalization was accomplished, an enlightened society would obviate the need for institutional care. When this emphasis on environmental determinism was applied to personality development, it laid the total weight of both praise and blame at the door of parents of the growing child.

This emphasis on psychological development and the social environment was a natural outgrowth of the spread of exciting ideas about the ramifications of upbringing, the elaboration of Freudian psychological/developmental concepts, and the development of skills and interest in observations of development in young children. But as Newton said, "To every action there is an equal and opposite reaction." Today the inroads of research have focused our attention on a different front, namely, the biological and genetic factors that seem to determine more of the nature and personality of the human being than we had thought. Not only personality style, discernible in earliest infancy as the baby interacts with the environment, but even such insignificant traits as a mannerism, a way of telling a joke have been identified through twin studies and the like as genetically determined, at least in part. Does an awareness of such evidently inborn characteristics sweep away the psychological/developmental view of personality formation? No, at least not yet—but like so much of our new knowledge, it gives us pause, and presents something further, and counter to some of our past perspectives, to integrate into our enormously complex mosaic of understanding of what makes a human being.

## PERSONALITY STYLE AND PERSONALITY DISORDER

Personality style becomes personality disorder when: (1) the person's characteristic way of relating to self and others is not merely stable, but fixed, rigid, and inflexible, and (2) it doesn't work. Those two criteria are really one: that is, a rigidly fixed style of relating that is not flexible and adaptable to different people and circumstances is, almost inevitably, a style that doesn't work. And the rigidity of the dysfunctional style, which becomes an obstacle to taking in new information and learning new ways, creates a snowball effect, a compounding of problems as the person moves through life without being able to utilize the corrective lessons of feedback from others.

One key to understanding the rigid, repetitive style of reaction and interaction that is implied by personality disorder is the concept of ego-syntonic versus ego-dystonic characteristics and behavior. Depression and anxiety are generally ego-dystonic—that is, they are not experienced as a normal, usual aspect of self, except in the case of entrenched, long-lasting depressions, but rather as "out of tune" with the person's normal way of being. But personality style and personality disorder are, by definition, egosyntonic, part of *me*, of the person's usual experience of self. Asked to reflect upon or change troublesome or self-sabotaging behavior, the person may shrug and say, "Well, that's just the way I am." Or the person may not even see his or her behavior as out of the ordinary—or may not care. As one woman said, in response to a comment that other clients didn't react so angrily to certain conditions of treatment in a mental health clinic: "Why should it matter to me how other people react?" Yet some of her life problems reflected exactly this attitude, which in turn was designed to protect her from pervasive feelings of low self-esteem, helplessness, and defeat as she tried to cope with other people and their demands. This is an example of how a dysfunctional personality style—which, if it is pervasive, rigid, and entrenched, we call a personality disorder—can interfere, not only with everyday problem solving, satisfaction, and relationships, but also with taking in new information in life or in treatment. The personality style or disorder may be part of the person's reaction to the mismatch between How I am/ What I need and What others offer and demand of me. But then it feeds on itself. If I feel: This is how I am, and I have no interest in considering my own patterns in comparison to others' or in learning how I affect others, I am in a poor position to consider change. If anything, the suggestion of changing my personality style and characteristic ways of behaving may feel like a threat to the self—to, as one person put it, "my basic being."

So another key to understanding personality disorder is the understanding of personality structure, to whatever degree it is a product of nurture rather than nature, as including an entrenched pattern of defenses that has been developed to try to protect the person against unmanageable feelings and disorganization. All people have characteristic defenses against unpleasant or even unbearable realities, within their own thoughts, wishes, and actions as well as those of others. The flexibility or rigidity of these defenses depends on the luck of their experiences and the other resources they have been able to draw upon. To look at personality disorder in this way does not deny the role of "inborn" or inherited characteristics, even in the form of discrete personality styles. Instead, we can reflect on how experience shapes and reinforces a person's "natural" or genetically determined tendencies.

Imagine, for instance, a person with an avoidant, detached, or mistrustful personality style. Examples would be Ted, with a diagnosis of schizoid personality disorder—a pattern of social and emotional detachment from others; Mavis, diagnosed with schizotypal personality disorder, a pattern of social and interpersonal deficits combined with eccentric perceptions and behavior; or Jim, with paranoid personality disorder, a pervasive attitude of distrust and suspiciousness of others. These are the personality disorders that are grouped as Cluster A in the DSM-IV, and that are sometimes antecedent to—and therefore may be seen as risk factors for—episodes of schizophrenia. Viewing them as personality styles, we can see how Ted's detachment and social avoidance, Mavis' eccentricity, and Jim's distrustful attitude might begin as a characterological trait and then become increasingly pronounced as each person's style interfered with the kind of social experience that could have been corrective. That is, a shy and avoidant person tends to avoid social interactions because they are not gratifying and/or arouse too much anxiety. Over time, each occasion of avoidance entrenches the avoidant pattern still more. The person who says, "I hate parties" . . . "I don't like long telephone calls" . . . "I don't feel comfortable talking to someone I don't know" naturally avoids these experiences. Instead of developing social skills and learning to feel more comfortable, as most people do during childhood and the early adult years, the person with these personality patterns tends to feel still more uncomfortable and avoidant over years of diminishing social experience.

Similar dynamics apply to the person with borderline personality disorder, who may react with unmanageable anxiety or rage to a variety of situations, alternating with total repression or numbing of these feelings, out of fear that they will quickly grow out of control. This kind of problem may be based on a biological deficit in the ability to modulate emotional states. But it has fallout in the form of a spiral of escalating experience in relationships, when the child or adult gives vent to intense emotions, only to receive an invalidating response, which in turn intensifies the emotion, which in turn is invalidated. (Linehan, 1987) The person who has this experience repeatedly when expressing feelings in close relationships will increasingly avoid closeness and emotional expression, and/or will become increasingly hypersensitive to occasions for feeling enraged, abandoned, or panicky. He may give in to agoraphobia and avoid going out and/or suffer from severe panic attacks. Whatever the exact pattern of symptoms, the tendency to respond with extremes of emotion will remain unmodified by experience for as long as the person avoids occasions for anger or anxiety or, alternatively, suffers panic attacks and rageful outbursts. What is missing is the experience of gradations of anger or anxiety and the opportunity to learn how to respond to these feelings in a moderate, yet expressive way. People who learn degrees of these feelings, and develop a repertoire of ways of expressing them, have a choice, and do not need to fear their rage or panic as if it were a monster in the closet, ready to spring out and devour them or the other person at any moment.

Personality disorder as a diagnosis is seen as a relatively fixed entity—a trait rather than state phenomenon—but these examples illustrate how the psychological and social aspects of experience can interact with a basic personality style that may be preprogrammed to an extent we do not yet know—and, if that style becomes both dysfunctional and rigidly entrenched as a defense, the personality style may take on the more negative and severe dimensions of personality disorder.

## PERSONALITY DISORDER AND IMMATURITY

In the case of Darrell we presented a man whose antisocial patterns became a diagnosis. But we saw in Darrell's story the clear outlines of psychological and social forces that taught, indeed overdetermined, antisocial behavior. And we also saw in the course of Darrell's treatment how behaviors that were at first viewed as symptoms of personality disorder could also be viewed as personality immaturity, in the sense that normal personality development and the emergence of a mature, adult self have not taken place. As Darrell was socialized to the treatment milieu, the therapeutic community, he learned and developed abilities—to wait, to endure frustration, to pursue goals over time—that had not been part of his social and psychological equipment. Again, the interaction of a personal deficit with a lack of corrective experience in the environment—experience that the deficit itself makes it steadily more difficult to gain—can transform a lack to a distortion of perceptions and a disorder of personality functioning. The same view can be taken of some people with borderline personality disorder who, in cognitive-behavioral therapy, learn coping skills for managing their emotions; we may view these skills as the lessons that were not offered or learned in the developmental process, and thus as a specific form of immaturity.

The importance of considering terminology in this way—personality style, structure, disorder, immaturity—lies partly in the effort to understand the causes of problems and partly in the search for a promising remedy. *Personality disorder*, for instance, speaks more neutrally of problems in functioning and sounds less entrenched than, for instance, the term *mental illness*, and it also sounds less like moralizing than the earlier term *character disorder*. But personality disorder still suggests pathology in many circles, and it relates historically to the notion that (1) personality disorders can't be treated, or (2) if they can, the treatment requires intensive psychodynamic psychotherapy with the intent of restructuring personality. Personality style sounds more malleable; style is something that can be put on and taken off. Personality immaturity suggests a particular relevance to cognitive-behavioral approaches to therapy—the teaching of unlearned skills and/or the correcting of unwarranted beliefs. It also reminds us, as a term and as a perspective, that while for many people life experiences have distorted, as trauma distorts, the person's emotions, thinking, behavior, and self-concept, for many others the experiences that would have led to full development have been blocked or lacking, so that emotion management, social skills, and interpersonal commitments have remained beyond the boundaries of the possible. For some people the problems lie, not in pathological psychological development, but in genetically programmed and/or substance-induced behavior, combined with failures of socialization on the part of family and community.

## PERSONALITY DEVELOPMENT: THE LOOP AND THE MAZE

Personality development can be seen as a constant progression of problem-solving efforts, in response to conflicts and demands, both internal and external, that arouse discordant feelings and press for some kind of action to relieve those feelings. The process is expressed, in a simplified way, in Figure 8.1. The problem/conflict/discordant feeling can be anything from the demand to get

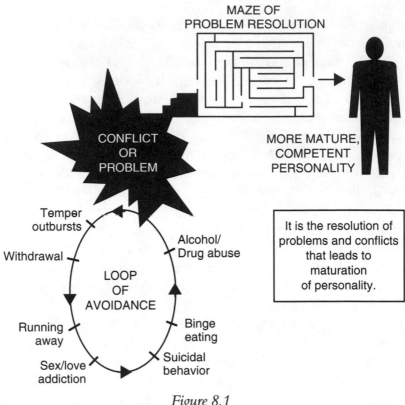

MAZE OF
PROBLEM RESOLUTION

CONFLICT
OR
PROBLEM

MORE MATURE,
COMPETENT
PERSONALITY

Temper
outbursts

Withdrawal

Alcohol/
Drug abuse

LOOP
OF
AVOIDANCE

Running
away

Binge
eating

Sex/love
addiction

Suicidal
behavior

It is the resolution of
problems and conflicts
that leads to
maturation
of personality.

*Figure 8.1*

out of bed in spite of fatigue, the demand to go to school or work in spite of anxiety and fear of humiliation, the conflict with a friend or family member that arouses a turmoil of bad feelings, and so on. The problem-solving or conflict resolution maze can mean a variety of actions and efforts to work out the problem, including meeting the demand despite one's feelings. The loop of evasion or avoidance may mean playing truant from school or work, avoiding a friend with whom one is embarrassed, having a temper outburst, going on an eating binge or a shopping spree, running away, using alcohol/other drugs, threatening or attempting suicide, giving up a task, or simply going back to sleep.

The point is that, if a person feels he has the basic equipment to be able to enter the maze of problem-solving and conflict-resolution efforts, and/or if the person has enough helping hands to lead him into that process—as good parents and teachers do for a child, or helping professionals for a client—then that process, repeated over and over throughout the years of growing up, leads to an ever more mature, more socialized and skilled and inwardly strong individual. If the door to the maze seems closed or the stairs to it too steep, or if the person feels he would be unable to find his way through, based on having little or no experience of success—and if the loop behaviors are ready to hand—then the easiest thing is to slip down the habit-greased slide, again and again, into whatever types of compulsive and self-destructive behavior are most familiar. Unfortunately, the loop behaviors only lead back into the feelings of low self-worth and shame, which become more global and pervasive with each incident.

The fundamental effort of parents, teachers, therapists, and people who are trying to develop themselves emotionally is to close off the behaviors of the loop of avoidance—to bar an inner door to alcohol/drug use, suicidal gestures, aggressive outbursts, withdrawal from situations—and to clear the way into the maze of resolution. These must be twin and intertwined processes in order to work well for the person struggling with the effort to master life experience. If the barriers to entering the maze are or appear to be too great—The cards are all stacked against me, My parents/teachers never listen, It's too complicated to figure out—or if the person feels or is too lacking in skills to make his way through—I can't keep my thoughts on track, I can't stand the way this makes me feel, I don't know how to do this, I feel stupid—and if the loop behaviors are familiar, accessible, and not firmly self-defined as "off limits"—then the likely outcome is obvious. The way to the maze is seen as up a steep flight of stairs; the way through is difficult to find. The path into the loop is all too familiar, and the slippery slope makes it a quick descent. Reversing the direction of a life pattern, once it is set in the process of growing up impaired, is a many-faceted effort. Once a person has begun to slip, again and again, into the loop, taking another path requires many helping hands.

## WISHFUL THINKING AND THE LOSS OF EXPECTATIONS

One of the major avoidant responses to be found in the loop is wishful thinking, daydreaming, or fantasy. All of us do this to some degree—in fact, one can view fantasy as a stepping-stone to desire, plan, intention, and finally action—that is, if a person feels able to put one foot in front of another, can see the direction to take, can find the next stepping-stone and dare to take a leap of faith occasionally if the distance from one stone to another is too great. Visualization—developing a visualized fantasy of oneself in a given situation, an increasingly elaborated plan of "how I would like it to be, what I would like to be doing"—has become a popularly discussed mode, both within and outside psychotherapy, of helping oneself to move forward, expand horizons, develop more creative approaches, and free up the more intuitive "right brain" for problem-solving efforts. So far, so good. Utilized in that way, consciously or otherwise, our capacity for fantasy is one of our most precious capabilities, and surely belongs in the maze of problem-solving and conflict-resolving activity.

Unless the dreaming is all we do . . . and then we find ourselves in the loop, endlessly circling around a favorite idea: *I'm going back to school one of these days . . . I'm going to be a famous rock star . . . When somebody gives me a job, I'll . . . God I wish I had a girlfriend . . . Maybe someday I'll be rich . . .* The loop becomes a holding pattern, and as long as we stay in it we never quite bump onto the ground of reality—or if we do, it hurts too much to bear.

Like all the avoidant behaviors in the loop, wishful thinking is not solely the province of young people with problems. All of us retreat temporarily into some form of avoidance, evasion, escape when we can't cope with finding and pushing our way into and through the maze. But for some young men and women with seriously disabling mental/emotional disorders, such wishful and escapist thinking becomes a way of life, and it has a tragic cast, for reasons that are not too hard to figure out. For Bill or Annie, in the absence of reality-based efforts on their part and support on the part of others, the episodes of acute illness may become increasingly frequent and severe, with even the respites between them allowing less return to a past level of functioning in life. For Ellen or Darrell, the patterns of personality immaturity and/or disorder may become ever more entrenched. For all four of these young men and women, the humiliation of a slipping-down life, especially against the backdrop of what we consider normal progress for young people in our society, may grow with each year until the empty fantasies of a successful or even a somewhat normal life become an intolerable mockery.

The key to avoiding that unhappy outcome lies in the development of some personal strengths, some sources of support, and some secure grounding in reality. For any of these young people, "getting real" implies compromise, sometimes very drastic compromise. Bill, for instance, has fallen off the path of normal, expectable adult development just at the time of one of the early expected accomplishments, leaving home for college, and although his path may not be downward if he has appropriate care and support, he is not likely to scale the heights that he and his family might have imagined in earlier days for the shy but intelligent young boy. In fact, if his path is only reasonably smooth, if it just doesn't take that downward direction, that will be cause for relief. If only he doesn't take on too much, if he doesn't get into a situation of too much pressure . . . If only he doesn't pick up a drink again, or get into marijuana, because, with his schizophrenia . . . If only he and his parents can focus on the little gains, the limited achievement of keeping the modest job he finally finds, keeping it a little longer and a little longer . . . If only the "break" and the hospitalization won't happen again.

Bill is more given to wishful thinking than Annie; what she does in the loop is to loop-the-loop with wild, self-destructive behavior, and she doesn't take much time to lie around and dream of how life could be, or how it really was, for that matter. But now and then, she meets someone from junior high school, someone who does a double-take and then says, "Aren't you . . . Didn't I know you in school?" and then she has to come up with some answer about what she's been doing, some wisecrack so they won't know whether it's a joke or not. Most people know, though, among the people she knew—and for her, as mostly for Bill, that life is all gone.

Ellen, in her wishful thinking, wishes for something we might think is reachable—freedom from the torment of flashbacks and panic attacks, freedom from surges of fear and rage, some sense of security in her relationships and within herself, allowing her to soothe her own emotional states, the traumatized child in herself.

Often she daydreams about having a home and family of her own, or of having a baby and raising it herself.

And Darrell? Darrell wishes aloud quite often—to win the lottery, to have a little red sports car, to travel to North Carolina where his aunt lives, or used to, or out to Indiana where a guy he knew in jail was going, where maybe he could work on a farm— only so far, he hasn't got it together to make any plans, and besides, he knows he'd get back onto drugs as soon as he walked out the door—so he's really as realistic as anybody, at least on that score, and he's afraid to go as far as the next corner at this time.

Wishing, dreaming, wishful thinking . . . all ways to keep hope alive, or to forget about real hopes . . . to imagine a life while failing to make it happen . . . to watch a kind of internal TV while you circle around and around in the holding pattern . . . *My sister's graduating from college . . . My brother's getting married . . . My buddy John, he's going West . . . I just turned thirty, what's in it for me? . . .* That's about it, thirty, that's about when Bill or Annie or Darrell comes to know this is no longer the troubles you got into in your twenties, this is your life.

That is surely one reason why so many young people with severe, ongoing psychiatric problems try suicide, and why so many try to get out of the pain by drinking and using drugs, and why so many rush into and out of things you'd know on the face of it wouldn't work—overly demanding jobs, impulsive marriages, stopping the medication, anything to deny or forget where it's at . . . Listen, says Bill, Annie, Darrell, I'm no different . . . I want the same things as anybody else you know.

THE LOOP OF COMPULSIVE BEHAVIOR

Some of the most difficult problems in the loop of avoidance are compulsive behaviors of many kinds, including some that are directly life-threatening, such as substance abuse/dependence, eating disorders, and suicidal acts. These are forms of avoidance, often frantic efforts to relieve tensions that feel intolerable; they generally begin as attempts to get out of a situation or a feeling and then progress to the status of a compulsion by being used, again and again, as a response, however ineffective. If the compulsive behavior is alcohol and/or other drug use, the person may also have a genetic heritage that preprograms the development of substance dependence such as alcoholism—so the use may quickly become compulsive and present, with the person's mental/emotional problems, one of the forms of dual disorder that we have discussed. This was Annie's case, and also Darrell's in his use of cocaine. For the person who has slipped into substance dependence or addiction, blocking off the loop of compulsive behavior may require intensive treatment in an inpatient or outpatient rehabilitation program. The same may be true for someone with an entrenched pattern of anorexia or bulimia, whose food avoidance or bingeing and purging may have taken on a life of its own, becoming so compelling an urge that treatment in an eating disorders rehabilitation unit is needed before the person can move on to develop other ways of responding to unbearable emotions. For the person with substance dependence or with an eating disorder, there are physiological changes that maintain the compulsive patterns, and there are also serious medical risks. The loop behavior becomes, in this situation, a magnet that perpetually pulls the person into the repetitive pattern, and special help is required—when the person is able to accept it—in order to resist its power and take a new direction toward coping with problems and intense emotions. Such help usually includes a treatment program specifically directed toward the problem, as well as involvement in a structured or "12-step" self-help program, in order to gain maximum support. But these routes to working on the problem are often not accepted initially, so that we often need to approach these problems indirectly until the person is motivated to acknowledge these behaviors and try to overcome them.

There are many other behaviors that are not compulsive in the same sense but are nonetheless so entrenched as ineffective patterns of coping that they are extremely tempting and difficult to overcome. It has become popular to use the concept of alcoholism to apply to a variety of such compulsive or dependent patterns— i.e., workaholism, sexaholism, compulsive gambling, and so forth. In a sense, these terms trivialize the true, physiologically based addictions to substances; and in another sense the comparison is apt, since any behavior that is used repeatedly and without regard for either its ineffectiveness as a means of coping or its damaging effects on the person's life may fairly be considered "compulsive."

For our purposes, the emphasis is on the loop behaviors as an obstacle to and distraction from taking on the tasks of personality development and the learning of more effective ways of coping with feelings and problems. For many young men and women, compulsive behavior patterns such as alcohol/drug use and eating disorders have begun early in adolescence or childhood, and not only have threatened their lives and safety as problems in themselves, but also have blocked the road of personality development, leaving them without many important learning and social experiences, and without the development of essential skills, even at the point in their adult lives when the substance abuse or eating disorder may be overcome. If the life-threatening loop behaviors do persist in the person's adult life, the loop itself may become the noose that threatens to cut off the ability to move and to grow and may bring life to an end before it has fully begun.

## WORKING OUT OF THE LOOP

If there is a way out of the loop of wishful thinking and compulsive, impulsive, and self-destructive behavior, it must lie in the development of personal strengths and coping skills as much as in the control of symptoms. Each of these young people—Bill, Annie, Ellen, Darrell—is not just a person with a mental illness, a personality disorder, a problem of antisocial behavior, or all of the above. Each is an individual, seeking a way to enter the maze of adult life and find a path of some measure of self-respect, stability, and fulfillment. Again, the crucial question is: Where are the gaps between what the person can do and what is demanded by his world, between what the person needs and what resources are available? And another, equally crucial question is: How far along the path of normal development—of personality, of learning, of social connection—was the person able to go before his problems and deficits blocked the way or caused him to fall or veer off the road? This second question tells us where the building blocks of support and new learning must begin.

This perspective points to an approach to treatment that includes skill building and personality development and builds on whatever strengths, achievements, and hopes the person has aspired to or attained. Today such approaches come in a number of forms that carry treatment beyond the limited framework of psychotropic medications and brief inpatient episodes for the acute stages of illness, conflict, and "acting-out" behavior, and the often unsupported, formless, or chaotic life that lies between episodes. Approaches that are more goal-directed and may replace or complement existing therapy and treatment programs include:

- Psychiatric rehabilitation directed toward specific skills;
- Cognitive-behavioral treatment focusing on specific problem areas in group or individual modalities;
- Family work of various kinds, offering support, coherence of approach, and communication with treatment staff;
- Ongoing supportive relationships with case managers, group and residential workers, and other members of a treatment/support network; and
- Self-help groups with 12-step or other, similar guidelines, offering the chance to overcome compulsive behavior and build personal, interpersonal, and spiritual strengths in the framework of a supportive community with clear values and guidelines for action.

A contemporary understanding of personality disorder and immaturity and their role in maintaining problematic functioning and behavior requires a multi-modal approach to treatment. Such an approach allows the person to work, not only on symptoms, but on underlying patterns of thinking, feeling, and behavior that tend to derail efforts to make a better life.

Chapter 9

# What About the Brain?

## *A Biopsychosocial/Organic Unity View of Thinking and Feelings*

We tend to think of the brain as the organ that does our thinking, but our thinking about this thinking organ has evolved in response to developing knowledge of how the brain works, as well as changing views of the human organism. There was a time, for instance, when the soul of a human being was thought of as having a physical reality and a specific location in the body, and death was conceived of as the soul leaving the body. Similarly, there is a long history of thinking of mind and brain as separate entities, connected in some way yet to be understood, with the brain as an incredibly complex neural network functioning as the servant of an executive entity, the mind. Also, references to "the head and the heart" as the seats of thinking and feeling, respectively, have persisted long beyond our growing knowledge of how those two organs actually work. But contemporary brain research has made it increasingly clear that body, brain, and mind are one organic unity, and, further, that the brain is the organ that generates not only our thinking but also our emotions. In fact, this familiar dichotomy between thinking and feeling must go the way of brain and mind, and of body and soul, as an outworn distinction that cannot be supported by contemporary knowledge of how the brain works.

146

In today's thinking about the brain, the nearest thing we have to the soul or a locus of consciousness is what might be called a "virtual center"—an imaginary integration point at which, according to researchers' speculations, the brain's complex of communication centers may send and receive messages. Clearly this is a chilly substitute for the imagined "soul" or "mind," and still more problematic is this conception's lack of fit with our subjective sense of self. If brain and mind are reduced to a set of technological abstractions and/or neurochemical formulas, how can we—caregivers and consumers, family members and human service practitioners—think about thinking and feelings in a humanly meaningful way? We need to adapt our common language to a new understanding of mental/emotional experience as a manifestation of brain process, with all that implies about the causes and treatment of specific disorders.

## BREAKTHROUGHS ABOUT THE BRAIN

Much of the knowledge to which we are currently adapting has emerged in the past 20 to 25 years, although the era of scientific research about brain structure and function began some 150 years ago. Since then, the process of mapping the brain's structures and gaining even a rudimentary grasp of its functioning has remained slow and tortuous, yielding many false leads and interesting speculations, but more questions than answers about how the brain works. But, thanks to developing technologies, the past two decades have been a particularly exciting period for researchers, offering some new developments and perspectives and opening the door to much more rapid progress in the future.

One major area of breakthrough in the field has been the development of imaging techniques that provide "still shots"—or even movies—of the brain in action. These techniques include: (1) the CAT (computerized axial tomographic) or CT (computerized tomographic) scan, which produces computerized images based on the relative densities of brain substance and fluid; (2) the MRI (magnetic resonance imaging) or NMR (nuclear magnetic response), which utilizes the electromagnetic responses of elements in brain and body cells; and (3) the RCBF (regional cerebral blood flow) and PET (positron-emission tomographic) scans, currently experimental and used primarily in research. Unlike the first two types of scan, which produce a static image of brain structure and contents, the RCBF and PET are able, through the use of radioactive tracers, to portray what areas of the brain are most active at a given time. Finally, (4) optical imaging is an even more recent development, using fiber-optic light and a special camera to see changes in the brain's surface that appear to correspond to the activity of neural cells.

These developments, each contributing to opening up a new world of possible observations, are seen by many scientists as only the beginning of the era of imaging the brain. The importance of these imaging techniques lies (1) in their ability to provide diagnostic information in individual cases—e.g., revealing a brain tumor or functional abnormality; (2) in the opportunity to research relationships between brain abnormalities and specific disorders—e.g., structural changes or functional anomalies in some forms of schizophrenia; and (3) in the development of general information about how the brain works, which contributes to the long-term effort to develop an accurate conceptual model of our thinking/feeling process.

Today, based on growing information, we can conceptualize the brain, as one prominent researcher puts it,

> ... as a very large network of different communication centers that can flash on and off and send messages to one another through electric impulses. The brain contains many different specialized information centers scattered throughout its three-dimensional space.... When [it] is working at its usual busy level of performance, it can be thought of as a three-dimensional layout of electrical switchboards in which many different areas are receiving messages, "lighting up," and sending messages back in response. (Andreason, 1984, pp. 90,91)

This metaphorical conception of the working brain may be overly simplistic, and in any case it builds upon more than 100 years of study and research to develop and explore the hypothesis of localization (specialization of functions of the various parts of the brain) and cerebral dominance (partly differential functioning of the two hemispheres). But it is only today, through the imaging techniques mentioned above, that scientists can begin to actually observe the working brain in action. One example of such an observation is the "lighting up" (reflecting increased metabolic activity) of the auditory centers of a psychiatric patient who is "hearing voices"—i.e., experiencing auditory hallucinations. This observation of brain process makes a clear link between the brain's neurochemical activity and the person's subjective experience. Such correlations do not necessarily tell us the direction of cause and effect between disorders of brain process and emotional experience, but they do open the way further to thinking about the brain and subjective experience as an organic unity. We may still fall into thinking and speaking of physical or mental process, mental or emotional disorder, or make such remarks as: It's all in your mind. But, after all, where else would "it" be?—since, as Andreason puts it, "The brain is the source of everything we are." (Ibid., p. 83)

Another major field of discovery in contemporary brain research is the brain's neurochemistry, and specifically the roles, functions, and importance of the neurotransmitters as the messengers that excite or inhibit the response of receptor neurons in the brain's transmission system. Here, we are in the amazing thicket of innumerable neurochemical connections and mini-events that actually produce or constitute a "state of mind," an action, a behavior pattern, an emotional response. The neurotransmitters—specifically dopamine, norepinephrine, and serotonin—and the more recently identified neuroactive peptides (regulatory hormones, endorphins, enkephalins) are emerging as keys to understanding and treating many of the symptoms of mental illness, alcoholism and other drug effects and addictions, and the specific functioning of psychotropic (mind- and mood-altering) medications in blocking unfavorable neurochemical processes.

Contemporary awareness of the role of neurotransmitters is reflected in both chemotherapy and other forms of treatment. For instance, the knowledge that prolonged use of cocaine depletes neurotransmitters that are natural neurochemical sources of feelings of pleasure, sheds new light on the severe depressions that accompany cocaine withdrawal and clarifies the person's treatment needs. Similarly, treatment programs for alcoholism now incorporate and teach awareness of the role of endorphins in producing natural, non-substance-induced euphoria.

Light spreads in both directions between knowledge and practice. Medications that affect neurotransmitter action may point to a new road of exploration into the nature and causes of an illness. As Kramer points out in *Listening to Prozac,* medications are often developed and their useful applications discovered by trial and error, analogy or fortunate circumstance; they do not necessarily spring from a full theoretical understanding of the causes of a disorder. Widespread response to the relatively new SSRI (selective serotonin reuptake inhibitor) family of antidepressant medications (Prozac, Zoloft, Paxil) may reflect the possible role of serotonin in maintaining euthymic or positive mood—but we are still not clear exactly what that role is. The neuroleptic medications used to control symptoms of schizophrenia, because they block neural receptors that are specific to dopamine, have suggested hypotheses relating that disorder to an excess of dopamine in the neural synapses—the loci of transmission of the brain's messages via the neurotransmitters. The investigation of chemical sequelae of drug use has shed new light on why some aspects and stages of withdrawal from drug use can be so difficult and fraught with the hazard of relapse; the body needs time to recover its own natural chemical balance. In addition, it has become common knowledge that some people who become substance-dependent have coexisting mood disorders that place them at serious risk of relapse when they are no longer able (or attempting) to self-medicate with alcohol or other drugs. These individuals may need to be medicated with antidepressants in order to maintain a normal mood and cope with the problems of everyday life, and the key to this specific treatment need may lie in their individual profile of neurotransmitter activity.

So we are gaining many glimpses into the organic unity of brain/mind/body/emotions—and at the same time having to decide what forms of treatment to provide, and how to respond with the right approach at the right time to human beings with various kinds of problems—and often with dual or multiple disorders.

THE BRAIN AND MENTAL ILLNESS

Until the explosion of knowledge about the brain in the past decade, scientists divided mental disorders into two categories: organic and functional. Organic disorders were conditions such as epilepsy or senile dementia, in which there was clearly something physically wrong with the brain. Functional disorders were thought to consist of psychological disorders occurring in a brain that was physically and chemically normal. Schizophrenia, bipolar illness, depression, and anxiety disorders were all thought to be functional disorders of a normal brain.

Thanks to the new diagnostic and research tools—CAT, PET, SPECT, and other scanning techniques that enable researchers to study brain activity in living people—we now recognize that every disorder of the brain is organic. We have moved beyond the artificial division between mind and body, between organic and functional. Every brain illness involves, at the very least, chemical and electrical alterations from normal patterns, and many also involve anatomical changes. Indeed, our current diagnostic guide, the DSM-IV, has eliminated the use of the term organic as redundant, since we know now that all brain disorders are "organic" in one way or another.

Broadly speaking, thought disorders are due to problems in the neocortex. For example, we can now locate both anatomical and electrochemical disorders in various areas of the neocortex of people who have been diagnosed with schizophrenia. In the normal brain, areas of the frontal lobe of the neocortex appear to function as new, high-order cognition centers that pull information from memory areas of the neocortex and the limbic system and, by projecting forward in time, allow us to imagine the future.

The frontal cortex is also responsible for much of our capacity to fantasize, abstract, and generalize, and predict the consequences of behavior. In many cases of schizophrenia—in which these very functions are diminished—scans show decreased activity of the frontal cortex. Nevertheless, patients with schizophrenia also often have limbic symptoms such as depression. So our contemporary picture of the brain's functioning, and of how its activity is expressed in what we call mental illness, remains complex and puzzling even as it is developed, clarified, and expanded by current research. What we do know is that we can no longer reasonably speak of problems such as schizophrenia and depression as if they were divorced from an organic unity with brain process and neurochemistry—so even the term *biopsychosocial,* to the extent that it implies separable elements of biology, psychology, and social factors, has the ring of a fast-disappearing time in our conceptualizing of mental disorders.

## THE FREUDIAN VERSION OF A BIOPSYCHOSOCIAL MODEL

The problem of integrating new conceptions of how we think (and feel) into our language and treatment is daunting but not new. A similar need was presented by Freud's exploration and unveiling of unconscious, preconscious, and conscious levels of thinking, awareness, and communication. Today, psychological testing has confirmed that what we call thinking and perception really involve multiple levels of cognition with varying degrees of conscious attention. We know, too, that what we do not know consciously affects our behavior more profoundly than the plain surface of what we "know" with conscious cognition. We do not have to be conscious of a sound in the night to "know" unconsciously that something unusual is happening. Changes in pulse, blood pressure, breathing, and brain activity instantly reflect awareness of a stimulus and a resulting state of alarm or hyperattention. The common experience of someone whose sleep is being interrupted—that the sound of a ringing telephone or the pressure of a full bladder is woven into a dream—tells us that our bodies "know" information that is transmitted to the brain but then may be processed in different ways, depending on our level of conscious awareness at a given time and on a variety of other factors such as emotional conflict and motivation. We rely, in our conscious, reality-based cognition and thought process, upon a variety of perceptions through our sensory and body systems. Yet we protect our sleep—and our emotionally based psychological defenses—by using a range of imaginative resources, and these too are produced by the complex apparatus of the brain.

Respect for these unconscious levels of awareness initially developed around the observations and psychological constructs of Sigmund Freud, whose initial observations of unconscious reasons for slips of the tongue and other seemingly meaningless phenomena of everyday life met with ridicule and denial in their time, and only gradually were accepted as specific instances of a fundamental aspect of our thought process—that cognition and cognitive functioning and expression are affected by emotion and motivation. This acknowledgment was fundamental to the understanding of human behavior proposed by Freud, which has profoundly affected our view of human problems in the twentieth century. Freud's original "topical theory" or "map" of types of awareness including conscious, preconscious, and unconscious, as well as his later formulation of id, ego, and superego, were powerful metaphors for the biological self (the id, with its primitive urges, or in the earlier theory the unconscious)—the social self or conscience (the superego), representing society or civilization, and the human psyche (or ego) mediating between the two in the process of development as well as in the present moment. For Freud as a biologist, the fundamental biological urges were of passionate interest, together with the ways in which conflict between biology and society was sometimes expressed in illness or neurosis. For his followers (or disciples), the latter became the more consuming interest, together with the translation (or sublimation) of these unconscious biological forces into socially tolerable behavior through the psychological growth and development of the personality.

As Freud conceived it, the preconscious contained thoughts that could be brought readily to mind; such thoughts were waiting in the wings of conscious awareness and were easily brought into full consciousness, since they were not emotionally threatening but merely not needed on a regular basis. The unconscious, on the other hand, contained content that would arouse anxiety if brought to conscious awareness. Such content was viewed by Freud as having been suppressed (consciously put away) or repressed (unconsciously or instinctively hidden from consciousness) because it was found unacceptable and could provoke emotional conflict.

Freud's later conceptualization of mental/psychological functions included concepts that have become generally familiar and functioned for a time as the basis for the psychoanalytic approach to treatment: the id as the source of primitive instinctual energy and desires, the superego as the internalized set of values and prohibitions that we call "conscience," and the ego as mediator between id and superego, and also between id and the reality of the outside world. This more dynamic formulation, brilliantly creative in its time, still offers a fruitful metaphor for understanding the development of personality and the dynamic forces at work in human behavior and experience, and it remains fundamental to approaches to psychotherapy that are still in widespread use in the mental health professions—especially for people not afflicted by major, biologically based mental disorders, but struggling with underlying emotional conflicts as well as situational problems. And, of course, this psychoanalytic formulation of human experience springing from Freudian theory has permeated modern literature and has profoundly affected our common myth of what it is to be a human being.

But Freud's model is only a metaphor, albeit a powerful one. Other hypotheses and constructs employed in Freud's thinking have been rendered obsolete by our contemporary knowledge. Interpretations of mental events and emotional problems in a purely Freudian framework—with its profound emphasis on early development and the methods of psychoanalysis used to access early experience—has become a specialty for the few in psychotherapy today. As exciting as is the territory of the mind as conceived by Freud, it is not to be found on the modern map of the brain. Instead the mental health professions are struggling to integrate current knowledge- and research-based biological perspectives in a total understanding of human problems—or, in too many cases, are simply hiding from the need to adopt a more inclusive and integrated viewpoint.

THE CONCEPT OF THE TRIUNE BRAIN

Another conceptualization of the brain and how it processes our experience was formulated long after Freud, by a researcher named Paul MacLean, who has been involved in animal research for over 30 or 40 years and whose most recent work was published only a few years ago. This concept of the brain as developed in the evolutionary process (of which MacLean's work is but one presentation) offers a useful way of understanding how we may react to events on different levels of awareness, and how some of our most intense reactions, such as anxiety or panic, seem to by-pass the more conscious and consciously controlled realm of our thought process.

MacLean discusses three "brains"—parts of subsystems of our total brain apparatus—as emerging at three different stages of evolutionary development. The first, Brain 1, is the instinctual brain—the brain stem at the upper end of the spinal cord that operates largely on reflexes—with no consciousness, no sense of self, no speech, no capacity for problem solving or reflection. This "first brain" controls respiration, pulse, body temperature, and the central alarm station (or *locus ceruleus*) that provokes the symptoms of panic in a mode of "fight or flight" when we are threatened. It is this brain that awakens us in the middle of the night to deal with a real or an imagined threat—that responds to the breaking glass that signals danger.

Brain 2, usually referred to as the limbic system, reflects a later development in evolution according to this conception and offers the emotional response to a stimulus—such as the infant's cry of distress, separation, or hunger—that works upon the mother. This response of the mammal to a cry of distress is required by a species whose young remain immature, unable at birth or for a time thereafter to care for and protect themselves. As human beings we respond with strong emotion to certain sounds, and some people believe that our often-profound response to music is based upon our responsivity to the cry of the infant and to the mother's voice.

These first two brains are often referred to together as the old brain. What is lacking between them is the higher-level cortical powers of Brain 3, the neocortex, which is a later development in evolution and is now known as the locus of our ability to solve cognitive problems, to think in the abstract, to envision the future and potential consequences of actions, to remember stimuli and people when they are absent, to exercise judgment and altruism, to maintain a commitment to other people and consciously held values, and so on—in other words, the abilities we think of as uniquely human. But we need to remember that, even though the "new brain," the neocortex, has developed and grown in both size and sophistication during our evolution, and is now a major source of our vanity in being human, it is still the "old brain," containing the instinctual and limbic systems, that remains dominant. Human beings can't think well when they are tired, hungry, sick, afraid, or in pain, and we need to remember that for our clients and ourselves.

Thinking of the brain in this way—as a triune system based on its evolutionary development—can help us to understand mental/emotional experience and problems on different levels, even as we appreciate their organic unity as aspects and messages of neurochemical process in our brains. Developing knowledge of the neurochemistry of our thinking and feeling processes doesn't mean that we must now view every problem as "a chemical imbalance," throwing away earlier models of psychological development and forgetting about psychodynamic and family/social systems perspectives on problems. Rather, as knowledge of the brain becomes more sophisticated and detailed, it can be integrated into an updated biopsychosocial model, offering a multi-lens view of human problems and experience.

## INTEGRATING MODELS OF PROBLEMS AND TREATMENT

Another look at three of the major mental/emotional problems we have discussed can illustrate the shift in perspective that is needed to inform contemporary treatment.

### A Biopsychosocial View of Sexual Abuse

Freud viewed child sexual abuse psychologically—at first as a type of early trauma that could profoundly affect adult mental process and behavior through the medium of unconscious mental process. He found that certain adult female patients with severe psychiatric symptoms could uncover memories of being sexually abused as children by close, trusted relatives. This finding, utilizing the techniques of hypnosis and then of free association—the basic technique of psychoanalysis as a form of psychotherapy—was, like so much of Freud's thinking, stunningly controversial in his time. The idea that such abuse of children took place was unacceptable then—just as the knowledge that it is widespread in our present society continues to be resisted by many people. Freud retreated from his own observations, adopting instead the view that his patients' emerging memories were merely fantasy material springing from their own infantile desires. The notion that it was traumatic experience that caused the adult symptoms—generally of a "hysterical" or avoidant nature and sometimes masquerading as a "physical" or "psychosomatic" problem—gave way to the substituted idea of early emotional conflict, perhaps resulting from a more general and seemingly innocuous overstimulation of the child, as the causative root.

Today, in view of our burgeoning awareness and acknowledgment of the sexual abuse and physical battering of both female and male children and of women that has run rampant in our society, this interpretation seems euphemistic. We know that traumatic and distorting experience is a fact of family life for many children. We also acknowledge Freud's conception of the effects of early overstimulation, combined with the child's own sexuality, as a less specific source of anxiety and conflict, driven underground into the realm of the unconscious to allow the individual to achieve a tenuous mental stability, and then reproduced as symptoms in child or adult life. These two conceptions can be applied differentially to people with different degrees of traumatic or disturbing childhood experience.

But what about the question of the validity of recovered memories of trauma and abuse? The objective truth of such memories becomes important if the person is seeking validation, justice, and perhaps compensation from or punishment of the alleged abuser. And certainly the recognition of child abuse, including sexual abuse, is an important issue for society. But in terms of treatment, the recognition of trauma and its aftermath may include a wide range of experiences, many of which may not have been abusive in a narrowly literal sense, but have been emotionally abusive for a particular child. The objective truth of exactly what happened in the past—whether overt abusive behavior or some other form of overstimulation—may not be possible to uncover, and it may not be the most important aspect of treatment, since, whatever the nature of the traumatic experiences, the problem for the adult survivor is only in part to rediscover the truth of abuse per se. Even more crucial to one's future life may be the development of a way of living with the undisputed truth of emotional injury and managing the levels of anxiety that are part of its aftermath.

The contribution of contemporary biology to the understanding of how trauma impacts upon emotional development, discussed in Ellen's case, is the knowledge that social/environmental stressors lead to biochemical changes—that is, that when a person is subjected to unbearable and inescapable stress—whether once, several times, or repeatedly—seemingly permanent changes take place in the brain. The relevant change for the traumatized child or adult, or child-become-adult, is damage to the alarm center of the brain—the locus ceruleus, located at the brain stem and having the function of releasing adrenaline in response to a perceived threat, so that the person can swiftly respond with fight or flight. When damaged by trauma, this internal alarm seems to lose its ability to modulate its response to a stimulus. The brain's response to a stimulus that recalls the original traumatizing experience is an all-or-nothing response—either a nonresponse or numbness, or an all-out panic attack resulting from a rapid release of excessive quantities of adrenaline. The capacity of the brain to produce gradations of anxiety as a signal of an impending threat or conflict, to identify the threat and thereby to help the person selectively to avoid or modify it, is severely limited and overdetermined, at least with regard to that type of stimulus. Several studies also have found physical and anatomical changes secondary to trauma, even when the trauma has not consisted of physical damage to either brain or body. (*Menninger Letter*, 1995)

Clearly, the effect of such a biological overadaptation, replacing the entire modulated range of anxiety signals with something akin to a shrieking smoke detector, has a tremendous impact on a person's freedom to experience life. This biologically based view of the consequences of the experience is certainly very different from Freud's conception of early trauma—and its consequences—but it is also profoundly congruent. This is an example of how developing knowledge of the brain's neurochemistry is fleshing out and complementing our previous psychologically based models. The most important implication for treatment of child sexual abuse or other traumatic history is that full attention must be given to the problem of regulating anxiety—a problem that impacts upon treatment itself, as well as perpetuating such avoidant or self-medicating behaviors as substance abuse. For the person suffering from PTSD (post-traumatic stress disorder), psychotherapy, with its usual mission of revisiting traumatic experience, is at least as much a minefield as is life itself. The person needs to develop ways of managing seemingly unmanageable feelings such as anxiety, shame, and helplessness. The attempt to revisit and "work through" the trauma may offer no benefit—in fact, may be impossible to undertake—unless it is preceded or accompanied by the development of effective skills for coping with and modulating these feelings. For this reason, the focus in treating post-traumatic stress has necessarily shifted from an approach based initially on Freudian theory, directly seeking a discharge of emotions related to the past trauma, to a much more gradual and sequenced approach to treatment, with the timing and stages determined by the person's growing ability to tolerate stressful emotions.

## A Biopsychosocial View of Schizophrenia

Even more marked changes in conception and approach to treatment have resulted from applying the biopsychosocial model, and specifically new knowledge of the brain, to the problem of schizophrenia. Today researchers are able to utilize very sophisticated methods of exploring what happens in the brain of the person with this illness—or rather, as we think today, one of this group of related illnesses. It has been possible to observe, for instance, that when a person free of this illness is confronted with an exercise in problem solving, metabolic activity in the frontal lobes of the cerebral cortex increases; in other words, that portion of the brain is activated to perform the function of thinking about the problem. When the person with schizophrenia is confronted with such a problem-solving exercise, that same portion of the brain shuts down—that is, the rate of blood flow and glucose metabolism in this portion of the brain, which governs much of the person's functioning in planning, abstract thought, and social judgment, is reduced. (MacFarlane, 1983, Beels, 1982)

Another important observation in recent years has been the finding that, in the brains of many people with schizophrenia, CT and MRI scans show evidence of atrophy—enlargement of the fluid-filled cavities known as ventricles—in the limbic system, affecting some aspects of emotion and memory, and in the cerebral cortex, affecting thinking. A third finding of interest, as noted above, is hyperactivity of pathways containing the neurotransmitter dopamine, suggesting that either the number or the sensitivity of receptors for this neurotransmitter is increased or, for some reason, the normal pattern of activity is disrupted.

This knowledge and the steadily increasing body of data from genetic studies have not produced a definitive understanding of the nature and causes of this type of mental illness. But the direction pointed by such findings has led us far away from the supposition that schizophrenia resulted from emotional conflict and/or problematic family dynamics. Yet the vulnerability observed in people with schizophrenia—the responsivity to stress and difficulty in both filtering and processing stimuli that is often found both in clinical experience and in studies using this latter-day technology of brain imaging—profoundly affects the person's capacity to interact with others and to cope with the demands of complex, stressful, confusing, and/or fast-moving social environments, as it may also have affected the person's ability to cope with any mixed messages and/or circumstantial "wild cards" in the process of development within the family.

How are we to integrate this biological knowledge with our understanding of the psychological developmental process? That body of conceptualizations has drawn upon our awareness of stages in development of the mental apparatus of the child—that children are ready and able to develop specific skills, functional abilities, social perceptions, attitudes and values, and specific stages of development. And it has drawn as well on observations, suppositions, and concepts dating back to Freud and elaborated in a vast, multifaceted development of many lines of thought about how we develop psychologically, the crucial influences of early and ongoing development, and so on. How are we to combine these perspectives with the findings of contemporary biology and genetic studies?

With regard to schizophrenia, the so-called stress/diathesis model offers a unifying perspective. This is the concept of a stress-responsive organism, the brain of the person with schizophrenia, subject to repeated episodes of overload of many kinds of stimulation—cognitive, emotional, physiological—that result from the major and minor events of everyday life. Like an overloaded switchboard—or, for that matter, an overburdened heart or other body organ—the brain shuts down, or produces a chaos of mis-perceptions, when it is overwhelmed with a quantity or quality of demands that exceed its capacity. The overstress can occur in connection with events in the person's own physiology, in the unfolding of relationships with others—both within and outside of the family—and/or in the encounters of everyday life. To the person with schizophrenia, as to any other person, change is stressful, and so is complexity, and so is ambiguity. The difference for the person with schizophrenia lies in that person's capacity to respond at a given time. It is the reciprocity between the person's own stress vulnerability—of the brain and of the developing personality—and the currently or cumulatively overstressing environment that creates the conditions for an acute episode of illness, and for the ongoing problems in functioning between such episodes.

The impact of developing contemporary knowledge of neuro-chemical and genetic factors in schizophrenia upon treatment and rehabilitation approaches can hardly be understated. The fundamental shift has been away from psychological and family systems interpretations of the illness itself, leading either to intensive psychodynamic psychotherapy or to family therapy. Instead, throughout most of the field of mental health service delivery, treatment for schizophrenia means a combination of (1) chemotherapy, (2) psychoeducation for clients and their families, and (3) rehabilitation approaches, including specific skills training for social and

vocational roles. Such treatment, when it is well informed by understanding of problems in brain process, is carefully planned to
avoid overstimulation, both cognitive and emotional, and relies
on a gradual and supportive process of building skills and ways of
compensating for what is now clearly regarded as a brain illness.
For many people with this major mental illness, psychotherapy
that is insight-oriented or confrontational rather than supportive
is useless at best, disruptive at worst. This still leaves room, however, for the practice of more intensive family or individual psychotherapy for specific clients, and at an appropriate stage of
treatment and rehabilitation. It should be noted also that, for
younger adults, "rehabilitation" really means habilitation—that
is, the building of skills and stress tolerance that the person has
not yet had an opportunity to develop, especially if that person
has attempted self-medication with alcohol and other drugs and
has taken the rocky path of a dual-disorder client, bypassing the
path of normal development.

## A Biopsychosocial View of Depression

A third example of the biopsychosocial model in action—the
combining of biological, psychological, and social perspectives on
our experiences of thinking and emotions—is our contemporary
understanding of depression. Psychiatrists have recognized for
more than 20 years that some people have recurrent or cyclical periods of depression that seem to be independent of life events.
Such episodes of depression might or might not involve psychotic
symptoms—that is, such a severe impact upon the person's
thoughts, emotions, and behavior that contact with reality is lost.
Psychotic depression was more readily recognized as having
chemical factors in its causation. Then the concept of endogenous—that is, internally/biologically based—as distinguished
from reactive or situationally caused depression was applied also
to less extreme depressive cycles. Except in such cases, episodes of
depression have been seen in psychological terms, as reactions to
loss, in many cases prolonged or complicated by underlying emotional conflict, or as "anger turned inward" by people unable to

exercise appropriate self-assertion and self-direction—for instance, some women in marital conflict.

Today our views of depression are much more variegated and complex, for we have had to incorporate new biological knowledge and a new awareness of genetic factors in mood disorders, as well as clinical experience with a rapidly increasing number of antidepressant medications that are found effective for many people. Here too the pendulum of thinking in the mental health professions has swung sharply toward the biological end of the spectrum as new knowledge has been gained—for example, the specific chemistry of some people who are suicidal, the relationship of blood levels of antidepressant medications to the retreat of the "psychological" experience of depression, and the role of certain neurotransmitters in our experience of pleasure.

How are we to process this kind of information and integrate it with our previous, more psychologically based understanding? It is tempting to begin to think of depression as essentially a chemical problem—and as we have noted, there are widespread efforts under way to educate the public about depression as a biologically based illness. But we need to remember that, just as biology can affect our subjective or "psychological" state of mind, psychological and social factors can influence our biology. In fact, we are speaking of one organic process, separated into its components only for the sake of discussion. In these terms, cause and effect in depression are best seen today, not as a one-way street but as a feedback loop, an interplay of biological, psychological and social influences on the mental/emotional/behavioral condition of a human being. This means that, in any group of people with diagnoses of depression, there is a wide range of interpretations to be made about the directions of cause and effect vectors. Among four people with diagnoses of major depression, there may be (a) one with a second or third episode of a cyclical affective illness such as bipolar or unipolar disorder; (b) another with a major depressive episode apparently precipitated by life events but now having a neurochemical aspect that makes it untreatable without antidepressant medication; (c) another with a severe reaction to withdrawal from alcohol and/or cocaine dependence; and (d) a fourth enmeshed in a destructive marriage. At least three of these four scenarios—(a), (b), and (c)—require or invite the use of medication, while (b) and (d) also call for individual or marital psychotherapy, and (a) and (c) for a rehabilitation approach that includes psychoeducation about the disorder and the use of a social support network in responding to the person's needs, as well as possible inpatient hospitalization or rehabilitation during an acute stage of treatment. In other words, the major depression episode, identified by similar symptoms in each case, may call for different though overlapping prescriptions for treatment, depending on the context of diagnosis and life course. That context in turn is determined by such additional information as family history, past psychiatric history, substance use history, current life stressors, and so on. The depression episode can be viewed through as many lenses as this information suggests and can be treated differentially at each relevant level of intervention.

Viewed in terms of the triune brain, depression seems related primarily to the limbic system, or "Brain 2." The cause may be external—for instance, a loved one is severely ill or has died—or it may be internal—reflecting an inherited (familial) pattern of unipolar or bipolar illness. The variable biopsychosocial origins of depression—and the interplay of the three brains described by MacLean—help to explain why the following five approaches to the treatment of depression are successful: (1) *Antidepressant medications* enhance the activity of chemical neurotransmitters that maintain a euthymic (nondepressed) mood. (2) *Traditional psychodynamic psychotherapy* focuses on feeling states in an attempt to "work through" presumed factors leading to or tending to maintain the depression. (3) *Cognitive-behavioral psychotherapy* uses the thinking capacity of the neocortex to correct cognitive distortions or "wrong messages" that provoke, express, and maintain the depression, leading to a change in behavior that, in turn, reduces negative activities and depressive feelings. (4) *Electroconvulsive (shock) therapy* (ECT) is used for severe, refractory depressions that have not responded to other forms of treatment, or in cases where certain hazards or side effects of medications may be of concern. In ECT, electrical currents passed through the brain bring about a seizure, which in turn, for reasons that are not clear, often relieves severe depression after a sequence of such treatments. (5) *Social treatments* such as support groups, religious or spiritual approaches, vocational activity, and/or artistic expression and experience may play an important role in helping some people master the sense of loneliness and alienation that often accompanies depression.

These five treatment approaches, each addressing a specific aspect of our thinking/feeling process, are not mutually exclusive. No one approach is likely to offer a cure in isolation from other approaches. But, used in combination, one modality can facilitate and augment the effectiveness of another, so that a positive synergy is brought to bear. Although few people need all five of these modes of treatment, most can benefit from a planned multimodal or sequential combination of two or three. Attention, through these and other approaches, to all aspects of a person's problem, reflects in treatment planning the multi-lens or biopsychosocial perspective on the presenting problem itself, in all its complexity.

WHAT KNOWLEDGE ABOUT THE BRAIN IMPLIES FOR TREATMENT

While research continues to push back the frontiers of knowledge about the brain, and about both neurochemical and genetic factors that are expressed in mental/emotional disorders, the most pressing question for caregivers remains: What is the most effective treatment for a given disorder? Today, for many or most problems, the answer includes chemotherapy to modify the brain's neurochemical process—neuroleptics, clozapine, or risperidone to eliminate or reduce the hallucinations and delusions that are so-called active symptoms of schizophrenia; lithium, or an anti-seizure medication to stabilize bipolar or unipolar disorder and reduce the likelihood of acute episodes; antidepressants to relieve symptoms of major or less serious depression; antianxiety agents to control generalized anxiety, obsessive-compulsive disorder, and/or panic attacks. It sometimes seems today that, no matter what the problem, there is a pill proposed that offers some potential for relief—although, all too often, the relief is inadequate and/or accompanied with troublesome side effects, so that the main emphasis of treatment falls upon some other modality. Even with this caveat, it is clear that contemporary knowledge of the brain goes hand in hand with—and is sometimes led by—new developments in psychopharmacology.

Another important set of implications for treatment spring from growing knowledge about how the brain learns, and about the mechanisms of alcohol and other drug dependence, as well as compulsive eating disorders. Persistent patterns of stimulation and response, and their familiar correlates in habitual patterns of behavior, are familiar to any of us who have tried to lose weight. Many people manage to lose a few or many pounds by months of earnest and persistent effort, and then find that, as soon as there is a relaxation of consciously enforced discipline, the old cravings regain their power, the former habit patterns reestablish themselves, and the person quickly returns to the unwanted weight, sometimes called the set point, established by the body's metabolism. Understanding the mechanism of the set point and the relationships of food cravings to neurotransmitter activity may not change the behavior patterns, but it at least relieves some of the burden of shame and self-blame for a lack of "willpower" and clarifies the addictive power of overeating and related disorders. Of course, such disorders can also be viewed in terms of their emotional and psychological meanings; as with all mental/emotional disorders, we believe a multi-lens perspective that integrates biological, psychological, and social aspects of the problem is most fruitful.

Biological research has clarified why people use drugs. Alcohol and other drugs of abuse act as exogenous neurochemicals—that is, chemicals that enter from outside the body but come to act as a substitute neurotransmitter, activating neuroreceptors and igniting a chain reaction of brain events. Or the drug may occupy the specific neuroreceptor sites and thus block the endogenous (natural) neuroreceptor from acting, bringing about a change in brain activity. Or the exogenous neurochemical (alcohol or other substance) may simply sit in the synaptic clef—the space between the active ends of nerve cells—and block the completion of a chemical/electrical action. This may be what happens when cocaine acts on stimulatory brain centers: the cells are forced by the presence of the cocaine molecules to continue firing until they are exhausted. This depletes the capacity for neurotransmitter action after the cocaine is withdrawn and apparently explains the depression, the crash which routinely follows the stimulation/excitement phase of cocaine use—the phase the user seeks in taking the drug.

Such developing knowledge is useful in treatment both for compulsive eating disorders and for alcohol and other substance abuse. Treatment may include medications that can block the effects of the drug of abuse, thereby decreasing craving. Treatment for the dual-disorder client with a concurrent problem of major depression may include use of antidepressant medications, once considered unacceptable in substance abuse programs. On the other hand, understanding of the crossover effects of alcohol with benzodiazepines both validates their temporary use in the process of detoxification and underlines the importance of *not* employing antianxiety agents for people with substance abuse problems, since this class of medications has a higher potential for addiction than antidepressants (which may also be used for anxiety because of their sedative side effects).

Still more to the point is the awareness of neurochemical aspects of alcohol and other drug dependence as a perspective upon relapse. The information gained helps treating professionals understand that the substance-abusing or substance-dependent person may not be able to recover and remain abstinent by the use of determination, support from Alcoholics Anonymous or another 12-step group, and only a brief period of detoxification and inpatient or other supervised care. Relapses do not necessarily occur because of a lack of motivation or a weakness of character. The problem of relapse is only partly "psychological"—that is, relating to the individual's conscious and/or "emotional" experience, conflicts, and decisions. The other part of the problem, and sometimes the more compelling, is biological, driven by relentless, yet unconscious brain messages, through mechanisms such as the conditioned reflex, now understood as the behavioral output of neurotransmitter/neuroreceptor activity patterns. This awareness also reinforces the perspective of the medical or disease model, underlines the requirement of total abstinence in order to avoid relapse, and clarifies our understanding of both Type I (habitually acquired) and Type II (genetically transmitted) patterns of alcoholism.

Finally, the awareness of biological/neurochemical substrates of disorders, and of the genetically determined patterns and ingrained stimulus-response sequences that drive some of our behavior, can help people to identify their risk factors, avoid situations likely to trigger unwanted behaviors, and compensate for their own behavioral tendencies. Examples of this kind of self-management are a person who avoids even recreational drinking because a family history of alcoholism inspires caution, or a person with past acute episodes of schizophrenia who is attentive to early warning signals of another episode, or a person with a tendency toward obesity or depression who consciously adopts a life-style that runs counter to that tendency and may function as a prophylactic. While it is humbling to acknowledge neurochemical processes as programming our human behavior, and may even add to a sense of helplessness, the good news is that we can utilize our knowledge of brain process and behavior patterns and even affect these patterns. Every word that is said in therapy, every word the reader reads on this page, and every message that we give ourselves, and repeat to ourselves, makes electrical/chemical changes in our brain—that is, changes the way we think and feel. We need not—and must not—think of thinking and feelings as biological *or* psychological *or* social, but rather as all three in one, and as a feedback loop into which information can enter at any point.

# PART III

# WHERE DO WE GO FROM HERE?

Chapter 10

# Entering the 21st Century

*Crosscurrents in Mental Health Care*

Anyone in the field of mental health services today is aware of forces that are pushing us this way and that, directing our efforts in ways that seem unrelated to the true goals of treatment. If mental health care were a river, it has never run smooth or straight, but has always followed a winding and complex course. But at least there has been a strong current moving more or less in one direction, gathering force and strength from developing knowledge and carrying us irresistibly—or so we have hoped—into a delta of increasingly enlightened and effective treatment approaches based on that knowledge.

Today, that current is still strong and still carries us on to new vistas in treatment. But there is a crosscurrent—the wind of change in the funding and organization of services—that is blowing us backward. This backwind turns our buffeted vessels in unexpected directions. Suddenly, in what might have been a river of progress, we are trying not so much to get somewhere as not to run aground. Our preoccupation with that effort is threatening some of our most valued concerns, at the level of front-line clinicians, treatment agencies, and our professions as a whole.

Those of us who choose to take an optimistic line may say that our field is confronting (nearly) "insurmountable opportunities" and that trying to bring intelligent planning to bear on the situation will actually lead to progress in providing effective treatment. Others, noting the past, present, and planned withdrawal of resources from the human service professions, focus on the rhetorical question: How will so few do so much for so many with so little—and so quickly?—and see only a dark future in which the need for treatment will be often ignored, and the agencies that have provided it will wither away. If there is truth in each position, the more positive truth will have to be snatched from the jaws of administrative and economic defeat. There will be no progress in treatment methods that does not make a viable peace with the current and coming circumstances of care. Therefore, while this book is directed primarily to front-line professional and family caregivers and consumers, and focuses on treatment issues and innovations, we cannot discuss the current directions of treatment in meaningful terms without first discussing its circumstances at the level of policy, administration, and the funding and reimbursement of services.

## THE PRESENT CRISIS IN MENTAL HEALTH CARE

It is important to understand that the problems of the mental health system do not begin and end with the present problem of shrinking resources, nor with the current ascendance of a majority in Congress that is intensely concerned with cutting the costs of human services.

Rather, these changes have highlighted and compounded problems that have been developing for a number of years. The mental health care system in the United States, like most human institutions, has developed over time in a haphazard way, and in most parts of our country has not been redesigned for present needs. In terms of service delivery, it is like a large, rambling building—in some cases a decaying mansion—with new wings and outbuildings tacked on or created with makeshift partitions. To the hapless consumer—wishing in vain for a floor plan and directory showing where to go, what to do, and how to get help—the reality in many cases is more like a maze, with many blind alleys, unfinished corridors, and DO NOT ENTER signs blocking the way.

This is not to say that community mental health agencies do not do a good job within the limits of their resources. Many are models of what people can do in modest settings and with a limited number of dedicated staff, and in most settings there is an earnest desire to provide care as effectively as possible to a changing clientele. But the total care system or nonsystem of which each agency is a part—the way in which agencies are related and do or don't work together—usually leaves much to be desired, and some of the people most in need—such as those with both psychiatric and substance abuse disorders—are going without adequate or appropriate care. We are living in a time of great promise in the technology of psychiatric treatment. Yet, except in a relatively few localities, the mental health care system has not yet been redesigned for the needs of our present client populations and the delivery of state-of-the-art services.

System change is very difficult, even though changing needs continually signal that change is required. In the past ten years, as the need to fuse services for dual-disorder clients has become obvious because of their increasing numbers, we still have been stuck in the traditional structure of separate mental health and substance abuse agencies, with all the related problems and conflicts in perspective and treatment methodology, and with an overarching problem of generally poor coordination. True, in some settings there has been enough interest to form a MICA, or dual-diagnosis, program and to institute some cross-training. But that sort of initiative is still at an early stage in most systems.

Meanwhile, the need for system redesign for purposes of better treatment and service delivery is overshadowed by our intense preoccupation with sheer survival of our agencies. The recent economic recession and the serious decline in tax revenues to support state governments in the hard-hit Northeast and elsewhere in the country has caused massive cutbacks in the service agency economy, which has been largely supported by state funds.

Now there is a new upsurge of concern and action in Congress around balancing the budget, reducing spending, overhauling entitlements, and transferring responsibility for human service delivery to the already overburdened states, which in turn are concerned with balancing budgets, reducing spending, and so on. In addition, the advent of managed care threatens agencies with the reduction of those third-party payments, including those made by public entitlement programs. The outlook for funding of mental health and substance abuse agencies is simply not good—and this at a time when breakthroughs in our knowledge base could open the door to real progress in effective treatment.

What should we do about this "fuel shortage" in the already run-down, sprawling, and problematic "building" of mental health and other human services? Should we close off some programs or "rooms," maybe entire wings—as has been done literally in many state hospitals—or just turn the thermostat down ten degrees for everyone, reducing service at all levels? Should we try to service the same rooms/programs with fewer staff, or keep only the core of the "building" in use, the emergency, inpatient, and other acute-care services? How proactive and creative can we be in redesigning and renovating our mental health house, instead of just closing the shutters and putting dust covers over the furniture?

So far, a popular strategy has been to retain state assistance for acute-care services, especially for people with major mental illness, while sharply limiting the length of stay for hospitalization. Inpatient care at least is seen as necessary, even as it is being cut to the bone. Many states have legitimately or illegitimately transferred costs to Medicare and Medicaid programs, which themselves may be threatened or limited in the near future. Meanwhile, two kinds of support for client populations have been cut dramatically: (1) outpatient clinic services for people who have not been diagnosed with a major mental illness, although they may, like Ellen, have ongoing and disabling problems; and (2) preventive and supportive services for people who do have a major mental illness diagnosis—which includes Bill and Annie but not Ellen and surely not Darrell, whose fate has already been transinstitutionalization into prison.

## THE MEANING OF "TRANSINSTITUTIONALIZATION"

In the context of a mental health system that was already not giving effective service to the populations these four young people represent, the burden of cost- and service-cutting changes is already weighing heavily on consumers, families, treatment agencies, and the larger society. It may come to weigh more heavily still. Darrell is currently the only one of these four young people who has broken any laws, and we do know that people with major mental illness are not generally found to be more prone to violence than the general population, and in fact are often victimized by others. However, the mixture of substance abuse/dependence with a mental/emotional disorder places the person in a more vulnerable position—in terms of impulse control, judgment, clarity of thinking, and stress management. From that viewpoint, it is becoming more common to find such young people, including sons and daughters of the middle class, committing acts that land them in jail and sometimes behind prison walls.

While we discuss the restructuring of mental health services, the economy of these services has already been restructured. There are now more mentally ill people in prison than in state hospitals. In the past 30 years, deinstitutionalization and its corollaries (admissions diversion and short-stay hospitalization) have reduced the population of psychiatric institutions from 550,000 to 90,000 nationwide, despite a 30 percent increase in the population of the country during this period. In addition, those occupying the 100,000 beds now available have an average length of hospitalization of perhaps two to four weeks—a length of stay that is twice that of most nongovernmental psychiatric hospitals. One can see that hospitalization as a location and form of treatment for mental disorders has declined dramatically. Meanwhile, since 1972 there has been a 750 percent increase in the number of jail and prison cells nationwide. In this same time period, problems of alcohol and other drug abuse, dependence, and addiction have become ever more widespread, and the population of people with dual psychiatric and substance use disorders has become a majority in most mental health programs.

It is well known to psychiatric hospital staff that episodes of alcohol and drug use/abuse account for a high proportion of psychiatric admissions, by either mimicking or triggering an episode of major mental illness. Yet there are typically no services in psychiatric hospitals that specifically address problems of substance abuse and dependence. It is equally well known to prison staff that a high proportion of inmates are mentally ill and/or drug-addicted. An estimated 80 percent of people in the prison population, designated as criminal by society, can be diagnosed as having a personality disorder and/or a major mental illness. An estimated 92 percent of these individuals also meet criteria for alcohol or drug abuse/dependence. Yet there are typically no or few services for mental and substance abuse disorders within prisons, and such services are extremely limited within the criminal justice system as a whole. This means that the person who is eventually released from prison and is out on the streets again, whether on parole or having served out his term, is neither treated nor truly "rehabilitated," because severe psychiatric and substance use problems have not been addressed. Add to this the recent and coming cuts in the provision of mental health, substance abuse, and other human services in the community, and it is clear that simply to build more and more prison beds will not solve our common social problem.

This phenomenon of transinstitutionalization is not generally recognized within the field, and still less by the general public. In New York, for instance, in 1970 there were 93,000 state psychiatric hospital beds and 13,000 prison beds. Now, with 66,000 state prison cells and 9,400 state hospital beds, there are some 9,800 incarcerated prisoners identified as SPMI—having a serious and persistent mental illness. By official count, there are more people with SPMI in prisons than in hospitals in New York City. In California, there are now 145,000 state prison beds and an estimated 40,000 jail cells, compared to 2,000 beds in state psychiatric hospitals. In effect, over the years since deinstitutionalization began in the 1970s, we have shifted the locus of care, first from the mental hospital to the streets, and now from the streets into the prison. Today's prison warden has become the director of a *de facto* mental health institution filled with drug-abusing, mentally ill people. Unfortunately this "program" lacks both trained staff and a coherent program design to deal with its new but unacknowledged population. There is evidence that mandated treatment can work in outpatient services, and it can certainly be provided within prisons, perhaps as a condition for release. The situation calls for innovative approaches, and for a comprehensive corrections/treatment approach that would require considerable system redesign and extensive retraining. But to accomplish this will in turn require funding, training of criminal justice personnel, coordination with mental health and substance abuse agencies, and an enlightened and imaginative approach that can carry us beyond the fear- and rage-driven demand for harsher punishments and more prisons. An irony of the present situation is that, like psychiatric hospitals, prisons are also reflecting the pressure for reduced stays and more rapid discharge from the institution, in order to accommodate the increasing demand for beds. It is unlikely that the construction of new beds can keep up with the demand. Rather, when short-stay incarceration is added to short-stay psychiatric hospitalization as a social phenomenon, our society as a whole becomes the institution, and we all remain at risk within its walls.

## THE PROMISE, CHALLENGE, AND TASKS OF COMMUNITY CARE

One way to put these changes in context is by reconsidering the original mandate of community care—that is, treatment of most mental disorders, most of the time, with community-based services. In the sixties the goal of "stamping out mental illness" seemed only a little overambitious, given appropriate outreach and prevention efforts. The hope was to offer the care and services mentally ill people need in the context of a normal life in the community. Deinstitutionalization flooded our streets and communities with people who had lived many years in institutions and needed extensive help and support in order to survive, let alone to fulfill the promise of life in the "least restrictive environment." In a few communities, model systems of care and services were developed. In many, there has been a valiant and partially successful effort to answer to the needs of mentally ill people. But in most localities across the country, and most conspicuously in major cities, people with chronic and severe mental disorders have been left to fend for themselves, with results that have mocked the original notion of "least restrictive" care.

At first the spotlight of public attention highlighted the older men and women—"shopping bag" persons—who had been deinstitutionalized after years in mental hospitals. But concern has focused more recently on younger people—such as Bill, Annie, Ellen, and Darrell—who are not *de*institutionalized but rather *un*institutionalized, spending most of their lives in community settings or in the streets as a result of policies of admissions diversion and short-stay hospitalization, or, as already noted, transinstitutionalized as revolving-door occupants of prison beds. The presence in our communities of these younger adults with severe mental disorders has aroused a variety of feelings, ranging from concern about their endangered lives to fear of their possible violent or criminal behavior.

A person with a major mental disorder—Bill, for instance, especially if he didn't have a family, or Annie, who is estranged from hers—has a number of strikes against him in trying to live an everyday life. Intense vulnerability to stress makes it terribly hazardous to try to make it in the world, with or without the complicating factor of alcohol and other drug use. Added to these problems are those of maintaining a connection with a therapist or an agency that can offer whatever help is needed, reliably and over time. Each of the young men and women we have described in this book—Bill, Annie, Ellen, Darrell—is capable of some degree of progress in managing a life that is hampered by a mental/emotional disorder. Yet each is greatly at risk of a slipping-down life, one in which successive episodes are more and more frequent and severe, and there is less and less chance of returning to a former level of functioning.

The difference between the positive and the far more negative outcome lies, for the most part, in what happens in the community, in the intervals between any episodes of inpatient care. The task of the inpatient unit, if there are acute episodes requiring hospitalization, is to manage, within the confines of a brief hospitalization, to restabilize and reengage the person in some form of outpatient treatment, rehabilitation, and support. The task of front-line staff in the community is to keep the person supported, motivated, and engaged in some sort of jointly planned effort on behalf of her own self-preservation and growth. That may mean maintaining sobriety and abstinence from alcohol and other drugs, with the help of an AA or other 12-step-oriented support group. It may mean remaining on psychotropic medication to control the active symptoms of a major mental illness. It may mean struggling to reduce emotional vulnerability and gain control over flashbacks and panic attacks resulting from post-traumatic stress. Sometimes it means all of the above. A major challenge for caregivers is to provide the "right" intensity of care and involvement at a given time, enough to help the young man or woman to stay afloat in the stressful seas of everyday events, and yet not so much as to take away the motivation for growth and independence. Sometimes, if a person is not receptive or trusting of mental health services and caregivers, the major challenge is that of maintaining a relationship at all.

## "ACUTE" AND "CHRONIC" CARE

The distinction between acute and chronic mental disorders and acute and chronic care sometimes creates confusion about these tasks. For one thing, people with chronic—that is, long-lasting or ongoing—mental disorders, such as Bill or Annie, do need support, services, and usually medication to maintain their stability, and in that sense they are chronically in need of care. But the level of care needed may vary a great deal. There may be acute episodes of illness requiring hospitalization and/or a partial hospital program, and these may be followed by a recovery period when the person needs a low-demand setting and more support than usual, from either family or case managers and residential counselors, just to manage everyday life. There may be other periods when the person is able to take on increasing independence, and when it is clear that personal and social growth is taking place; the person is taking more initiative, taking a more active role in treatment and/or in social life, work, advocacy groups, or other activities.

Such periods generally increase if the person is able to break out of the mental disorder/substance abuse cycle and manage both problems more effectively.

A person like Ellen, with post-traumatic stress and personality disorder, may have very different needs from those of Bill and Annie, but still may show a pattern of periods of turbulence and other periods of more steady progress. Each of these periods may be punctuated by times when the stressful emotions are overwhelming and crisis intervention or even a brief hospitalization is required because of suicidal gestures and/or an episode of substance abuse. A man like Darrell needs something more specialized—an extensive period in a close, containing milieu modeled on a TC (therapeutic community) as well as help with his cognitive and self-management skills, and he too may have episodes of suicidal or dangerous behavior including relapses into substance abuse.

In other words, a major mental or emotional disorder—especially when combined with substance abuse—blurs the distinction between chronic and acute and implies the need for a range of services that are (1) flexible and adaptable to the person's current level of needs, (2) reliably available both as ongoing support and in crises, (3) user-friendly, nonstigmatizing, and responsive to the person as she develops increasing independence, and (4) informed by a coherent philosophy of treatment and a continuous commitment to maintaining care. Our next question is: To what degree are these criteria satisfied under the current conditions of mental health care, and will they be met in the future?

## THE MEANING OF COHERENT TREATMENT

In his seminal book on psychotherapy *Persuasion and Healing* (1963), Jerome Frank pointed out that it is a congruence of belief and value system between "treater" and "treated" that leads to a positive outcome. The specifics of the beliefs and value systems do not seem to be as important as the agreement between clinician and client. This congruence of shared values is implied by the phrase "therapeutic alliance."

How likely is it that such congruence, and the sense of a real therapeutic alliance, will survive as a person moves through a complicated treatment system or nonsystem, in which each program and/or clinician has a different treatment philosophy and set of values? The first challenge, for the agency provider and for the individual caregiver, is how to create and maintain that initial sense of human connection, the *sine qua non*—without which, nothing. In a locality that has not developed an integrated treatment system, continuity may be a problem. But it does not cease to be a problem in a sophisticated, comprehensive, and fine-tuned treatment system. In a well-developed system with a range of treatment programs, a consumer with dual (psychiatric/substance abuse) problems may pass through, in quick succession, (1) a crisis intervention program focused on immediate life-preserving measures such as medication and behavior management; (2) a general hospital inpatient unit for rapid stabilization, where there is often an expectation that clients share personal and often painful feelings in group therapy sessions with virtual strangers; (3) a long-term day program that serves people with very different histories, levels of functioning, and treatment needs; (4) an outpatient program for substance abuse with a high-demand, confrontational approach focusing on the effects of alcohol/drug use and withdrawal; (5) a residence with a mixed population and a low level of staff training in both psychiatric and substance abuse issues. It would be unfair to call this "bad treatment," when such a system offers an array of choices and programs, with each individual unit fine-tuned to its own particular purposes and intended population. Yet, in this unintentional potpourri of individual treatment settings, there may be little to be found of shared beliefs and value systems in the everyday sense, but rather a bewildering array of expectations and attitudes toward the person and her problems. Like the fragmented state of service delivery, the fragmented presentation of treatment itself cries out for a more coherent approach. Such an approach would involve a level of communication and joint planning among units requiring considerably more time and attention than most of us have to give to such efforts today, and that would only begin to create a more coherent picture for the individual consumer.

To the degree that there is that communication and mutual understanding of goals and methods between treatment programs in a community, the consumer is well served. There is, then, a general coherence between the various treatment approaches, and the consumer can experience being on a path of treatment that is leading toward discernible goals and markers of progress. The system that is able to achieve that, and translate it into some degree of predictability and reliability for the individual in treatment, is fulfilling the original mission of community care. This makes it possible for the consumer to rely on and make sense of a connection with the system as a whole. What the person needs at a given time, the system is reliably able and willing to provide; that is the meaning of the once-familiar buzz-phrase "continuity of care." Unfortunately, it is more common for the person in need to have strong connections with particular caregivers, but feel only a marginal connection with the program or treatment system as a whole, meaning that the therapeutic safety net is only as strong as the therapist's tenure in the agency. Whatever walls and gaps exist between discrete treatment programs—hospital, crisis service, outpatient clinic, substance abuse agency, court system—threaten this continuity and make it less likely that the person will be able to pursue a coherent path of stabilization, recovery, and personal growth.

All of these considerations speak for the need for case managers in the community who can broker services, advocate for clients, and, most important, maintain a sense of one continuously involved, caring person who knows the client/consumer and is experienced as "on my side." This role assumes a case management connection that is independent of what level of care or treatment program the person happens to be involved in at a given time. The value of the continuous case manager as a human resource cannot be overstated. All the kinds of clients we have discussed have difficulty leaving relationships and making new ones under any circumstances. To do so while under stress and disorganized, and to pass from one program or level of care to another without a single thread of continuity in their sources of help, is simply too much to expect.

## OTHER THREATS TO CONTINUITY OF CARE

Another threat to the ideal of community treatment is the dramatic reduction in the duration and intensity of treatment available in the past five years, as a result of fiscal changes in both the public and the private sector. As we have noted, publicly funded mental health services have suffered substantial cutbacks in most states as well as from federal forces. The reduction in beds and length of stay in public psychiatric institutions is an obvious example. As we have also noted, transinstitutionalization into prison is one of the consequences for many young men and women. An increasing burden upon families and community treatment agencies is certainly another.

Outpatient and day treatment mental health services for mentally ill people have certainly increased in the past couple of decades, but these community services—including outpatient clinics, day treatment centers, and case managers to assist people in handling their affairs in the community—probably peaked, in terms of quantity available, in the mid-1980s and have shown a steady decline since, largely due to fiscal reduction based on budget shortfalls.

An even more dramatic decrease in the availability of mental health treatment has taken place in the private sector, where such treatment is funded by health insurance for employed people and their families. Over the past five years many employers have switched from relatively generous coverage for mental health inpatient and outpatient care to dramatically reduced coverage. Patients with chronic anxiety and depressive disorders, for example, who were able to see a mental health professional on an as-needed basis every week for two or three years, and thus were able to maintain their employment and functioning, may now be restricted by cutbacks in their insurance to six visits a year. This reduced amount of treatment availability may be inadequate to maintain someone in the workforce, let alone as a productive member of family and society.

And then, there are the uninsured. By 1994 it was estimated that 39,000,000 Americans had neither public nor private health coverage. Of course, this group has no mental health coverage either. And there are additional millions of people who have some health coverage but little or no mental health coverage, which means that they are eligible only for publicly funded services, which, especially as agencies become more hard-pressed, may become limited to brief crisis intervention in a life-threatening emergency.

It is a regrettable paradox that, as our knowledge and capability for improving treatment have increased, the availability of treatment has been dramatically decreasing. As we know more, we are able to do less.

## TIME FRAMES FOR TREATMENT: HOW LONG IS LONG ENOUGH?

The particular crunch that treatment professionals are now experiencing is that the public and private payment mechanisms are insisting on funding only episodic treatment, even though most of the symptoms and conditions to be treated are long-term— chronic mental/emotional disorders with acute episodes punctuating periods of remission, increased stability, and progress. We can see this pattern, and the problems it presents in planning treatment today, not only for major mental disorders (Bill, Annie) and severe substance dependence (Darrell), but across the full range of mental/emotional problems as well as chronic physical health problems.

Depression, for instance, is a disorder that can be treated effectively with medication, psychotherapy, or both; however, it tends to be a relapsing disorder. People with anxiety and panic disorders can be well treated with medications and cognitive/behavioral as well as other psychotherapeutic techniques. However, when there is an increase in their life stress they are likely to have a return of symptoms and again need treatment, so that here too remission and relapse are part of the pattern. Substance abuse disorders can equally well be characterized as long-term conditions which tend to be treatable, with significant improvement of the functioning and life satisfaction of the person. However, they are also conditions that are prone to relapse. The nature of the anxiety, depressive, and confusional disorders that make up the bulk of serious mental conditions requiring treatment is that they tend to be long-term conditions with a course characterized by recovery or remission when treated, but with relapse when treatment is discontinued or there are added stresses in the person's life. The same comment can be made about alcoholism and other addictive disorders.

Does the paradigm of relapse and recovery that we are describing here mean that everyone who once has a problem needs to be treated forever? Certainly not. However, there are certain implications that we must accept if we are to live in the real world. As an individual goes from a state of wellness into acute illness for the first time, or into a relapse to a severe level of a problem, acute and intensive treatment is necessary. If there is danger to self or others at the time of this episode, then hospitalization may be required, and this is very expensive. However, the most economical use of hospitalization, which has come into vogue in the past ten years, is to use it in a focused way to achieve crisis stabilization, do a necessary diagnostic assessment and the beginning of a treatment plan, and get the person ready to leave the hospital in order to be treated as an outpatient or day patient just as soon as partial recovery from the severe episode has been accomplished.

Effective treatment today can now shorten the period of acute illness and distress from months to days—or a few weeks, in the majority of cases. Here are a few examples: (1) An episode of schizophrenic psychosis, untreated, might keep the patient in the hospital for several months or even years. Treatment with neuroleptic medications may allow that same person to safely leave the hospital and enter a day program in two to four weeks. (2) A severe depressive episode with suicidal thoughts may require, if untreated with medication, a two- to four-month hospitalization before the natural healing process might or might not bring the person out of that deep depression and enable him to leave the hospital. With the antidepressant medications available today— and, in cases of unusual and refractory depression, the use of electroconvulsive therapy—that same person may be able to leave the hospital in two to three weeks.

Despite such advances, it is clear that none of these patients, even when treated with the best methods we have today, is likely to be ready to leave the hospital within six days. Yet that is the demand that is being pressed upon treating personnel by more and more insurance and managed-care companies. While the effort to achieve a rapid return to community life is positive, the pressure for shorter and shorter hospital stays often does a disservice both to the individual patient and to the quality of care.

The paragraphs above describe the availability of effective treatment for severe episodes. What next? Does treatment end when the person is discharged from the hospital after a few weeks? Not if we wish to care for the person and assist in his recovery. The hospital has been limited, because of time constraints, to crisis stabilization. Treatment must then be picked up in a community setting, be it an outpatient clinic or day treatment program. These locations of treatment are also far less expensive than hospitalization. A single day of psychiatric hospitalization can cost, today, between $500 and $1,000. A day program may cost $80–$150 a day, and an outpatient visit may cost $60–$130. What is commonly lacking in discussion of the costs of community services, and in the budgeting for such services at all levels, is a clear realization that recovery not expended on services that may appear "luxurious" in community care is spent, in the end, many times over—in the budgets of public psychiatric hospitals, in the criminal justice system, on welfare, on shelters for the homeless. No matter how we try to evade the reality of human needs, truth will out—they will not disappear.

## THE CHALLENGE OF MANAGED CARE

In this struggle to contain the constantly escalating costs of both mental health and other health care, combined with the urgent need for cost containment, it is not surprising that the concept and practice of managed care has taken hold. What is disturbing is the degree to which managed care threatens to dominate both the public and the private practice of psychotherapy from a position that is often remote from the close, individualized knowledge of each person and circumstance. Many practitioners feel or fear that managed care means a Procrustean bed into which real human beings now have to try to fit—or be cut off at the point where their extremities hang over the edge.

Basically, managed care is an attempt to strictly control the costs of care for employers and their health insurance carriers, while seeking to ensure what is regarded as good-quality and appropriate treatment. The managed-care company serves as a clinical and economic mediator between the employer/insurance carrier and the employee/client and his therapist. For the legion of people who do not have health/mental health care insurance at all—because they are unemployed or lack these benefits on their jobs—this is no concern, since they cannot be reimbursed for psychotherapy in any case. For those who do have insurance, and for both private practitioners and public agencies, the concern is extreme. For the client/patient the danger is being cut off from more than a very limited number of treatment visits, regardless of the pace of responding to therapy and the persistence of a given mental/emotional condition. For the private practitioner and the public, private, or private-not-for-profit agency the concern is survival; for third-party payers, both private insurance companies and Medicaid/Medicare entitlements are an indispensable support. This is particularly true in an economic downturn, because the irony is that, when people lose their jobs or experience other overwhelming financial stress, they commonly see therapy as a luxury and something they cannot have if they have to pay for it themselves. Yet research shows that unemployment and related family stress lead to both first episodes of illness and relapse of existing disorders.

Most people will not seek treatment unless they are in pain or otherwise in need of treatment. Most of the people therapists see in treatment, in both the public and the private sector, are there because they need to be there, because they desperately need to solve problems that are causing them great emotional stress and, in many cases, serious problems in health, employment, personal and social responsibility, and often the ability to live with and take care of their families. The so-called "worried well"—a dismissing label sometimes used in community mental health to distinguish people who have "just problems in living" from those who suffer from major mental disorders—is really both a misnomer and an expression of disrespect for human stress and striving. Many of the so-called "worried well" are the people who, despite their problems, keep society going—who work, raise children, take care of elderly parents and mentally ill adult children, and struggle to keep their marriages together or to keep from going under with an eating disorder, a panic disorder, or a long-lasting period of depression or agoraphobia. Some of them are abused women or adult survivors of abuse. Some of them are depressed, unemployed older men who have been, in effect, kicked out of society. Some of them are "displaced homemakers" trying, after being widowed or divorced, to find a new place for themselves in which they can function and contribute to society. Many of the "worried well" have good reason to be worried—about their jobs, their health, their futures, about young children they are struggling to raise or adult children they are struggling to save—such as the mentally ill and emotionally troubled young people described in this book.

We cannot divide people into neat, mutually exclusive categories of acute or chronic, mentally ill or substance-abusing, troubled or delinquent, depressed or just having marital problems—except for the most immediate purposes of triage. No (wo)man is an island, and people and problems interact and, without appropriate help, grow more severely troubled and "dysfunctional." Managed care is a good idea in principle, and it is not that different from the idea of planned, integrated, coherent treatment, centralized intake, and so on—all crucial aspects of a comprehensive and well-coordinated community care system. In principle, it should be very positive to have an outside "expert" to monitor treatment planning and require therapists to approach their work with sound, carefully thought-out plans. But the focus of managed care so far is economic more than clinical; it is basically a drastic and often shortsighted attempt to control costs. Where it may function to limit care with undue severity, to diminish people's chances of finding and choosing the therapist they need and pursuing a course of treatment to an end that is determined by improvement of their condition or relief of their problem—there it will work against both individuals and our society. There is always danger when the people who make treatment and reimbursement decisions are too far removed from the people whose lives are affected—whether the latter are individuals in therapy or communities trying to plan for their own populations.

At the same time, we have a serious need for more controls on the runaway engine of health care costs in our society. We need to find some ways of limiting the wildly escalating costs of treatment, in all sectors of the health care system. Open-ended support for some long-term psychotherapy needs to be limited or at least questioned, for clinical as well as economic reasons, and, as difficult as it is to change gears and perspectives, such questioning may be long overdue. Certainly there is a valid need for time-limited and time-effective treatment in today's economy, and certainly brief, focused therapy can offer not only financial but genuine clinical benefits.

It remains to be seen whether managed care can provide a humane, enlightened mechanism for both clinical and economic review and control. One hopeful thought is that, as we get into the second generation of managed care, employers are beginning to ask for employee satisfaction surveys regarding their treatment. At the same time, outcome studies on treatment are revealing the benefits of treatment for the employee. Probably we will see some easing of the extreme constraints on length of treatment that we have seen in the early days of managed care, in which case there may be more room for potential positive benefits of the system. Of one thing we are quite certain: the time frames now being approved for reimbursement—by insurance carriers, managed-care companies, Medicaid—are too short for the processes of recovery, change, and growth, even in terms of brief treatment with limited goals.

## CRISIS AND OPPORTUNITY

The current crisis in the conditions of mental health care is very real, but it should not lead us to despair or passive resignation to the decline of treatment. This is rather the crucible of change, in which we will now struggle to achieve a more positive chemistry. One way of looking at this crisis is as a genuine opportunity to "seize the day" and bring about long-needed changes in traditional treatment. It is not an exaggeration to say that our responses to this challenge and opportunity will determine, not only our present survival, but the future development of human service programs in our country.

Redesigning a system or even a single program must go beyond simply cutting staff. More radical change is needed and is the healthiest response to crisis, and by not only cutting back but also changing philosophy and restructuring programs we can make a new foundation for future growth. The good news is that the crisis—like an individual life crisis—can create a more promising climate for innovation. The economic state of the mental health/human services system has sunk beyond the help of minor adjustments and cost reductions. New conceptual models and coping strategies are needed—not as the luxurious experiments of a surplus economy, but as urgently needed strategies for survival.

Chapter 11

# What Do We Do Now?

*A Guide for Clinicians and Agencies*

With all the problems confronting today's mental health system and practitioners, it is important to recognize some of the positive trends in contemporary treatment. Some of the trends we see as progress have already become standard practice, while others are on the cutting edge of developments in the field. All of these new or more established trends are among our resources as we struggle to enter the 21st century in mental health care. A nonexhaustive list includes:

- Integrated/team treatment on the biopsychosocial model
- New medications for specific mental/emotional disorders
- Specific guidelines for treatment and everyday management of many mental/emotional disorders
- Psychiatric rehabilitation techniques to meet the need for coping skills and remedial learning of all kinds
- Brief, problem-focused therapy and crisis intervention
- Cognitive and behavioral approaches to many problems
- Psychoeducational approaches for specific problems and populations
- Use of computers in assessment and treatment

- Family involvement in both education and treatment
- A growing awareness of dual (psychiatric/substance abuse) and multiple disorders and how they affect treatment needs
- A growing sensitivity to men's and women's developmental issues and social roles
- A growing awareness of childhood trauma and abuse and of post-traumatic stress disorders affecting adult survivors, both women and men
- A growing body of research showing causative clusters for specific disorders
- A growing body of knowledge about the brain based on brain imaging and other modern technologies
- A growing awareness among health care professionals of the need for cost containment through cost-effectiveness, and of the advantages of self-regulation and self-direction in this effort

Together with these promising trends in treatment and assessment, we are seeing important developments on the part of client/consumers and family members:

- A higher percentage of people with problems partaking of treatment services
- Growth in consumer advocacy, empowerment and input into programs
- Growth of self-help/mutual support groups
- Outstanding growth of political advocacy, education and empowerment of family members through NAMI (National Alliance for the Mentally Ill) and other organizations
- Increasing knowledge about mental, emotional, and substance use disorders in local communities and among the general public

In our view these are trends and developments that offer many possibilities for delivering good treatment. There is also hope to be found in the increasingly widespread knowledge about mental and substance use disorders, resulting at least in more open discussion of problems, with increased information and awareness countering some of the substantial stigma that still remains. The challenge for agencies and individual caregivers is to find ways of delivering services of a level and quality that match contemporary knowledge in the field, and at the same time to work successfully with the requirements and limitations of the new health care environment.

In the past, improvements in mental health and substance abuse treatment services have consisted primarily of enhancement of existing programs. We have not tended to retire or drastically alter traditional programs or approaches that were no longer useful. Rather, existing programs have been maintained, while new programs have been put on hold until they could be funded with new money. Often new program models have been introduced as demonstration projects, only to disappear as their original funding ran out. Few administrators have been willing to face the hard choices involved in the concept of starting from ground zero at the beginning of each budget year and planning for programs only on the basis of current need and demonstrated outcomes. Of course, there is something to be said for the stability and predictability provided by programs and methods that are ongoing, even though they may stand in the path of positive change. The appeal of the new should not automatically result in the casting off of what has been done in the past. Besides, any sweeping or fundamental change does not come cheap in terms of temporary disruption and stress. But the lag between developing knowledge and its translation into practice has been a serious problem in the field of mental health, and so has the lag between awareness of new populations and the development of programs designed to meet their needs.

Now, the situation has changed, for good or ill. The bad news is obvious enough. The good news is that the time is ripe for a more direct approach to building or rebuilding services in a more coherent, need-based manner. To the extent that this occurs, the current crisis can offer new ways of delivering good treatment by those providers and front-line caregivers who survive and are ready to meet the future.

Of course there will be continued disagreement about whether the changes to be made are good or bad, and about what are the best and most effective forms of treatment. These differences reflect both our disparate backgrounds as caregivers and the state of rapidly developing knowledge and creativity in a field that has always been at least as much an art as a science. The constant desire to grow and to expand our repertoire of interventions is reflected in the wealth of advertisements for workshops promising this or that creative new approach to human problems. We are always hungry for information about new ways to work, even though a healthy or cynical skepticism may modify the appetite, and even as, like all human beings, we remain wedded to our own ways and deeply resistant to change.

In practical terms, a provider's response to a person seeking treatment turns on three questions: (1) What does the person need at this time? (2) What does the person want, or choose to accept? and (3) What services are available? We do continue to explore, both in research and in the daily experience of practice, the more ambitious question: What is the most effective treatment for a given disorder—or for dual or multiple disorders? But in most cases our program design and treatment offerings represent a compromise between what we believe would be the best course of treatment and, on the other hand, the limits of our resources, the person's motivation, and the funds available.

In the present climate these compromises may be increasingly painful. But two essential things we can do, and these are: (1) to conceptualize and offer an extended care and treatment plan— that is, as long and varied a sequence of interventions as would be helpful for a specific disorder, regardless of any limitations upon care, and at the same time (2) provide something meaningful at the front door, and at every stage along the way, even if treatment turns out to end there.

## THE TRAIN OF TREATMENT AND SERVICES

One way of thinking about this is to envision treatment as a train passing through the landscape of the larger community, bringing supplies and carrying passengers from one stop to another, according to their diverse and changing needs. The locomotive pulls the entire train along a track running through the current terrain of health care.

This train of treatment and services has many passenger cars (treatment modules), connected to one another with easily sliding doors. At each stop, passengers get on and off the train, and some may take two or three or many more rides. For a single passenger—Bill, for instance—the first ride may be in the first car, designed for acute inpatient treatment of people who temporarily need protection and crisis stabilization. Bill might finish this first ride in the first car—a brief period of inpatient care—and get off at the next stop. Later he or his case manager might flag down the train again, and he might enter that same passenger car for another short ride—another brief stay on an inpatient unit. Or, even during the first ride, Bill might agree to move on into the second car, a brief, intensive day treatment program, and continue the train ride a little longer before getting off. In fact, depending on how many cars the train has in his particular community, he might move from one car to another, according to his own readiness for one or another level of care and form of treatment. The length of the train of treatment and services, and the number and variety of "cars" or forms of treatment, depends on the resources available in a specific community. How long Bill stays on the train depends on (1) his own willingness or commitment, (2) his clinical needs, and (3) the limits set by whoever is paying for the ride.

Some passengers don't need a long ride on the mental health train; they only need help in getting to a better emotional place during a life crisis. Others may need a longer time on the treatment train, but are willing or able to take only short rides, as if they get motion sickness and have to step off for a while—or, in some cases, feel that they can move along better on foot. Some people settle in and seem to feel at home on the train of mental health treatment and services, and may not want to get off. A person can request a ride in any car of the train—but in the new era of managed care each person has to speak to the driver/conductor first, to learn what kind of ticket he has to ride, and for how long. Bill's ticket might cover him for (1) six days in the inpatient car/module, followed by (2) 21 days in the day treatment car, and (3) limited periods in outpatient psychotherapy, (4) ongoing medication clinic, and/or (5) two visits a week to a psychosocial club, (6) two months of intensive psychiatric rehabilitation, (7) six months of supported education, and/or (8) supported work. Or the ticket might pay only for the first ride on the first car, so that Bill would have to step right off the train again and find his way on foot through the larger community. Annie might be willing to take only short rides until she has stepped on and off the train so many times that she has begun to realize these interrupted rides get her nowhere. Ellen might come onto the train to ride in car 3, outpatient psychotherapy, but might need to move into car 2, acute day treatment, for short periods while she rode through the landscape of past and present trauma. Darrell might step straight onto the train at car 9, cognitive retraining, and/or 10, the modified therapeutic community for people with both substance use and mental illness. Our best hope is that the train will have all the cars needed to accommodate all of its passengers and take them where they want to go, and that their time-limited rides will have some coherent purpose and direction. Our worst fear is that these short rides or treatment episodes will be only brief, random, and abortive interruptions in an essentially unsupported life.

## THE ASSESSMENT EXPRESS: INTAKE, TREATMENT PLANNING, AND MONITORING

Thinking of treatment in this way, as a linked sequence of modules offering different types and levels of care, implies (1) an integrated treatment "train" or mental health service delivery system, with at least enough linkage and communication among passenger cars that all are moving in the same direction. It also implies (2) a way of handling intake, planning, and monitoring of treatment that tickets each ride in terms of (a) how long the ride will be, (b) what car(s) of the train the person will occupy, and (c) what will be the station or checkpoint at which the person can (or must) get off. It also supposes that the train's driver/conductor will have a record of the person's former rides. In fact, some passengers such as Bill and Annie must have a coupon book rather than a single ticket, the assumption being that there will be many rides in various cars, with new or repeated points of destination.

This metaphor is not suggested idly, but because we believe that, because of the new restrictions imposed by managed care and other service delivery constraints, we must now reconceptualize mental health/substance abuse treatment for ongoing problems in just this way—as moving toward a sequence of destinations, and with specific lengths of time for each ride and each treatment episode. As long-term treatment has been often interrupted by an unwilling client, it is now made episodic by the treatment system as well. How can we make discontinuous care work for continuous, ongoing disorders? As long as we think of our programs as buildings set in one place and separate from one another (as they may be physically), we may view short episodes and interruptions in treatment as nothing but fragmentation. But the idea of people in motion toward their goals—riding a train with easy access between cars, and able to enter and leave the train as their own motivations and the limits on treatment require—may help us also to remember that the larger landscape of the community can offer some resources of its own.

Without activating such community resources—the schools, workplaces, churches, residences, community centers, criminal justice staff, families, and consumer advocacy and self-help organizations, as well as consumer-run psychosocial clubs and drop-in centers—we will not manage to deliver the continuity of support that Bill, Annie, Ellen, and Darrell need. Major mental illness, dual psychiatric and substance use disorders, post-traumatic stress disorder and major depression, and antisocial behavior with drug abuse are all long-lasting and relapsing disorders. Since we now must treat them episodically, we must ensure that passengers stepping off the treatment train can live in a receptive, aware, and compassionate environment, and that the early warning signals of another acute episode are recognized and responded to reliably as signals to flag down the treatment train for another ride. This means that our treatment teams must now include both the training of personnel and community contacts with some knowledge of early warning signals of episodes, and also some awareness of aftercare needs.

ESSENTIAL COMPONENTS OF ASSESSMENT

The essential components of service for the "assessment express" engine of the treatment train can be grouped as follows:

*Acute Care Services*

- *Triage*—identifying those cases that are urgent because of life-threatening or other emergency aspects
- *Crisis intervention*—and in some cases hospitalization—for people in urgent need
- *Referral to acute care services* for those who need a ride in the passenger cars of psychiatric hospitalization, detoxification for substance use, and/or partial (day or evening) hospital or day program
- *Referral to other services* outside the mental health system, such as emergency medical evaluation and treatment, housing, food, income maintenance, and/or child protective and family support services

*Problem Identification and Brief Treatment*

- *Assessment of problems* for which people seek psychotherapy
- *Referral to appropriate mental health and substance abuse treatment services*—the cars of the treatment train where specific lengths and types of outpatient treatment are provided, whether for crisis intervention or solution-focused brief treatment
- *Education/psychoeducation about the problems presented*—e.g., anxiety, depression, substance use/abuse, eating disorders, marital and child/family problems—in a group or individual format, and as part of the intake or the brief treatment services
- *Referral to other community resources* such as self-help groups and educational programs to follow a brief episode of treatment—i.e., services for the point at which the person gets off the train

*Ongoing Treatment Planning and Monitoring*

Assessment, treatment planning, and monitoring for care episodes result in a longer course of treatment for people—such as Bill, Annie, or Darrell—who have a major mental illness and/or substance abuse disorder and require extended forms of treatment and support. It is usual for the person with one or more severe and ongoing problems to pass through different levels and types of service—different "passenger cars" of the treatment train. This is true for two reasons: (1) The person's needs change markedly from one phase of the disorder to another—from acute episodes through convalescence to remission and rehabilitation, and back again in another acute episode. (2) The person's progress toward goals commonly takes place gradually, over a long period of time. Also, (3) the person may be unwilling or unable to enter one or another of the passenger cars of treatment at a given time or may have worn out her welcome in that particular segment of the treatment train.

For all of these reasons, the ongoing monitoring of treatment is an important—perhaps the most important—aspect of the assessment express functions for people with long-term and severe disorders, and especially for those such as Bill, Annie, Darrell, and perhaps Ellen with dual or multiple disorders. Only through long-term treatment planning and monitoring can we keep the many cars of the treatment train coupled and moving in the same general direction.

THE DUAL-DISORDER TREATMENT TRIP

One of the major problems in treating dual psychiatric and substance use disorders has been the routing of mental health and substance abuse clients onto separate trains, sometimes on different tracks—most commonly those of separate agencies—and sometimes on a one-track collision course. We believe that there should be only one train, and that the subgroups of dual-disorder clients should be offered the seats in cars that correspond to their specific combination of problems. If there is to be a special car—a MICA program—it can be only a part of the total approach to dual-disorder treatment, which is generally agreed to require concurrent treatment of coexisting disorders and a flexible approach to individualized treatment planning, as well as a psychoeducational car (treatment module) for premotivated and preabstinent clients. These are specialized services in one sense—but they are basic in another; that is, they need to be offered across the board to the majority of younger adults who are in mental health treatment and/or the criminal justice system, since within each of these two systems there is a majority of people whose psychiatric and behavioral problems are aggravated by some form of substance use.

Here, too, the treatment train itself must relate to a series of stops in the community, at which self-help groups such as AA (Alcoholics Anonymous), NA (Narcotics Anonymous), GA (Gamblers Anonymous), DRA (Dual Recovery Anonymous), and others are major resources. Family support organizations and multifamily groups also need to be developed as community resources to carry forward the work of recovery both in major mental illness and in substance use. But the treatment and self-help services that are directed toward "recovery" from an identified and acknowledged substance abuse disorder are not sufficient to address the need for education in the larger community of clients with dual or multiple problems and others who may develop these problems. Such education is needed about alcohol and other drug effects, and about the many forms and stages of substance abuse as it applies to especially vulnerable people, such as those who are very young or psychiatrically fragile. From this viewpoint, it makes sense for *any* young adult passenger on the treatment plan at least to pass through a car/module that provides a psychoeducational approach to the basic facts and issues of substance use and dual disorders.

INSIDE THE TREATMENT MODULE

If we do conceptualize treatment as a linked series of specialized passenger cars, what is inside each "car" or treatment module, and what determines what happens during the ride? Ideally, a person would enter each treatment car with a clearly defined goal or agenda for what should be accomplished during the trip. In reality, people usually enter treatment cars or modules with symptoms and problems; the goal is to be relieved of these, but often there is no clear idea about how this goal can be achieved. The first task of the clinician is to greet the person at the door of the treatment car, invite her in, and create a dialog about what needs to be accomplished, what this particular treatment "car" has to offer, and what can and cannot be worked on within the limits of the treatment car's offerings and the length of the ride. The treatment plan that results from this dialogue should reflect both the person's needs and wants as she sees them, and the clinician's understanding of the dynamics of the problem(s) and of the treatment process. For instance, if the person presents the symptoms of major depression, she has a wealth of information about how this depression feels, its specific symptoms, how it began, what has been its course, as well as her personal and family history and the context of life circumstances and relationships in which the depression has taken root. The clinician has another relevant body of information: what medications may be useful, what forms of individual and/or group treatment can help, and how interventions designed for specific problems can be brought into play for this particular person, in this life situation, riding in this particular treatment car for a given length of time.

If Bill, for instance, gets onto the treatment train at the time of his first inpatient episode, he will find in the inpatient car/module (1) a relatively safe place, where keeping him safe during an episode of confusion, poor judgment, or unmanageably intense moods is a primary function of care—and for this reason the doors of this car are locked at both ends; (2) an entrance booth where his problem is diagnosed as a specific illness or disorder, and where medication to control its symptoms is prescribed, administered, and monitored; (3) a space for meeting with family, residential staff, case managers, and other people involved with Bill, to develop an understanding of the episode and appropriate plans for where Bill will go upon leaving this treatment car/module; (4) a group space where the diverse population of other passengers gathers to focus on the causes of their psychiatric and/or life crisis and what they can do to manage the present episode and try to prevent or short-circuit episodes in the future; (5) spaces for social, recreational, physical, and artistic experience to help in restoring a sense of normalcy and connection; and finally, (6) a space at the exit door where the discharge plan, begun when Bill entered the car, can be looked at, modified, and put into action, with further input from family and any other significant others. These are the essential functions of inpatient care in our time.

The most obvious change from historical conceptions of what happens in a psychiatric hospital is the shift from the goal of "cure" to the goal of stabilization of an acute psychiatric crisis. Some of the activities may be similar, but they need to be accomplished in a very—sometimes an absurdly—short time. The passenger/patient used to get off the train when he was cured. Bill will get off the train when the time allotted to his inpatient episode is over, provided he is minimally able to step down from the train or walk into another car/treatment module.

The next treatment car that Bill might enter (if he is willing and also lucky enough to live where such a program is offered) is an intensive, time-limited day treatment or partial hospital program, where many of the same services described in the inpatient car would be taking place. Such a program serves as an alternative to hospitalization or as a transition from the hospital back into the community. The partial hospital module continues to provide safety, in a somewhat different form from that offered in the hospital; the safety here lies in close contact and following up on any signs of impending relapse. The other crucial aspect of the intensive day program or partial hospital is its focus on crisis stabilization, individual problem assessment, and goal setting. For Bill, the focus might be on providing education for him and his family about (1) his illness, (2) his medication, (3) the effects of alcohol and drug use in interaction with both, (4) possible early warning signals of any future acute episode, (5) how to modify any stressors that might contribute to an episode, (6) the probable timing of a complete recovery, and (7) how to set goals appropriate to the stages of recovery and of further development. For Annie, many of the same subjects would be appropriate for the time-limited day program. For Ellen, the work of the day program or partial hospital module would include addressing her symptoms of post-traumatic stress disorder, but addressing them might mean, in this module, only acknowledging them and the need to work on them in a future module or episode of treatment. Or it might mean identifying the task of modulating the intensity of flashbacks or panic attacks as a direct subject of treatment by cognitive-behavioral methods. Education and psychoeducation about emotion management, like similar approaches about alcohol/drug effects, can be provided in time-limited segments in the inpatient and partial hospital/day program cars of the treatment train, as well as in other cars such as outpatient clinic and long-term day program. In fact, it is useful to have some components consistently present in sequence in these different cars/modules, since this contributes to the task of providing continuity and a progression of treatment experiences, both for those who are willing and able to stay on the train for an extended period of time and move through a number of treatment cars and for those who get on and off the train a number of times.

Part of the challenge of inpatient and partial hospital or acute day program care lies in managing a diverse population within a single closely knit program, making appropriate use of the group modality. The outpatient clinic treatment car, divided into separate spaces for individual, group, and family treatment, can offer a still more focused approach to a given problem or problem dynamic of a person in a life situation, entering this particular treatment car with a ticket for a specified length of ride. Some clinics are developing time-limited groups focused on specific problems, psychoeducational classes to address targeted topics, and a new emphasis on brief and cognitive therapies in order to cope with the demand of managed care for time-limited and outcome-oriented treatment.

## SPECIAL CARS ON THE TREATMENT TRAIN

The length of the treatment/services train and the number and variety of its passenger cars will depend, in the coming era, upon each community's capabilities and level of concern for troubled people. We have spent the past three or four decades learning more and more about the services that are needed and can be used by people who are to some degree impaired or disabled by mental/emotional/substance abuse problems. Clearly it is in the interest of local communities and the larger society to ensure that people with problems have the forms of help they need to put their feet on the path of productive life. Otherwise Bill, Annie, Ellen, and Darrell remain dependent on society's shrinking and waning services and remain at risk for self-destructive and criminal behavior. With the kinds of help that can be offered, both in the basic cars of the treatment/services train—assessment, acute care, brief treatment and rehabilitation programs, day and outpatient treatment—and in cars with special services such as supported work and education, such troubled lives can be redirected onto a new and more promising track.

Such specialized passenger cars on the treatment train might include:

- *Intensive psychiatric rehabilitation* directed to developing specific skills for coping with various aspects of life—such as "ADL" skills—activities of daily living and self-care; prevocational skills—e.g., how to get up in the morning and prepare for work, how to relate to supervisors and co-workers, and so on; communication and relationship skills—how to express feelings, how to ask for what one needs, how to compromise, how to manage conflict and work out problems, how to develop good friendships and family relationships, and so on.

- *Psychoeducational curricula and motivational interviewing* to educate and engage people who are not yet identifying ongoing problems in their functioning and are not yet ready or willing to enter passenger cars labeled as treatment.

- *Cognitive-behavioral and problem-focused treatment* in group and/or individual modules for such problems as depression, panic disorder, phobias, alexithymia (lack of a language for feelings), low self-esteem, aggressiveness and violence, and so on.

- *Cognitive-behavioral and problem-focused treatment* (as described above) in segments of flexible length—with renewable or transfer tickets on the treatment train—for people with ongoing personality disorders who need to learn to manage high levels of anxiety, anger, depression, and other problematic responses in life situations.

- *Cognitive retraining targeted to specific skills* such as attention, memory, information processing, problem identification and problem solving, as well as building a sense of mastery and competence.

- *Intensive substance abuse treatment* for certain passengers who have a clear-cut substance use disorder that was misdiagnosed or obscured by symptoms of mental illness.

- *Supported education* for younger adults interested in college and/or vocational training.
- *Supported work* for people who are able to take on work roles—if they have appropriate supervision and support along the way.
- *Family education and support* to inform and assist family members in their struggles with mental disorders of their children, adult children, siblings, spouses, or parents—preferably in the form of groups tailored to lower anxiety through both education and support.
- *Consumer empowerment and advocacy* through the development of consumer self-help groups and organizations.
- *Case managers.* This is not really a separate car of the treatment train, but rather a cadre of passenger companions and guides, to ensure that the passenger cars are effectively coupled, to help people find their way from one car/module to another, and to access the kinds of help they need in getting on and off the treatment train. As most of us know, case managers are often crucial to client/passengers' progress.
- *Residential services.* This too may not appear as a regular treatment car but is clearly a necessary resource for young men and women who need support and supervision, and who may be able to use a supportive residence as the setting for growth and development into their adulthood. The range of such residences should include fully staffed group homes as well as shared and individual apartments with various levels of supervision and support.

Given these examples of possible special cars on the treatment/services train, how many can be provided, and how long each ride can be, depends on complex factors of planning, funding, and community concern. But there is no question that such services are meaningful in changing the course of endangered lives onto a track of growth and productive membership in society. We have yet to explore the degree to which some of these services can be provided through other agencies in the community—such as family and consumer groups, public school systems, community colleges, churches, state offices of vocational rehabilitation, supported workshops sponsored by corporations or employer organizations, in the spirit of the Americans with Disabilities Act (ADA), intended to ensure full participation in society for people whose functioning is compromised. But it is clearly in our interest as a society to provide, in one form or another, the kinds of services that can help young men and women to stay out of hospitals, off drugs of abuse, and on the track of a stable and potentially productive adult life.

Is the treatment train a perverse metaphor? It would be more familiar, certainly, to think of each treatment program or level or component of care as a station, a program site, and the train as carrying Bill from one to another. But we believe that this form of the metaphor is better suited to how care and treatment must work in the present and forthcoming era. Treatment modules cannot be, so to speak, separate buildings, each fixed in a particular spot and only incidentally related to one another; they must be securely linked, so that passengers can move freely back and forth, from one car/treatment module to another, and they must be in motion, carrying each person forward, and moving in one consistent direction—the direction of progress, whatever its specific meaning for that individual. In the course of that progress, the person at times will be moving through the train to other levels of care and forms of intervention. At other times some will retreat back to the more protective and intensive car/module of inpatient care or acute day treatment. Such movements from one car to another, and the steps off and onto the treatment train itself, should be easy to accomplish and informed by a coherent, long-term, overall treatment and life plan to which treatment episodes and modules each contribute. Only in that way can care and treatment be more than a collection of fragments, each of which is inadequate to meet the demands of one or more ongoing disorders and related needs.

Chapter 12

# Person to Person

*What Clinicians, Family, Other Caregivers,
and Consumers Can Do to Help*

To understand the complexity of mental/emotional problems
and design programs to treat them is a good beginning, but of
course it is only the beginning for the front-line caregiver. In the
everyday life of care and treatment, many issues and questions remain: How can I get her to keep appointments? . . . How can I
help him learn to trust me? . . . Is he suicidal today? . . . Has she
been using drugs again? . . . Should I let her keep on coming to
the day program? . . . How can I stop him from harassing other
clients? . . . Is there any point to what we're trying to do? . . . How
do I treat someone for "dual diagnosis"? . . .

Who is the caregiver asking these questions? Increasingly people in the mental health field are recognizing that the term *caregivers* means many people in addition to psychiatrists or other
therapists. It means people in many other working roles—case
managers, group home staff, substance abuse counselors, school
guidance personnel, DSS caseworkers, law enforcement people. It
also means family members and the support network of friends,
neighbors, and community. In a very real sense, we are all in this
together—this frustrating, alarming, and sometimes devastating

effort to help a troubled young man or woman—and of course, this effort is more likely to bear fruit when the formal treatment team and the informal social network can work together and support and guide one another.

The questions that arise are endless and diverse for people who take responsibility for a troubled person. Care in its broadest sense includes caring and attention as well as treatment, services, protection, and its demands are shared by professional providers of service and family members. The duties, problems, responsibility, and anxiety of caregiving vary with the mental status and functioning of the troubled person. Many young people reject both care and treatment at times, and attention, concern, or advice from family members also may be vehemently refused. *Leave me alone . . . It's my business what I do . . . Don't treat me like a kid . . . I'll do it when I'm ready . . . It's my life, isn't it? . . .* The demand for self-determination is persistent and has its own inherent validity, even when it raises vexing issues of personal rights, competence, social responsibility, and control. But both professional caregivers and family members have an inescapable responsibility for the troubled person when that person is unable to manage alone.

For the provider, that responsibility is defined in detail. It is a heavy responsibility in both human and legal terms—and it may be terminated when a therapist or agency decides to "give up" on the client. For the family member, especially the parent, the burden of responsibility, fear, and sorrow is global and lasts forever. Because of this difference, and because different issues arise for the provider and the family member as each tries to help the person in need of care and support, we will address these two groups of caregivers separately and offer somewhat different, though overlapping, guidelines. However, we see professional caregivers as members of the same treatment team with family members and other concerned people in the community, as well as case managers, residential counselors, child protective and family support workers, probation officers, and everyone else who is working with the troubled person. Only through close communication and teamwork can we offer help that makes sense to the person and family.

## HOW CAN I HELP MY CLIENT? SOME GUIDELINES FOR CLINICIANS AND OTHER CAREGIVERS

1. *Look at and speak to the normal person within the person you meet.* The troubled person may come to you in a state of psychiatric undress—frantic and fragmented with anxiety, suffused with rage, in a psychotic state of confusion. Try to make contact with the normal human being who is inside this desperate exterior, wanting what all human beings want—to be listened to with respect, to gain reassurance and safety, to get a handle on what to do next. It is your calm and openness to direct contact that helps the person get back to reality, self-control, and self-direction. Until the person can do that, your reassurance takes the form of providing safety and security by taking charge of the situation as needed.

2. *Consider the full range of the client/consumer's needs.* The person may come to you in a general hospital emergency room, a psychiatric inpatient unit, an outpatient mental health or substance abuse clinic, a group home, a police court, a college guidance office. You may have limited time to assess the person's problems and situation. But it is vital to get a sense of the range of problems, since the person may need services from others, not necessarily instead of, but in addition to, your own agency. The point here is not to exclude the person from service, but rather to figure out how to link together all the services needed—to obtain psychiatric help for the person who has shown up in prison or with a medical problem, substance abuse treatment for the dual-disorder client in a psychiatric clinic, housing and financial help for a young street person brought in by the police, or psychotherapy for a college student who is looking for career guidance. Disturbed young people often show up at the wrong door for the kind of help they need, or need more than one agency can provide. As the rides offered on the treatment-and-services train become more brief, it is all the more important to have easy access between cars.

3. *Consider the limits and extent of your own role and responsibility in a total plan of care.* How long can you be involved with this person? What resources can you provide, and what has to come

from somewhere else? If your time is short or your role is limited, what can you try to provide that will be meaningful and helpful? Sometimes the best help you can offer is your view, as an informed consultant, of the situation and what needs to be done.

4. *Focus on specific, limited goals, chosen in terms of what the person wants and sees as important right now.* This should consist of the first steps in a long-range, comprehensive plan for getting on with life. Part of the work of your initial contact(s) with the person is to make a link between what the person is looking for—for example, I have to get out of this hospital . . . I want my driver's license back . . . I need a job . . . I want you to get my wife to come back to me—and a broader view of what is needed in terms of internal and behavioral change. An appropriate question is: After you get your driver's license back, then what? What will be different, and what do you need to do? Partial recovery or convalescence from an acute episode gives rise to new needs and new possible goals in the long-term process of recovery and growth.

5. *Pursue these goals, updating and redefining them with your client as needed, during whatever time you have together.* If you are working with someone for a longer period, touch base often about the person's progress and set new goals together when earlier goals are achieved. The point of this way of thinking is to achieve a sense of progress, however slow, limited, or uneven it may be, and to combat a demoralizing sense of "hanging out" in the mental health or other human service system—or an equally demoralizing experience of attending short episodes of treatment and then being pushed off the train again, without any coherent plan or sense of progress and direction.

6. *If goals aren't being achieved or seem to be overwhelming, cut them down to smaller steps and praise progress wherever you see it.* It is progress, for instance, to stay out of the hospital six months rather than three, or to hold a job for two months rather than two weeks. The troubled person will say, "You see, I can't succeed at anything, because now I've lost another job." It's up to you to

point out the stations being reached along the track to successful functioning.

7. *Recognize that some of the goals are emotional or interpersonal.* Learning to trust you, to tolerate anger and disappointment, to manage emotions and conflicts without dangerous and self-destructive acting out—these are goals as important as sticking it out with a job or getting an AA sponsor. The emotional/interpersonal goals are fundamental—but they, too, can be framed in small steps. We need to identify progress in these terms, too: You got angry just now, but you didn't blow up at me . . . You waited half an hour instead of storming out in five minutes . . . You made that phone call even though it was hard to pick up the phone . . . You felt suicidal, but this time you talked about it, you didn't act it out . . . These observations are antidotes to the toxic judgments of the troubled person (and sometimes other people): There I go again . . . I've lost it again . . . I'll never change.

8. *Try to tap into your client's and your own sense of humor.* Humor—and especially being able to laugh at our mistakes, rationalizations, and disappointments—is very important in our lives. Humor accepts and tolerates our common condition of imperfection. Humor shared with your client helps the person know that: We're both human beings here, and we can share some things on a basis of equality. Humor helps to counter the feeling: I'm the therapist, you're the patient . . . I'm the winner, you're the loser . . . I'm the helper, you're the needy one. But, a word of caution: Be careful about how, when, and with whom you use humor, so that it never comes out as a trivializing or putdown of your client's problems. And, don't confuse humor with sarcasm. Many clients, as well as other people, need protection from and increased awareness of the use of cutting sarcasm as a defensive attack upon others or oneself.

9. *Respect the pain, grief, and difficulty of the person's life.* It is often very difficult to feel what it means to be looked at as mentally ill or a bum, to feel helpless with alcohol and other drugs, to be

afraid of your own thoughts—or to live in a furnished room, live in danger in the streets, take the bus to the program every day (if you have the money), stand out in the rain. . . . Even (or especially) in the helping professions, it is easy to fall into an unthinking arrogance based on having a more comfortable life than many of our clients—and then to think: She missed the last two appointments and claimed the car broke down or the babysitter didn't come; she's resisting . . . He flew into a rage when I asked him about sexual abuse; he's in denial . . . That client's mother is on the phone every day demanding something; she's driving me crazy! If you find yourself looking down on someone for her problems, try to imagine walking in that person's shoes.

10. *Always assess for alcohol and other drug use/abuse/dependency.* A problem with substance use often goes unnoticed in mental health or other kinds of agencies—especially if the use is "not that much," but the person is vulnerable to alcohol/drug effects. Alcohol and other drugs can cause or mimic any psychiatric symptom and can play an ongoing role in a person's troubles with life and with mental health treatment. It is essential to know and address your client's habits of use or abuse, and what kind of education, treatment, or other services are needed.

11. *Treat the "dual-disorder" or "multi-problem" client as best you can, providing education and consistent feedback for the person who is not yet motivated to consider substance use as a problem.* The premotivated, preabstinent, or "not yet" client needs special attention to substance use, usually within the mental health system. It isn't a solution to withhold treatment—except on days when the person is actively drunk or stoned, or in situations where medication, for instance, may be life-threatening when combined with drug use. Most people with dual disorders—psychiatric and substance use problems—need time to learn about the effects of alcohol and drugs in a low-key, educational framework before they are ready to undertake abstinence. In our view, the treatment program's responsibility is (1) to confront the issue, and not to enable substance abuse by avoiding the subject of alcohol/drug effects and their meaning for someone with mental/emotional problems; (2) to provide needed education about alcohol/drug effects in a non-

judgmental framework, with encouragement toward abstinence as an eventual goal; but (3) not to reject or judge the person for not being ready yet to take on the goal of abstinence; and (4) to continue to provide other mental health services that are needed. A dual-disorder or multi-problem client commonly needs time to come around to considering abstinence.

12. *Involve family members and other significant others in your treatment whenever possible.* Family and other important people in your client's life may be valuable resources, unintentional saboteurs, or both. Often they are people your client needs to turn to or to come to terms with in the course of developing a stable adult life. While concerns about confidentiality and the rights of client/consumers to refuse family involvement are often raised, we believe that responsible treatment includes encouraging young men and women to recognize that family meetings, mutual education, and communication are appropriate and important to their progress, especially if the person lives with or has contact with parents. In recent years many family members have become very well informed about mental illness, and family education or "psychoeducation" has emerged as an important component of treatment, particularly for schizophrenia and other major mental illness, including dual disorders. It is vital to frame family involvement as supportive to both the consumer and family members, and to focus on meaningful issues in managing everyday life. It is also important to avoid unnecessary conflict, reproaches about past events, and long, stressful sessions of "letting it all hang out," even around the traditional issues of family therapy. While dealing with the past (and particularly with past or present physical or sexual abuse) can be essential to creating a healthy future, the timing of such interventions must be chosen carefully. If a young woman or man is very fragile or is in the process of recovering from an acute episode, it is wise to postpone any confrontations and focus on creating the conditions for safety and growth. We believe it is also important, for the sake of the client as much as for the family, to prevent sessions from deteriorating into verbal bashing and recriminations to no purpose, by or toward any family members. Blame is not what family work is about, and relieving useless self-

blame, guilt, and anxiety is a primary responsibility of clinicians who work with families. Instead of focusing on who did what to whom, try to help family members and others to maintain a sense of hope and optimism, tempered with realistic awareness of the severity of many mental and dual disorders, and of the difficulty and hazards of the tasks of recovery. Remember that family members are also your clients and deserve your help and support.

## HOW CAN I HELP MY SON/DAUGHTER? SOME GUIDELINES FOR FAMILIES

If you are a parent of someone with a major mental illness or a severe personality problem, you probably have gone through a long, painful process in recognizing that the problem will not just go away. When a young person has had one or more episodes of mental illness requiring hospital care, or has shown over time that he or she is unable to get started with a stable adult life, you will have gone through many moments of hope: Maybe this time he'll make it . . . Maybe she'll stay on medication . . . Maybe he'll never have to go back to the hospital . . . And many fears: I think he's getting sick again, this is how it was before . . . Maybe she'll never be well . . . Maybe he'll commit suicide or overdose on drugs . . . Maybe she'll hit the streets and we won't know if she's alive or dead . . . Maybe . . . Maybe . . . Along with these hopes and fears go many other feelings—anger and resentment, shame and blame and self-blame. Parents and other family members need support as they struggle with these feelings. Clinicians can and should work with the families of their clients, and a family member can and should ask for such help—for family meetings and education programs as well as direct communication about everyday situations. Still, there is really no way for mental health professionals to fully understand what family members experience, and therefore the most useful support is often within the family movement—through self-help groups, many of which are affiliated with NAMI (National Alliance for the Mentally Ill), a powerful support and advocacy group for families. Of course this does not relieve people working in the field of their responsibility to offer whatever support, help, and understanding they can to family members of their clients. The suggestions made here are offered in humility and with awareness that they are only a beginning and are often "more easily said than done."

1. *Learn all you can about your son's or daughter's problem.* The first step in this learning may be to find out the diagnosis, if one has been made. If not, you can still gain understanding by reading and learning about the range of mental, personality, and substance use disorders and considering how the symptoms and patterns described may fit your adult child's behavior. There are many books and articles about these disorders today, and your local mental health center, your local library, and/or a family self-help group may be a good source of information. If you know someone in the field or can call a mental health or family service agency, you may be able to get some feedback over the telephone.

2. *Seek professional advice and information about the problem.* Of course, if your adult child has been treated or is in treatment, your best source of information is the treatment team, and the best way to get the information may be to ask for a family meeting. Enlightened mental health and substance abuse services today include family conferences so that aspects of a mental/emotional/substance use disorder can be openly discussed. But if your family member has not been either willing or obliged to have treatment, and yet you feel that there is something seriously wrong, you can start with a phone call to a mental health clinic, mental health association, or other agency, just to try to get some information and guidance. A word of caution: if you are not sure what the problem is and/or have not been told a diagnosis, try not to jump to conclusions based on reading and hearsay alone, but keep an open mind and seek the advice of someone in the field.

3. *Encourage your son or daughter to see a qualified therapist*—a psychiatrist or other trained mental health caregiver—as a first step to getting help. The first step into treatment for your son or daughter may result from a crisis and an emergency evaluation, perhaps an involuntary hospitalization if he is out of control mentally or emotionally and needs protection. But, of course, you would

rather see your adult child get treatment by an easier route. Unfortunately, many very troubled people, younger people in particular, are unwilling to seek therapy. If the person has a mental illness or personality disorder, part of the problem may be an attitude of suspicion and defensiveness that itself stands in the way of being willing to get help. In that case, you may have to live with frustration and dread until a crisis does develop. If your adult child does need to be hospitalized at some point, at least the crisis may serve as the first step in getting into treatment.

4. *Try to accept your son's or daughter's illness or disorder, and to gradually come to terms with your own feelings about it.* Of course, such acceptance is overwhelmingly difficult, and for many people it takes years of emotional struggle. Most parents who are able to get the support and understanding they need are able to achieve some acceptance of a mental illness. Crucial to that acceptance is relieving yourself of self-blame, and even of the need to ask: Why did this happen? We still do not know what causes mental illness, but enough is known about biological and genetic aspects of such illness to show that the idea that parents are "to blame" for such illnesses is simplistic and unfair. Most evidence points to the concept of a person who is vulnerable to a major mental illness and likely to develop an episode under levels of stress that another person without such vulnerability would be able to tolerate. Other kinds of problems may indeed result from the circumstances of growing up. Early alcohol and other drug use is a common factor today in the development of young people who show a lack of personal and interpersonal skills and strengths and the immature or dysfunctional patterns of behavior that prevent them from effectively managing their lives. In certain kinds of mental illness (e.g., schizophrenia), the good news is that family members generally can play an important part in limiting the course of the mental disorders and contributing to a more positive outcome than the person could achieve without family understanding and support. In other cases, some kinds of behavior problems may call for a rigorous attention to setting limits and expectations; while in still other situations, encouragement and empathy, combined with help in gaining specific skills and new sources of confidence

and self-esteem, may be the most fruitful response. That is why understanding the nature of a specific disorder and gaining some knowledge and perspective on the problem are so important. The importance lies not in assigning blame or self-blame, but in figuring out what to do in response to the problem that exists in the life of your adult child. And in some cases the only response available to you, difficult as it is, may be simply to wait for your adult son or daughter to accept treatment.

5. *Inform yourself thoroughly about alcohol/drug use.* Because so many younger adults with mental/emotional disorders also have problems of substance use, misuse, abuse, or dependence, both clinicians and family members need to be thoroughly educated about alcohol and drug effects and their interplay with psychiatric symptoms. Your son or daughter may not be using alcohol and other drugs in a way you would consider substance abuse, but may be especially vulnerable to their effects, and these may be responsible for the person's slipping back into a self-defeating behavior pattern such as oversleeping, missing appointments, slacking off on responsibilities, developing delusional ideas or other symptoms, losing control of anger. If you believe that alcohol/ drug use at any level is complicating your son's or daughter's life and treatment and may be threatening his or her mental stability, you owe it to your adult child and yourself to try to confront the issue and set limits. If you can't get your son or daughter to listen, to seek help, or to pay attention to your concern about substance use, you may be able to get some suggestions from the person's therapist or from other professional sources. Bear in mind, however, that you need to avoid pushing your adult child away by using heavy confrontation or lecturing. A low-key, yet persistent reminder of what you think and feel about how substance use is affecting the person's life and functioning is more in order, plus any limits you need to set to protect the serenity of your own home and relationships. If there is someone else in your home or family who drinks or uses other drugs—or if you do, yourself— you need to think carefully about the effects of this behavior pattern on your adult son or daughter with a mental/emotional problem, and perhaps to make some changes, since what is familiar,

even if distressing, behavior for you may be overly stressful and arousing for your adult child with a mental illness and/or a substance use problem as well.

6. *Try to involve your son or daughter in a daytime treatment program or some other structured activity*—such as a job, a school program, a volunteer responsibility. Your adult child may not be able to manage work or school without extensive support; if there is no supported work or college program available in your area, it still may be useful to look for something to do that will give shape to the day. No mental/emotional problem that we know of is helped by being idle, except in periods of recovery from an acute episode.

7. *If your son or daughter lives with you and there are problems, consider other arrangements.* It is extremely difficult for most parents to tell a troubled son or daughter that she has to live elsewhere, and certainly good living alternatives may not be available, so there are no easy answers to the problem. But a group home or community residence, if available, may be the best possible place to learn to take care of oneself and to manage everyday life. If you do find and can make use of such a resource, remember that good parenting does not always mean the close holding of childhood, and that launching a troubled young adult with appropriate support may be the most important thing you can do to help your son or daughter move forward.

8. *Do not tolerate violence or abuse, and set firm limits on any abusive behavior.* This principle applies whether or not your adult child lives with you. Mental/emotional problems, including major mental illness, do not give your son or daughter the right to speak and behave abusively. You and he may not always be able to keep such out-of-bounds behavior under control, but at least you can firmly state and set the limits you feel are appropriate in your own home, and you can also decide how much and what kind of contact with your adult child is best for all of you.

9. *Suit your expectations to your son's or daughter's ability to meet them, and to the nature of his or her mental disorder.* Except in the case of violence and abuse, try not to set up expectations and demands that your adult child seems unable to meet. You may be able to move

toward the standard of behavior and level of responsibility that you want to establish, but you may need to move in very small steps toward what you would like, and you can't make too many changes at once, even if you feel you have been too lenient and undemanding. You may be able to get some understanding and guidance from treating clinicians and other workers about what kinds of expectations are reasonable. What is good and viable in one situation may have nothing to do with another, so try to rely on what you can learn of your adult child's diagnosis and ability to function—and on what you know does and doesn't work.

10. *Appoint yourself a member of the treatment team.* You may need to work hard to get across the message to your son's or daughter's clinicians that you need and expect to be involved in decisions about treatment, placement, and so on, and that you have substantial knowledge and expertise to contribute. Keep trying. The trend today is to recognize parents' need for information and the importance of their input and participation, especially when changes in level of care or other aspects of treatment and services are being made.

11. *Take good care of yourself whenever possible.* It is common for devoted parents, many of whom have good reason to be anxious, to gradually focus more and more of their lives and attention on a troubled son or daughter. In a crisis, of course, it is natural and necessary to devote all your energies to the situation, and even between crises many parents find themselves trying to meet ongoing needs and demands that are overwhelming; yet there seem to be no alternatives. But in the long run it is vital, for the sake of your adult child as well as yourselves, to continue to lead as normal a life as possible, and to maintain interests and activities that take you outside the boundaries of a son's or daughter's illness.

12. *Don't give up hope.* For one thing, there are always new medications and approaches coming down the road. While family members shouldn't put all their hopes into waiting for the magic potion, it is still encouraging that the development of new medications continues. In addition, your family member may be able to make progress over time, becoming more stable and better able

to manage the stress of life. For both the person in treatment and the one who has so far refused treatment, there is always some hope for the future.

## HOW CAN I HELP MYSELF? SOME GUIDELINES FOR CLIENT/CONSUMERS

Today we are learning that it is not only professional and family caregivers who can impact on a person's mental disorder. Rather, the most important caregiver may be the person himself. If you are a client/consumer of mental health services (or feel that you have serious problems), you, yourself, are in the best position to know who you are, who you want to be, what you would like to do in your life, and what stands in the way. You know more than anyone else about what you think about, how you feel, and what you do, because you know it from the inside. What you may not know as much about is how others see you and why people may see you as "troubled," "disturbed," "out of control," or failing at life. You can't see *all* of yourself the way you can be seen in the mirror of another person's point of view. This means that you and the people around you both have something important to offer in thinking about what kinds of help you might need.

In the same way, you are the person in the best position to change what you do, how you think and feel, and how you get along in life. In fact, you are the only person who can change your own behavior. Yet you may feel helpless and powerless to change, as many people do, for one reason or another. Some people have thoughts that come to mind even though they don't want to think them, such as: I'm no good . . . I can't win . . . They're talking about me . . . They're out to get me . . . Some people even hear such thoughts as voices inside their heads, giving them bad messages. Some people feel frightened and confused when they try to go out of the house or to do something new or find that they just can't activate themselves to do anything in the course of the day. Some people have trouble controlling their tempers and lose control whenever they get angry. Some people have a problem of substance abuse or dependence or simply have gotten used to making use of alcohol or other drugs whenever they're tense and want to relax—even if it leaves them more confused and anxious than before.

If you have had any of these experiences, you may feel: I can't change myself or anything about my life. So, although you have a major part to play in changing your troubled thoughts or feelings or behavior—and making your life better—you also may need some help and collaboration from others, both in figuring out what your problems are and in planning some steps and directions for change. Most of all, you may need some encouragement and support from people who know you (or get to know you) and can be there for you when it seems too difficult to move forward.

This is a time when many people are concerned about client/consumers' rights—the right to have good treatment, to have input into their treatment, and to learn as much as they can about their disorder, as well as the right to confidentiality, the right to refuse treatment, and so on. Most of us in the field believe that these rights are important and that the increasing role of client/consumers in their own treatment and in giving feedback to treatment programs is a very positive development. You may want to take part in a consumer self-help group and/or to get involved in consumer advocacy, either locally or in the form of political advocacy for support of mental health programs. Whatever you choose to do as a client/consumer, we believe it is important to remember your responsibilities as well as your rights—that is, your responsibility to take charge of yourself as much as you can, to follow through on the treatment you choose, and to work for the good of other client/consumers and support them as much as you can. With a balance of consumer rights and responsibilities, consumers can be strong in working for their own welfare and that of others and can gain the greatest benefit from whatever help they need from their mental health/substance abuse treatment and services.

The suggestions that follow are some thoughts about how you can go about helping yourself to set your feet on a good path and to take charge of your own adult life:

1. *Recognize and honor yourself for your strengths.* You are not just a walking collection of problems; you are also a unique human

being with wishes, hopes, interests, and talents, and with some qualities that are good and special to you. You may not be able to think, offhand, of anything good about yourself. Keep thinking. What do you like and respect about yourself? Maybe the fact that you try to be thoughtful of others. Maybe you see yourself as a loyal friend. Maybe you are persistent and struggle hard to reach your goals. If you can't think of anything to honor in yourself, ask your family or other people who know you. Maybe the one thing you can find to like about yourself is your hope for the future, your aspirations for yourself and your desire to change. What is important is to realize that your problems are not your *self*, and that there is more to know and value about you. This knowledge can help you to have the strength to try to change what you don't like about yourself and your life.

2. *Look at yourself honestly and recognize your problems.* This is probably the most important thing you can do for yourself. Many people fail in their efforts to make a good life because they can't see their own problems and shortcomings, and therefore they don't know where to start in making changes and may also fight off other people's efforts to help. You take a major step toward taking charge of your own life when you recognize what kinds of problems you have. If you feel confused about your problems or feel frightened and upset when you think about them, you could ask your therapist, your family, or a good friend to discuss what they notice about you and what they think you can do to help yourself.

3. *Start to make a plan for becoming more like the person you want to be and making a life more like the life you want.* First, think about what would be the first step in such a plan. Maybe finding a therapist or an AA sponsor? Maybe going outside for a walk every day, or talking to your therapist about something you've been afraid to talk about. Maybe just talking to someone you've seen in the day program or deciding to attend your treatment program every day. Maybe you would want to take up a hobby you've thought about vaguely as: I wish I could . . . or: Someday I might . . . Maybe you would start by trying to do something—go to a meeting or a class, or listen to music with a friend, or read or write something—that

you haven't felt able to do for a while. Think about two or three things you could choose to do as a "first step" and choose one. Make it something you feel you really can do, even though it might be difficult or scary.

Second, think some more about the end-point of a plan to become more like the person you want to be and do what you want to do. What would be your ultimate goal or direction? That is, what would you like to be doing in a year or so that you aren't doing now? Does your "first step" point you a little way in that direction? For instance, if your goal is to make some friends and have a better social life or not be as lonely, does your first step do something to help you move toward that goal? Is it the beginning of learning a skill you might need, such as making small talk or planning something to do with a friend? If your first step is to say a friendly "Good morning" to someone you've been arguing with, that would relate to a goal of having fewer arguments and having more friendly relationships or a more peaceful life. If your goal is to stop using alcohol or other drugs, then to go one day without picking up would be a reasonable first step. (Notice, though, that this isn't the same as the 12 steps of Alcoholics Anonymous. The steps we're talking about here are not big, global decisions; they are very specific things that you can do to help you move in the direction of your goal.)

4. *Take the first step you decided upon,* to make your life just a little bit different from how it was yesterday, or to do something a little bit different from what you did before. If you can take that one step today, that's all you have to do. On the other hand, you could take another step tomorrow, and then you would be two steps down a new path in your life.

5. *Structure your days.* If you don't already have something you do each day, such as attending classes, working at a job, going to a day treatment or supported work program, or doing some kind of volunteer work on a regular schedule, plan to take on some activity, commitment, or schedule that you follow each day or several times a week. This will help you to focus your attention on realistic goals, to interact with other people, and to form the habits you

need in order to keep your mood and thinking stable. These habits will also help you to be ready to go to school, work at a job, or do whatever you hope to do in the future.

6. *Be realistic in setting your goals and expectations.* Think carefully about what you can and can't do for now, what you have to offer and what your problems are. Choose your next steps in life according to these realities, even if they are just beginning steps on a long road to where you want to go. Sometimes people work at a job they don't like, just to form the habit of going to work every day and sticking it out in a situation. That makes it easier to get and keep the job you *do* want when you are ready.

7. *If you're having trouble taking your first steps or making progress toward your goals, cut them down to mini-steps and mini-goals.* Learn to work on making progress in small ways, toward limited goals. Talk with the people around you about what kinds of mini-goals and steps would make sense for you.

8. *Consider all areas of your life*—where you are in school, work, living arrangements, your relationships with family and friends, your social life and how you spend your time, and what kind of treatment you are having. Think about each area and how you would like to make it better, so that you can plan for more changes as you go along.

9. *Think about your medications.* If you are taking medication for mental/emotional problems, do you understand what it is and what it is supposed to do to help you? Are you worried about side effects? Do you understand your dosage and remember to take the meds reliably? If there is a problem in any of these ways, you may need to have more communication with your doctor, and perhaps to ask about possible changes in your meds if needed. The point is to be sure that you are getting the maximum benefit from any medication you are taking, and that you are taking responsibility for taking it in the best way to make it work for you.

10. *Think and learn about alcohol and drug use and its effects.* Many people find that the interaction between mental/emotional prob-

lems and alcohol/drug use makes it more difficult to cope with everyday life. Some also find that their medications don't work well with alcohol and drug use. You may feel that this concern doesn't apply to you. Find out. See what you can learn and how you can share that learning with others.

11. *Join the consumer self-help movement.* Get together with other people who have mental/emotional and/or substance use problems. People have more strength when they can work together and try to help one another.

12. *Don't give up hope for the future.* You may sometimes feel like giving up on yourself. This happens because progress can be very slow, and it can be very discouraging to try to cope with mental/emotional disorders. Keep trying, remember your strengths and your value as a person, and never stop thinking about your goals for yourself and your hopes for the future.

These few suggestions for caregivers, family members, and client/consumers are offered with humility and the awareness that there is no simple answer to these very complex problems in human behavior. We hope that these general guidelines may be of some help to some of you along the way, and that you will add to them from your own experience.

Chapter 13

# The Ragged Interface Between Mental Disorder and Society

## Toward New Paradigms of Treatment

From whatever role and perspective we look at Bill, Annie, Ellen, Darrell, and their innumerable sisters and brothers, we are bound to step back at some point and think again of the questions that began this book: Who are these young people? Where have they all come from? And: What is happening in our society to produce so many young men and women with serious mental disorder and substance use problems?

In our first chapter we suggested four major factors that may contribute to this virtual tidal wave of troubled young people:

1. *An increasingly complex, competitive, and fast-paced society,* resulting in high levels of stimulation and demand, with reduced need and tolerance for people seen as marginal, with low skills and high vulnerability to stress;

2. *Increased numbers of people with mental illness and/or alcohol/drug abuse who are treated—or untreated—in the community,* because of reduced use of inpatient care for mental illness, lack of availability of treatment slots for alcohol and drug abuse, and lack of involuntary commitment to drug rehabilitation facilities, with an increased risk of and reliance upon prison as a re-

sponse to these disorders as they are expressed in aggressive
and disorganized behavior;

3. *Widespread availability and use of alcohol and other drugs in all socioeconomic groups,* affecting vulnerable people such as young
children and adolescents, and also people with mental/emo-
tional disorders.

4. *Major changes in family structure and the nurturing, socialization,
and supervision of children,* resulting in more stress and less
support for families and for vulnerable family members.

Associated with these four major factors, and aggravating their
impact upon people with mental and substance use disorders, are
such factors as stigma, backlash, blaming the victim, concern
about shrinking resources in an economic downturn, increasing
cultural diversity, and increased dangers in once-safe places, combined with loss of a shared sense of social values, purpose, compassion, and responsibility.

Some of these factors—stigma, deinstitutionalization, availability of drugs to young and vulnerable people—affect how
people express their mental/emotional disorders, and how those
with mental disorders fare in our communities. Other factors,
such as failures in the nurturing and socialization of children,
directly affect the development of personality disorder, alco-
hol/drug use and abuse, and criminal behavior. For many of us
the question, "Is there anything we can do to make it better?" is
a haunting one. It reflects not only in our concern for individuals we already know but for the wave we see advancing, what appears to be a rising, even a towering wave of mental disorder,
uncontrolled and violent behavior, and children and adults who
are failing at life—and this in a society where failure or success,
alienation or inclusion, dropping out or making it, tend to define the difference between a decent life and one that is barely
livable.

## MENTAL DISORDER AS WAVE AND PARTICLE

For many years physicists discussed the nature of light: Does it
consist of discrete particles, or is it composed of some continuous

material that has a wave form? Each model has been useful, and it is now commonly recognized that they are complementary rather than competitive. In a similar way, we can look at mental/emotional and substance use disorders as discrete illnesses, as we do when making an individual diagnosis. Or we can take all the particles together and see them as a continuum, or wave, that gathers force as it spreads through society.

When we look at schizophrenia, for example, we are looking at a definable form of serious mental disorder that afflicts approximately 1 percent of the population of every nation on earth. Subparticle analysis tells us that there are different forms of schizophrenia that we can identify within that 1 percent group. Some forms of schizophrenia have partial genetic transmission. Others may be triggered in otherwise healthy individuals by heavy use of marijuana during adolescence, according to a pathbreaking Swedish study. Some people with certain personality characteristics may be predisposed to develop schizophrenia under the influence of more-than-ordinary life stress or simply from the usual pressures and conflicts of young adult life in our communities. So even within one diagnosis we are faced with extreme variations in causes and profiles of functioning.

In other words, we can't speak realistically of mental disorder as if it were a single homogeneous problem, nor should we speak of substance abuse as one entity, nor of MICA or dual-disorder patients as one population. What we can say is that mental disorders are common—again, the Epidemiological Catchment Area (ECA) study data suggest that 29.5 percent of the total population of the United States will experience at least an episode of a diagnosable psychiatric problem—whether that problem is a major mental illness like schizophrenia (and can be expected to remain a factor in the person's life after the first "break" or episode) or a bout of depression that may or may not recur throughout the person's lifetime. The more recent National Comorbidity Study found that 48 percent of Americans have had a mental disorder and/or a substance abuse disorder within their lifetime, and 35 percent have had at least one of these disorders during the past year.

One implication of these findings is that "normal people" and "the mentally ill" are not in an us-and-them relationship. Rather, the two populations mix and mingle, and a very large minority of us spend some time "over the line"—that is, seriously affected by a mental/emotional and/or substance use disorder—in one way or another. These periods may not divorce us from our real lives—or alternatively they may place us in a psychiatric hospital to spend a brief period in the care and control of others. If we look around at our neighbors and friends and our own extended families, we are surprisingly likely to find some Annie or Bill or Darrell or Ellen, someone with a serious problem that severely hampers healthy growth and the development of a steady adult life.

Mental health professionals tend to be interested in the particle perspective on the mental disorders; they are most interested in the individuals who suffer from the conditions that they prefer or happen to treat as clinicians. Public policy interests lean more to the wave phenomenon—to the general interface between people with these disorders and society as a whole. People outside the mental health field often ask: "Is mental illness becoming more common in our society?" An appropriate answer is: *"Which* mental illnesses?" or "What do you mean by mental illness?" Certain forms of schizophrenia, such as the catatonic type, may be seen less commonly than was the case 25 years ago. On the other hand, substance abuse, which is also categorized as a psychiatric disorder, has clearly risen in the past two decades. Since, other than through the ECA and NCS studies, it is very difficult to get aggregate figures of the wave form of mental disorder in our society, the overall question is virtually unanswerable. Even if we could decide what we are counting, exactly—that is, what are the boundaries of mental disorder—and if we could accurately count all of the individuals who have it at a given time, the figures would not hold for long: For some it would be gone tomorrow, and for others it would be a lifetime affliction.

Another problem in measuring the current size of the wave is that some disorders are diagnosed more frequently today, but they may not necessarily have become more common. Borderline personality disorder, narcissistic disorder, bulimia, anorexia, and other eating disorders are all diagnosed more commonly now than they were 25 years ago. Post-traumatic stress disorder is a new diagnosis. Are these problems actually occurring more frequently, or are clinicians looking for them and picking them out more accurately through the more sophisticated criteria of DSM-IV? This question is rhetorical because every culture looks through its own lenses at mental/emotional disorders, and each new set of lenses reveals new outlines and dimensions in what we see. With all the sophistication of our contemporary lenses, we still can assess mental/emotional, personality, and substance use disorders only in terms of our own society's current definitions of what is normal or abnormal, pathological, or merely reflective of the process of social change.

But to these authors the most important concern is not that one or another mental disorder may be more or less commonly diagnosed. The much more disturbing concern is the percentage of young men and women who—through some combination of specific mental/emotional disorder, past and/or current use of alcohol and other drugs, related immaturities and personality/developmental problems, and resulting lack of personal and interpersonal strengths and skills—are unable to find a fulfilling and productive place in our society. That percentage is certainly increasing; according to the National Comorbidity Study, there are now between 60 and 70 million young men and women with mental and/or substance abuse disorders in the United States alone, of whom close to 10 million currently have both disorders, and we see all around us the individuals who are tumbled in this swelling wave.

Unfortunately, there is no single source of this wave that we can point to; like most social phenomena, it results from a confluence of forces, and we must stop trying simplistically to blame such troubles on a single enemy or on social change itself. The problem is not families who no longer find time or do not have the resources to raise their children. It is not the coddling or intrusion, nor the failure or abdication, of government and other institutions. It is not the sweeping changes in mental health treatment, nor the lack of such changes and treatment. It is not simply a more technologically advanced and less forgiving society, nor simply the abandonment of a shared community ethic. It is not only the widespread turning to substances of abuse as an ill-chosen effort to cope with unmanageable stress. Rather, it is *all* of the above to some degree, and more.

## LOSING HOME: THE STRESSING OF FAMILY AND CHILD

Among the various undersea earthquakes producing the growing tidal wave of mental disorder, there is one to which our society must pay close attention if it is to survive. That is the increasing stress upon and fragmentation of families, and the multiple resulting threats to the nurturing and socializing of children. A fundamental meaning of "home" is a place of safety in which children are protected while they grow to be young adult men and women, able to live reasonably well in a reasonably safe world. Home in this sense is threatened from all sides—from within and from outside—for many children. For children of abuse and neglect, home holds no safety, but is rather the seat of danger. Children of families riddled with alcoholism and other drug abuse are chronically at risk. Some, like Darrell, go unfed, physically and/or emotionally, and some fear for their lives. For children of poverty, the family itself, however devoted, is a ship in danger of sinking. For children of divorce, the destruction of a safe world is part of the territory of their lives. For children of single, divorced or widowed working mothers as well as those of two working parents, the empty house, the frequent lack of a constant parental presence demands, for good and/or ill, a precocious independence. For children as young as eight or ten, drugs are at hand, as accessible as the junk food or the cigarettes in the vending machine. For children of whom high achievement is expected, the burden of this expectation may be overwhelming, given a lack of sufficient attention, tutelage, and support. For children who are vulnerable, as for adults, the temptation is great to run away—from any or all of these conditions—into drugs, delinquency, passive withdrawal, blind defiance, unstable behavior, psychotic or near-psychotic fantasy, and/or suicide.

These thoughts about the swelling of the wave relate in different ways and degrees to the stories of Bill, Annie, Ellen, Darrell, and other troubled individuals. Most important, they describe a social/cultural ground on which many children and their families live, a rolling deck where you have to be fast and steady on your feet to stay aboard, and where consistent and trustworthy models of how to live as an adult man or woman are often hard to come by. Families, parents, try in varying degrees, and with varying degrees of success, to provide such models. Children are fortunate if they are raised by adults who can offer love, concern, closeness, a sense of value and vitality in the life to be lived. Many such parents are able to provide additional child care and resources for their children, compensating for absence that may be dictated by economics and/or the sometimes competing needs and crises of adult development. But parents rendered helpless by poverty, mental disorder, substance abuse, illness, family crisis, or their own childhood sufferings are not likely to have these gifts to give, and even luckier parents may be hard pressed to give them consistently.

If home is no longer a reliably safe place, or if it never was, the world beyond the home is fraught with overwhelming danger for many children, and the loss of safety in schools, in the streets and subways, in drug- and crime-ridden neighborhoods is an obvious aspect of that danger. A more subtle hazard of the course is the world of the media, of TV and movies that bombard children and adults with overstimulating, trivializing, and sometimes near-psychotic material, offering up the familiar trio of sex, drugs, and violence as constant themes, together with coverage of bizarre news items, tragic and deadly conflicts and famines happening elsewhere in the world, yet present in the living room, and so on. The nature of this highly stimulating, yet often depersonalized material—combined with the ease and consistency of its dissemination through the mass media, whether as fact or as fiction—has created a shared social world full of what we might call psychotic content, dominated by primitive, untrammeled urges and by extremes of violence, terror, and aggression. When the medium of this message is the movies, then parental guidance is suggested. But what if there are no parents, or their guidance is meaningless to children who spend their fantasy lives in such a world?

In *Children Without Childhood*, Marie Winn (1984) wrote of what she called the loss of childhood—the widespread change in parental and societal attitudes that has converted childhood from a time to be protected from adult life to a time to be "prepared" for it through constant, repetitive, full exposure to supposedly adult experiences and concerns. But precocious experience does not prepare children for the integration of conflict and trauma in adult life. We know from studies of post-traumatic stress that exposure to stimulation exceeding the child's or adult's capacity to cope with it leads to numbing desensitization and acting out of troubling conflicts and confusing messages. For some children, these numbing and traumatizing experiences take place within the home. Some children also are especially vulnerable to the images of adult behavior that come from outside, offering inappropriate and destructive models beyond a context of parental guidance or learned values in which the child might be able to receive and neutralize them. In fact, even the adult ego may be overwhelmed by these images as they come forth from the evening news or the daytime talk show. Adults too may be reduced to apathy, indifference, cynicism, non-response, and gallows humor, treating the news, the domestic horror story, and the anxiety of each day as if they were not real.

The impact of social change cannot be denied—and the clock cannot be turned back to some era that in any case was golden only for some people and in some ways. There was a time when children were handmade by parents—that is, hand-raised, hand-fed, and always under the watchful eye of a parent, teacher, or other familiar, responsible adult. That time is gone for a variety of reasons, and many of today's children in every socioeconomic class are on their own, self- or sibling-raised for much of the day, fast-food-fed, and always watching the flickering eye of the TV screen. In many, perhaps most, cases, this is not because parents choose to be neglectful or to give short shrift to the needs of their children. Often it is because parents themselves are hard pressed to fulfill their roles, especially their breadwinner roles, in a hard-pressing society. And it is because, with each new task we have taken on while being parents—whether economic or in the interest of other demands and personal needs—we have given up a little more of the home ground, aided by the microwave, the kitchen timer, the fast-food restaurant, the forces of burgeoning technology.

For many families this means that what was once seen as an important family ritual—the gathering of all family members for a leisurely dinner that structured the day by securing its end point and ensured one reliable time each day for family communication and sharing—has receded to the status of an American myth. Not that there aren't many families, communities, parts of the country where it takes place quite dependably. But, given that only 7 in 10 American children live in two-parent households, and only 4 in 10 children in families below the poverty line live with married parents, one may wonder how many family dinners are still going on; and in how many kitchens the family pressure cooker is the dinner hour itself, traversed in haste between the day's work and the night shift; and for how many single mothers the "family dinner" means McDonald's eaten in the car on the way to the shopping center to buy sneakers. Does it matter? At the least, a once-familiar family ritual, one that ideally helped to instill a sense of belonging and reliability, a value system and a time of daily touching base, is missing from many homes. How many other sources of family socialization have vanished? The answer depends upon the family's circumstances, setting, and socioeconomic level. But, whether the culture is one of poverty or workaholism, or both, and whether the family has options or not in the ways it grows its children, the loss of family ritual and togetherness in the rush of a pressured life has a hidden cost in failures of socialization and nurturing.

Such failures, or missed opportunities, of which the family dinner is only one example, have a meaning at whatever level they occur, whether the care and tending is totally or only partially absent. The child who is not adequately nurtured and socialized is at greater risk of failing to develop adequate tolerance of frustration, anxiety, and distress. The more vulnerable the child, the greater the risk that he will turn to substance use or other self-destructive behavior as a quick source of stimulation, relief, and short-lived pleasure. The ability to postpone gratification, tolerate painful feelings, and work effectively toward long-term goals is a fruit of long, careful nurturing, training, and support of the very complex, very fragile individual child. The tempting assumption that we can raise children in a microwave oven, with a few minutes' warming at a time, is, alas, incorrect.

But these thoughts are not intended as an argument for a return to conservative "family values" of another time. We can't go home again in that respect, any more than we can go home to the era of institutional care for mental illness. As families are stressed, fragmented, and in many cases destroyed, we must find ways to support these frequently overstressed and less stable structures, so that the needs of children and parents can be more adequately met. The question is not whether to punish or reward the single mother or the divorcing family. It is rather how the community can support the parent(s) so that the parent(s) can raise the child well enough to make a viable life. A wild card of biologically determined mental illness, family crisis and/or child developmental problems may turn up on the family's table anyway—but at least we must ensure that more children have the basic nurturing they need for healthy personality development, and that more children are more reliably socialized to the values we want to maintain in the community.

One way to frame the situation is to admit that the economic and social roles of adults, both women and men, and the demands upon time and energy in the world outside the home, have been so expanded that many parents are less available for their caregiving role. This social change has had an enormous impact on the care of not only children but also elderly persons and other vulnerable family members. The resulting role conflicts create extreme distress and burden for families touched by mental illness, as well as those whose structure is altered by death, serious illness, or divorce. Other changes in and pressures upon families include unemployment, retraining, relocation; transition to new developmental stages in the lives of both children and adults; and elective, yet important and valuable, initiatives such as adult education and mid-life career changes. All such predictable and unpredictable crises and transitions take their toll in time and energy even as they may open the way to new developmental opportunities. The devaluation of child care as a focus, and the preoccupation of many adults with the unrelenting demands of the outside world, and sometimes of their own inner world, pose serious hazards to children in an increasingly complex and shifting context of everyday life.

Many parents are aware of these conflicts and of the inroads upon their caregiving roles, yet are helpless to alter life circumstances that are overdetermined by economic needs. Many of us, deeply involved in work roles, place our trust in our ability to model adult development and independence, recognizing that the parent who is always at home to teach and nurture children can-not also, and simultaneously, be the parent who earns income, achieves, and creates sources of meaning in the world of work. What we have lost in freeing at least some women from the as-sumption that the caregiving tasks are always and only theirs, we have certainly gained in creating a more ambitious model of what it is to be a fully developed adult woman or man. But this gain in the abstract is only imperfectly translated into the daily lives of children and adults, and the image of superwoman has become, for many parents, as much persecutory as liberating. For a child who is vulnerable, and/or for parents who are overstressed, the loss of reliable, predictable, continuous family life may be disas-trous. For the legion of single working mothers (the majority se-verely disadvantaged in economic terms) and for divorced fathers as well, the attempt to raise children safely and well often feels like a doomed effort, the luxury of another time.

Add to these stressors the crushing burdens of mental illness, alcohol and other drug dependence, child developmental disor-ders, and—often most salient—the deficits in what parents them-selves have been given as children, and it is clear why nurturing and socialization of children has become so problematic, and why we are currently raising another high-risk generation, highly vul-nerable to the development of dual mental/emotional and sub-stance use disorders. What can help us to reduce the size of this advancing wave?

In our view, our society must return to viewing children as a re-sponsibility of the entire community. In a time when the nurtur-ing and socialization once provided by the extended family, then by the idealized nuclear family, are no longer reliably available, we need to adopt the model of the African village, the notion that it takes an entire village to raise a child. Our society, our total com-munity, is the parent of last resort for all our children, and like other parents it will bear the brunt of whatever parenting respon-sibilities are not fulfilled. It is true that some mental disorders cannot fairly be ascribed to unsuccessful parenting, and that not every shortcoming of parenting results in mental disorder or sub-stance abuse. But surely there is more to child rearing, and more to a growing young person, than a mere absence of mental illness, and surely, for the child who is extra-vulnerable, the need for supportive attention is especially acute. We cannot afford to evade the responsibility for affirmative action of parents on behalf of children, and of society on behalf of both parent and child. When parents cannot fulfill their responsibility to nurture and protect the children they have brought into the world, the community as a whole must respond to the need.

## MENTAL DISORDER AND THE MEDICAL MODEL

Another question needs to be raised with regard to psychiatric and substance abuse disorders, which is: How should we define illness as distinguished from antisocial behavior or willful choice of an alternative lifestyle? In the case of major mental illness such as schizophrenia, the answer is usually easy. When a person shows clear evidence of psychotic thinking, hallucinations, or delusions, most people see psychiatric treatment, preferably in a hospital, as the appropriate response. But for people with dual psychiatric and substance use disorders, especially with the addition of any kind of trouble with the law, the answer is much less clear, and the person is quite likely to land in jail. As we have noted, a recent study found that 80 percent of people in a prison population were substance-abusing, and 80 percent of the substance-abusing prisoners were also mentally ill. The study also found that 83 percent of people with dual diagnosis had been given their Axis I diagnosis first, usually several years earlier. This study highlights the problem of transinstitutionalization into prison for people with dual disorders whose behavior is aggressive, disorganized, illegal, and/or drug-seeking at any cost—and who frequently turn out to have an underlying psychiatric illness. With so much blurring of the boundaries between once-discrete problems, and with so much dumping and so little coordination between the treatment and criminal justice systems, where are the guidelines to ensure that a person with an illness will be treated, a criminal will be incarcerated and/or punished, and someone who merely marches to a different drummer may do so in peace?

These questions are profound for any society. That is, they cut to the bone of our values and reflect our fundamental conceptions of what "disturbed" behavior or "psychiatric problems" are all about, and where individual and societal rights and responsibilities begin and end. A discussion of the many issues involved in mental illness and legal responsibility, or of the insanity defense or related matters, and so on is beyond the scope of this book. But we should note that the medical model of troublesome behavior as a manifestation of mental illness has certain implications:

1. Major mental illnesses are defined as public health problems once they are seen to be widespread in society.
2. The focus of research is on the biochemical, neurological, and genetic aspects of such an illness as the most appropriate paths toward effective treatment and prevention.
3. The person with the illness is viewed to some degree as a victim, not a perpetrator of problems.
4. To that degree, the person's family members may also be viewed as victims, not perpetrators of the illness.
5. Insofar as the person is seen as having an illness, there is an implication of social responsibility for responding to that illness by protecting the individual and the community and by providing treatment.
6. In the case of mental illness, because of its effects upon patterns of thinking, feeling, and behavior, there is an implication of less or even *no* personal responsibility for some kinds of socially damaging actions.
7. The other side of the coin is the limitations or inroads upon the civil rights of the person with mental illness, as in the case of involuntary hospitalization. The "patient" is placed in a passive and sometimes helpless position; the word "invalid" has a double meaning that is all too appropriate, and the person diagnosed with a mental illness is automatically deprived of the role of family soothsayer or social critic.

These and other implications of the medical model of major mental illness give rise to a number of issues and questions in the treatment of mental disorders. For instance, Bill, sitting on a bed in his college dormitory, dressed in a sheet and chanting, once he is seen as mentally ill, becomes a concern to his parents and to campus authorities. The police come and take him to a hospital, against his will as expressed by passive resistance. Do they have a right to take him where he doesn't want to go? Do we have the right to ignore the increasing signs of mental illness and withdrawal? Surely the college authorities, *in loco parentis,* have the responsibility to exercise judgment about a student's behavior and what needs to be done. But what if he were living in a furnished room in a small town, or perhaps in New York City? Who has the right, and why, to bring him to treatment? And what if he were crouching on a city sidewalk or set up housekeeping in a packing case in a doorway in winter? Such questions arise again and again, whenever someone dies of the cold or commits a crime under the apparent influence of a mental illness. With what authority does the system step in, and who is to blame if it does not? Is a suicidal or homicidal person automatically to be considered mentally ill and in need of hospitalization? Where does the danger begin and end?

These questions lie along the ragged edge between mental disorder and social responsibility, and probably that edge must always continue to shift, sometimes in one direction, sometimes in another. Meanwhile, the right to refuse treatment, both as an inpatient and in outpatient services, remains a major stumbling block in maintaining continuity of treatment and follow-up for young men and women with mental illness, especially those with concurrent substance abuse disorders, and a major reason why many become revolving-door patients in psychiatric hospitals and revolving-door inmates in jails and prisons.

To the degree that psychiatric and substance use disorders are viewed in terms of the medical model, two points stand out as essential: (1) It is crucial for the well-being of the total community that enough funding be provided to allow for prevention of disorders at all levels: primary prevention, directed to reducing the number of new cases of illness that are bred in the community; secondary prevention, directed to intervening early enough at the onset of disorders to prevent them from becoming chronic, severe, and disabling; and tertiary prevention, directed toward providing a ground floor of treatment and services for people who are struggling to live with severe, persistent mental illness and substance abuse disorders. And (2) it is also essential to decide, as a total community, at what point and by what criteria we will consider a developing crisis to require emergency intervention. The person who dies in a packing box on a city street is at the end point of a long, long downward path. We need to be much more clear in our collective minds about when we can or must look the other way and when and how we must intervene.

## SOCIAL RESPONSIBILITY AND SOCIAL CONTROL: IN SEARCH OF A NEW PARADIGM

To take a somewhat more sweeping view of these issues, we may reflect that every society has to decide how to treat people who deviate in one way or another from what is considered normal— people who are vulnerable and can't care for themselves, those who are handicapped or disabled in some way, those whose behavior crosses the boundaries of what we consider acceptable, in social and/or legal terms. The most useful questions today are about: (1) why mental disorders and substance abuse are increasing, (2) what we can do about prevention and intervention, and (3) whether our present paradigm of social responsibility, treatment, and control is suited to the present situation.

Each new situation created by the forces of social change presents the opportunity for a new experiment in social responsibility and control. The attitude of a society—the degree of responsibility it bears for its vulnerable people, as well as the responsibility it demands from those whose behavior deviates from the norm for whatever reason—is like a searchlight slowly scanning a wall. As the light moves to one extreme or the other of concerned or indifferent treatment, or of forgiving or harsh consequences, it throws up the images of failed excess—of an attitude or policy carried too far—that belong to that end of the wall. Every good intention results in unintended consequences. We could not experience the mixed consequences of the welfare system, for instance, until we had established and used it, nor come to know the evils of mental institutions until too many people had been confined in them for too long. In turn, we could not taste the results of deinstitutionalization until we had discharged the vast numbers of chronically mentally ill people into the streets. Similarly, in the ethics and mores of personal life, we could not know the consequences of divorce until it had become rampant in our society, nor the fallout from authoritarian or permissive parenting until we had experienced each. As human beings, we need to chafe against repression in order to rebel, and to have freedom in order to appreciate the dangers of license. These truths, if they are truths, go with the territory of human thought and experience.

Thomas Kuhn, in his book *The Nature of Scientific Revolutions*, points out that science proceeds, not by theory, but by means of natural experiments, new situations that are offered by circumstance and that ultimately result in major paradigm shifts in our thinking about and responses to a problem. In the eighteenth century the major institution of social control and responsibility for people seen as having deviant behavior was the jail. In the nineteenth century, some behavior was reconceptualized as mental illness, and a new paradigm for its care was confinement in the mental institution. In the twentieth century, as substance abuse/dependence has challenged the relevance of both the jail and the mental hospital, a new paradigm has been found in the firm grasp of the therapeutic community for substance abuse, and in the loose embrace of community care for mental and emotional problems. And now, what new paradigm shift is required for the drug-using, nonpsychotic, quasi-psychotic, or newly psychotic individual who becomes dangerous and disrupts society? As psychiatric hospital beds disappear and more prisons are built, we seem to have come around full circle to the jail/prison system as the repository of such people and incarceration as our major instrument of social control. But the jail of the eighteenth (or the twenty-first) century, the mental hospital of the nineteenth and the therapeutic community and community care models of the twentieth are all inadequate. We need a new response to social deviance that will integrate the best aspects of the mental health, substance abuse, criminal justice, education, family support, and social service paradigms and transform them into an integrated system of care for people who are most persistently in need of both restraint and protection, both limits and support.

One possibility we can envision for these new "consumers," "patients," or "inmates" with dual or multiple disorders—these young people with lives at risk who break the old paradigms—is a new kind of institution that is like the new kind of museum—without walls. What if people most severely at risk to themselves or others, who look most urgently to society's searchlight of responsibility/control, could receive long-term commitment, not to a hospital or a prison, but to a team consisting of a community-based case manager, probation worker, substance abuse and mental health counselor, with access to a psychiatrist and any other relevant personnel? What if the required contact with this team—like the contacts of mental health case managers, AA sponsors, and probation or parole officers—were to ebb and flow according to the need for each person, with fully collaborative relationships among professional, paraprofessional, and community people, and among the currently existing systems of service? What if the team had access to a closed setting at one end of the spectrum of care and an open one at the other, consisting of a complex of community residences and school, work, social and recreational settings? Such a network, incorporating the services of many systems with some ongoing control, would be an institution without walls. It would avoid the abuses and restrictions of the nineteenth century institution or the eighteenth (or twenty-first) century jail, and yet would offer some elements of structure and boundaries to support over time the safety and growth of the troubled individual.

This is but one of many possibilities that need to be explored in this new era in which our old paradigms of treatment and care are being overthrown. Our familiar approaches are too limited for the young men and women who become patients, clients, consumers, inmates, or survivors of the separate psychiatric, substance abuse, and criminal justice systems today. And they are too limited for the chaotic, fast-changing, and newly constricting circumstances of care in the twenty-first century. The need to develop new and more imaginative paradigms places the responsibility and burden of social thought and advocacy upon every citizen. The old order and the old assumptions are fading fast, and we are in the midst of the disorder from which new structures must be made.

# REFERENCES

American Psychiatric Association. *Diagnostic and Statistical Manual of Mental Disorders.* Fourth Edition. Washington, DC: American Psychiatric Association, 1994.

Andreason, N. C. *The Broken Brain: The Biological Revolution in Psychiatry.* New York: Harper & Row, 1984.

Beels, C. C. Family treatments of schizophrenia: Background and state of the art. *Hospital and Community Psychiatry,* Vol. 33, No. 7 (1982), pp. 541–550.

Frank, J. *Persuasion and Healing: A Comparative Study of Psychotherapy.* Rev. Ed. Baltimore: Johns Hopkins University Press, 1973.

Herman, J. L. *Trauma and Recovery.* New York: Basic Books, 1992.

Kessler, R. C., et al. Lifetime and 12-month prevalence of DSMIII-R psychiatric disorders in the United States: results from the comorbidity survey. *Archives of General Psychiatry,* Vol. 51 (January 1994).

Knop, J., et al. A 30-year follow-up study of the sons of alcoholic men. *Acta Psychiatr. Scand. Suppl.* (1W3), Vol. 370 (1993), pp. 48–53.

Kramer, P. D. *Listening to Prozac: A Psychiatrist Explores Antidepressant Drugs and the Remaking of the Self.* New York: Penguin Books, 1994 (paperback); New York: Viking Penguin, 1993.

Linehan, M. M. *Cognitive-Behavioral Treatment of Borderline Personality Disorder* and *Skills Training Manual for Treating Borderline Personality Disorder.* New York: Guilford Press, 1993.

Linehan, M. M. Dialectical behavior therapy for borderline personality disorder: theory and method. *Bulletin of the Menninger Clinic,* Vol. 51, No. 3 (1987), pp. 162–176.

MacLean, Paul. *The Triune Brain in Evolution.* New York: Plenum, 1990.

McFarlane, W. R. Multiple family therapy in schizophrenia. In W. R. McFarlane (Ed.), *Family Therapy in Schizophrenia.* New York: Guilford Press, 1983.

*The Menninger Letter,* Vol. 3, No. 9 (1995).

Osher, F. C. and Kofoed, L. L. Treatment of patients with psychiatric and psychoactive substance abuse disorders. *Hospital and Community Psychiatry,* Vol. 40, pp. 1025–1030.

Rosenblatt, Roger. The society that pretends to love children. In "What grown-ups don't understand: A special issue on childhood in America," *The New York Times Magazine,* October 8, 1995.

Sacks, Oliver. *The Man Who Mistook His Wife for a Hat.* New York: Summit Books, 1985.

Saunders, E. A. and Arnold, F. A critique of conceptual and treatment approaches to borderline psychopathology in light of findings about childhood abuse. *Psychiatry,* Vol. 56 (May 1993).

Scheflen, A. E., *Levels of Schizophrenia.* New York: Brunner/Mazel, 1981.

Sweeney, C. Portrait of the American child, 1995. In "What grown-ups don't understand: A special issue on childhood in America," *The New York Times Magazine,* October 8, 1995.

Winn, Marie. *Children Without Childhood: Growing Up Too Fast in a World of Sex and Drugs.* New York: Viking Penguin, 1965.

Winnicott, D. W. The capacity to be alone. In *The Maturational Process and the Facilitating Environment.* The International Psycho-Analytical Library. London: Hogarth Press; New York: International Universities Press, 1965.

# SELECTED BIBLIOGRAPHY

MENTAL DISORDER IN SOCIETY

American Psychiatric Association. *Diagnostic and Statistical Manual of Mental Disorders.* Fourth Edition. Washington, DC: American Psychiatric Association, 1994.

Bernikow, L. *Alone in America: The Search for Companionship.* New York: Harper & Row, 1986.

Dean, A., Kraft, A. M., and Pepper, B. (Eds.) *The Social Setting of Mental Health.* New York: Basic Books, 1976.

Gruenberg, E. M. Social breakdown in young adults: keeping crises from becoming chronic. In B. Pepper and H. Ryglewicz (Eds.), *The Young Adult Chronic Patient.* New Directions for Mental Health Services, No. 14. San Francisco: Jossey-Bass, 1982.

Haley, J. *Leaving Home: The Therapy of Disturbed Young People.* New York: McGraw-Hill, 1980.

Hopper, K., Baxter, E., and Cox, S. Not making it crazy: the young homeless patients in New York City. In B. Pepper and H. Ryglewicz, (Eds.), *The Young Adult Chronic Patient.* New Directions for Mental Health Services, No. 14. San Francisco: Jossey-Bass, 1982.

Kessler, R. C. et al. Lifetime and 12-month prevalence of DSMIII-R psychiatric disorders in the United States: Results from the comorbidity survey. *Archives of General Psychiatry*, Vol. 51 (January 1994).

Lamb, H. Richard (Ed.) *The Homeless Mentally Ill: A Task Force Report of the American Psychiatric Association.* Washington, DC: American Psychiatric Association, 1984.

Lasch, C. *The Culture of Narcissism: American Life in an Age of Diminishing Expectations.* New York: W. W. Norton, 1979.

Pepper, B. and Ryglewicz, H. The uninstitutionalized generation: A new breed of psychiatric patient. In B. Pepper and H. Ryglewicz (Eds.), *The Young Adult Chronic Patient.* New Directions for Mental Health Services, No. 14. San Francisco: Jossey-Bass, 1982.

Rinsley, D. B. The adolescent, the family, and the culture of narcissism: A psychosocial commentary (1986). In F. C. Feinstein (Ed.), *Adolescent Psychiatry,* Vol. 13, pp. 7–28.

Robins, L. N. and Regier, D. A. (Eds.) *Psychiatric Disorders in America: The Epidemiologic Catchment Area Study.* New York: The Free Press, 1991.

THE BRAIN AND THE BIOPSYCHOSOCIAL MODEL

Andreason, N. C. *The Broken Brain: The Biological Revolution in Psychiatry.* New York: Harper & Row, 1984.

Dennett, D. C. *Consciousness Explained.* Boston: Little, Brown and Company, 1991.

Edelman, G. *Bright Air, Brilliant Fire: On the Matter of the Mind.* New York: Basic Books, 1995.

Edelman, G. *The Remembered Present: A Biological Theory of Consciousness.* New York: Basic Books, 1995.

Gazzaniga, M. S. *Mind Matters: How Mind and Brain Interact to Create Our Conscious Lives.* Boston: Houghton Mifflin, 1988.

Sagan, C. *Broca's Brain: Reflections on the Romance of Science.* New York: Random House, 1979.

Searle, John R. The mystery of consciousness. *The New York Review of Books,* Vol. XLII, Nos. 17 and 18, November 2 and 16, 1995.

Thompson, R. F. *The Brain: An Introduction to Neuroscience.* New York: W. H. Freeman and Company, 1985.

## SCHIZOPHRENIA AND THE FAMILY

Anderson, C. M.; Reiss, D. J., and Hogarty, G. E. *Schizophrenia and the Family: A Practitioner's Guide to Psychoeducation and Management.* New York: Guilford Press, 1984.

Beels, C. C. Family treatments of schizophrenia: Background and state of the art. *Hospital and Community Psychiatry,* Vol. 33, No. 7, pp. 541–550.

Bernheim, K. F., Lewine, R. R., and Beale, C. T. *The Caring Family: Living with Chronic Mental Illness.* Chicago: Contemporary Books, 1982.

Falloon, I. R. H., Boyd, J. L. and McGill, C. W. *Family Care of Schizophrenia.* New York: Guilford Press, 1984.

Lefley, H. P. and Wasow, M. (Eds.) *Helping Families Cope with Mental Illness.* Chronic Mental Illness Series, Vol. 1. Baltimore, MD: Harwood Academic Publishers, 1994.

McFarlane, W. R. (Ed.). *Family Therapy in Schizophrenia.* New York: Guilford Press, 1983.

Scheflen, A. E. *Levels of Schizophrenia.* New York: Brunner/Mazel, 1981.

Torrey, E. F. *Surviving Schizophrenia: A Family Manual.* New York: Harper & Row, 1988.


## MAJOR AFFECTIVE (MOOD) DISORDERS

Arieti, S. and Bemporad, J. *Severe and Mild Depression.* New York: Basic Books, 1978.

Beck, A. T., Rush, A. J., Shaw, B. F., and Emery, G. *Cognitive Therapy of Depression.* New York: Guilford Press, 1979.

Goodwin, F. C. and Jamison, K. R. *Manic-Depressive Illness.* New York: Oxford University Press, 1990.

Gut, E. *Productive and Unproductive Depression.* New York: Basic Books, 1989.

Jamison, K. R. *Touched with Fire: Manic-Depressive Illness and the Artistic Temperament.* New York: Free Press, 1993.

Jamison, K. R. *An Unquiet Mind: A Memoir of Moods and Madness.* New York: Alfred A. Knopf, 1995.

248 Selected Bibliography

Kramer, P. D. *Listening to Prozac: A Psychiatrist Explores Antidepressant Drugs and the Remaking of the Self.* New York: Penguin, 1994 (paperback); New York: Viking Penguin, 1993.

Thompson, T. *The Beast: A Reckoning With Depression.* New York: G.P. Putnam's Sons, 1995.


## BORDERLINE AND OTHER PERSONALITY DISORDERS

Adler, G. *Borderline Psychopathology and Its Treatment.* New York: Jason Aronson, 1985.

Beck, A. T., Freeman, A. and Associates. *Cognitive Therapy of Personality Disorders.* New York: Guilford Press, 1990.

Clarkin, J. F., Marziali, E. and Munroe-Blum, H. *Borderline Personality Disorder: Clinical and Empirical Perspectives.* New York: Guilford Press, 1992.

Freeman, A. *Cognitive Therapy of Personality Disorders,* 1990.

Gunderson, J. *Borderline Personality Disorder.* Washington, DC: American Psychiatric Association Press, 1984.

Kernberg, O. *Borderline Conditions and Pathological Narcissism.* New York: Jason Aronson, 1975.

Kernberg, O., Selzer, M. A., Koenigsberg, H. W., Carr, A. C., and Appelbaum, A. H. *Psychodynamic Psychotherapy of Borderline Patients.* New York: Basic Books, 1989.

Kohut, H. *The Restoration of the Self.* New York: International Universities Press, 1977.

Linehan, M. M. *Cognitive-Behavioral Treatment of Borderline Personality Disorder and Skills Training Manual for Treating Borderline Personality Disorder.* New York: Guilford Press, 1993.

Masterson, J. F. *The Search for the Real Self: Unmasking the Personality Disorders of Our Age.* New York: The Free Press, 1988.

Masterson, J. F. and Klein, R. *Psychotherapy of the Disorders of the Self: The Masterson Approach.* New York: Brunner/Mazel, 1989.

Stone, M. H. *The Fate of Borderline Patients: Successful Outcome and Psychiatric Practice.* New York: Guilford Press, 1990.

Young, J. E. *Cognitive Therapy of Personality Disorders: A Schema-Focused Approach.* Rev. Ed. Sarasota, FL: Professional Resource Press, 1994.

## POST-TRAUMATIC STRESS DISORDER

Herman, J. L. *Trauma and Recovery.* New York: Basic Books, 1992.

Shapiro, F. *Eye Movement Desensitization and Reprocessing.* New York: Guilford Press, 1995.

Simonds, S. L. *Bridging the Silence: Nonverbal Modalities in the Treatment of Adult Survivors of Childhood Sexual Abuse.* New York: W. W. Norton, 1994.


## ANXIETY DISORDERS

Barlow, D. H. *Anxiety and Its Disorders: The Nature and Treatment of Anxiety and Panic.* New York: Guilford Press, 1988.

Beck, A. T., Emery, G. with Greenberg, R. L. *Anxiety Disorders and Phobias: A Cognitive Perspective.* New York: Basic Books, 1985.

McNally, R. J. *Panic Disorder: A Critical Analysis.* New York: Guilford Press, 1994.

Rapee, R. M. and Barlow, D. H. *Chronic Anxiety: Generalized Anxiety Disorder and Mixed Anxiety-Depression.* New York: Guilford Press, 1991.


## PERSONALITY DEVELOPMENT: YOUNG ADULTS AND ADOLESCENTS

Blos, P. *The Adolescent Passage: Developmental Issues.* New York: International Universities Press, 1979.

Feinstein, S. C. (Ed.) *Adolescent Psychiatry,* Volume 16: *Developmental and Clinical Studies.* Chicago: The University of Chicago Press, 1989.

Rinsley, D. B. The adolescent, the family, and the culture of narcissism: A psychosocial commentary. In S. C. Feinstein (Ed.), *Adolescent Psychiatry*, Vol. 13, pp. 7–28.

Ryglewicz, H., and Pepper, B. Compromised development: the complex plight of young adults with mental/emotional disorders. In S. C. Feinstein (Ed.), *Adolescent Psychiatry,* Volume 16: *Developmental and Clinical Studies.* Chicago: The University of Chicago Press, 1989.

TREATMENT AND SERVICES FOR DUAL DISORDERS

Alterman, A. I. (Ed.). *Substance Abuse and Psychopathology.* New York: Plenum Books, 1985.

Baker, F. *Coordination of Alcohol, Drug Abuse, and Mental Health Services.* Technical Assistance Publication Series No. 4. Rockville, MD: U.S. Department of Health and Human Services, Public Health Service, Substance Abuse and Mental Health Services Administration, Center for Substance Abuse Treatment, DHHS Publication No. (SMA) 93-1742.

Crowe, A. H. and Reeves, R. *Treatment for Alcohol and Other Drug Abuse: Opportunities for Coordination.* Technical Assistance Publication Series, No. 11. Rockville, MD: U.S. Department of Health and Human Services, DHHS Publication No. (SMA) 94-2075. Printed 1994.

Daley, D. C., Moss. H., and Campbell, F. *Dual Disorders: Counseling Clients with Chemical Dependency and Mental Illness.* Center City, MN: Hazelden Educational Materials, 1987.

Donovan, D. M. and Marlatt, G. A. *Assessment of Addictive Behaviors.* New York: Guilford Press, 1988.

Drake, R. E., McLaughlin, P., Pepper, B., and Minkoff, K. Dual diagnosis of major mental illness and substance disorder: An overview. In K. Minkoff and R. E. Drake (Eds.), *Dual Diagnosis of Major Mental Illness and Substance Disorder.* New Directions for Mental Health Services, No. 50. San Francisco: Jossey-Bass, 1991.

Evans, K. and Sullivan, J. M. *Dual Diagnosis: Counseling the Mentally Ill Substance Abuser.* New York: Guilford Press, 1990.

Fleisch, B. *Approaches in the Treatment of Adolescents with Emotional and Substance Abuse Problems.* Technical Assistance Publication Series No. 1. Rockville, MD: U.S. Department of Health and Human Services, DHHS Publication No. (SMA) 93-1744. Reprinted 1993.

Gottheil, E., McLellan, A. T., and Druly, K. A. *Substance Abuse and Psychiatric Illness.* New York: Pergamon, 1980.

Kessler, R. C., Nelson, C. B., McGonagle, K. A., and Edlund, M. J. The epidemiology of co-occurring mental disorders and substance use disorders in the national comorbidity survey: Implications for prevention and service utilization. *American Journal of Orthopsychiatry*, in press.

Kostcn, T. R. and Kleber, H. D. *Clinician's Guide to Cocaine Addiction: Theory, Research and Treatment.* New York: Guilford Press, 1992.

Meyer, R. C. *Psychopathology and Addictive Disorders.* New York: Guilford Press, 1986.

Miller, W. R. and Rollnick, S. *Motivational Interviewing: Preparing People to Change Addictive Behavior.* New York: Guilford Press, 1991.

Minkoff, K. and Drake, R. E. (Eds.) *Dual Diagnosis of Major Mental Illness and Substance Disorder.* New Directions for Mental Health Services, No. 50. San Francisco: Jossey-Bass, 1991.

Mitchell, J. L., Consensus Panel Chair. *Pregnant, Substance-Using Women.* Treatment Improvement Protocol (TIP) Series, No. 2. Rockville, MD: U.S. Department of Health and Human Services, DHHS Publication No. (SMA) 93-1998. Printed 1993.

Nowinski, J. *Substance Abuse in Adolescents and Young Adults: A Guide to Treatment.* New York: W. W. Norton, 1990.

Pepper, B., Ryglewicz, H., and Massaro, J. *Alcohol, Street Drugs and Emotional Problems: What You Need to Know.* Rev. Ed. Center City, MN: Hazelden Educational Materials, 1994. An information booklet for consumers; formerly Ryglewicz, H. and Pepper, B. *Alcohol and Street Drugs: Time for a Change.* New City, NY: The Information Exchange, 1992.

Ridgely, M. S., Goldman, H. H., and Talbott, J. A. Treatment of Chronic Mentally Ill Young Adults with Substance Abuse Problems: Emerging National Trends. In S. C. Feinstein (Ed.), *Adolescent Psychiatry,* Volume 16: *Developmental and Clinical Studies.* Chicago: The University of Chicago Press, 1989.

Ries, R. *Consensus Panel Chair: Assessment and Treatment of Patients with Coexisting Mental Illness and Alcohol and Other Drug Abuse.* Treatment Improvement Protocol (TIP) Series. Rockville, MD: U.S. Department of Health and Human Services, DHHS Publication No. (SMA) 94-1078. Printed 1994.

Ryglewicz, H. Massaro, J., and Pepper, B. *Alcohol, Street Drugs and Emotional Problems: What the Family Needs To Know.* Center City, MN: Hazelden Educational Materials, 1996. Rev. Ed; formerly *Alcohol and*

*Street Drugs: What Parents Need To Know.*. New City, NY: The Information Exchange (TIE), 1992. Rev. Ed. with J. Massaro, 1992.

Ryglewicz, H. and Pepper, B. *Alcohol, Drugs, and Mental/Emotional Problems: What You Need To Know To Help Your Dual Disorder Client.* Rev. Ed. New City, NY: The Information Exchange, 1991.

Ryglewicz, H. Psychoeducation for clients and families: A way in, out, and through in working with people with dual disorders. *Psycho-social Rehabilitation Journal,* Vol. 15, No. 2 (October 1991).

Ryglewicz, H. and Pepper, B. The dual-disorder client: Mental disorder and substance use. In S. Cooper and T. H. Lentner (Eds.), *Innovations in Community Mental Health.* Sarasota, FL: Professional Resources Press, 1992.

*The Dual Disorders Recovery Book.* Center City, MN: Hazelden Educational Materials, 1993.

Wallace, B. C. (Ed.) *The Chemically Dependent: Phases of Treatment and Recovery.* New York: Brunner/Mazel, 1992.

# OTHER PUBLICATIONS
# BY THE AUTHORS

## BOOKS

*Advances in Treating the Young Adult Chronic Patient.* Bert Pepper and Hilary Ryglewicz (Eds.). New Directions in Mental Health Services, No. 21. San Francisco: Jossey-Bass, 1984.

*The Young Adult Chronic Patient.* Bert Pepper and Hilary Ryglewicz (Eds.). New Directions in Mental Health Services, No. 14. San Francisco: Jossey-Bass, 1982.

*The Social Setting of Mental Health.* Alfred Dean, Alan M. Kraft, and Bert Pepper (Eds.). New York: Basic Books, 1976.

*Working Couples: How To Cope with Two Jobs and One Home.* Hilary Ryglewicz and Pat Koch Thaler. New York: Sovereign Books, 1980.

*Feeling Safe: Making Space for the Self.* Stephen Shapiro and Hilary Ryglewicz. Englewood Cliffs, NJ: Prentice-Hall, 1976.

*Trusting Yourself: Psychotherapy as a Beginning.* Stephen Shapiro and Hilary Tyrka. Englewood Cliffs, NJ: Prentice-Hall, 1975.

## EDUCATIONAL BOOKLETS

*Alcohol, Drugs and Mental/Emotional Problems: What You Need To Know To Help Your Dual-Disorder Client* (Clinicians' version). Hilary Ryglewicz and Bert Pepper. New City, NY: The Information Exchange (TIE), Inc. Rev. Ed. with Jackie Massaro.

*Alcohol and Street Drugs: What Parents Need To Know* (Parents' version). Hilary Ryglewicz and Bert Pepper. New City, NY: The Information Exchange (TIE), Inc. Rev. Ed. with Jackie Massaro. Republished by Hazelden Educational Materials, Center City, MN, as *Alcohol, Street Drugs and Emotional Problems: What the Family Needs to Know* (1996).

*Alcohol and Street Drugs: Time for a Choice* (Client/consumers' version). Hilary Ryglewicz and Bert Pepper. New City, NY: The Information Exchange (TIE). Rev. Ed. with Jackie Massaro. Republished by Hazelden Educational Materials, Center City, MN, as *Alcohol, Street Drugs and Emotional Problems: What You Need to Know* (1994).

# ABOUT THE
# INFORMATION EXCHANGE

The Information Exchange (TIE), Inc. is a private, not-for-profit organization founded in 1983 by Bert Pepper, M.D., its Executive Director. TIE's purpose is to provide education nationwide about young adults with serious mental/emotional and substance disorders and to disseminate new ideas and information about treatment.

TIE has developed a variety of training and consultation services and educational materials designed to help providers develop comprehensive, unified, accessible, and humane systems of treatment for young people with mental/emotional disorders and/or alcohol and drug problems. The authors and other staff are available to provide modular training and consultation to help clinicians and agencies to function positively with managed care and other contemporary conditions of treatment. TIE also has published a quarterly bulletin, TIE-Lines, since 1983, with topical articles on many related subjects. All issues and other publications, as well as further information, are available from: The Information Exchange (TIE), Inc., 20 Squadron Blvd., Suite 400, New City, New York 10956. (TEL: 914-634-0050; FAX: 914-634-1690).

# INDEX

AA, xiv, 34, 35, 77, 78, 80, 91, 98, 109, 167, 179, 200, 223, 242
Abuse, 49–54, 156–59
ACOAs, 58
Acute care, 179–80, 198
Acute day programs. *See* Day programs
ADA (Americans with Disabilities Act), 206
Addictions: crack/cocaine babies, 103–08; plus psychiatric symptoms, 75, 79–80, 97–123. *See also* Alcohol use and alcoholism; Drug use and abuse; Eating disorders
ADL skills, 204
Adult child of abuse, 49–54
Adult child of alcoholic parents, 48–54, 58
Affective disorders. *See* Mood disorders
Alcohol use and alcoholism: assessment for, 212; bipolar disorder and, 31–40, 74–78, 80, 87, 90–92; borderline personality disorder and, 48–54, 56; brain and, 166–68; case example of, 31–34; client/consumer guidelines on, 224–25; education and counseling on, 30, 86, 87, 90; families and, 217–18; genetic causes of alcoholism, 36; increased availability and impact of, 8, 73, 225–26; and levels of motivation and denial,

81–83; and loop of compulsive behavior, 142–44; major mood disorders and, 31–40, 52; plus psychiatric symptoms, 75, 79–80; post-traumatic stress disorder and, 57–58. *See also* Drug use and abuse; Dual disorders
Alcoholics Anonymous (AA), xiv, 34, 35, 77, 78, 80, 91, 98, 109, 167, 179, 200, 223, 242
Alexithymia, 204
American Psychiatric Association, 15, 62
Americans with Disabilities Act (ADA), 206
Amphetamines, 38
Annie (case example), 31–40, 74–75, 77–78, 80, 87, 90–92, 129, 140–41, 143, 144, 174, 178, 179, 184, 196, 202, 231
Antianxiety agents, 165
Antidepressants, 163, 164, 165
Antisocial personality disorder, 100–101, 112
Anxiety, 127–28, 165, 183, 184
Assessment, 196–99, 212
Avoidance, loop of, 137–44

Bill (case example), 11–15, 19–20, 39–40, 75, 77, 80, 128–29, 140–41, 144, 174, 178, 179, 184, 195–96, 201–02, 231